The New Foundations
of Management
Accounting

THE NEW FOUNDATIONS OF MANAGEMENT ACCOUNTING

Ahmed Riahi-Belkaoui

QUORUM BOOKS

New York • Westport, Connecticut • London

Library of Congress Cataloging-in-Publication Data

Riahi-Belkaoui, Ahmed
    The new foundations of management accounting / Ahmed Riahi-Belkaoui.
      p.   cm.
    Includes bibliographical references and index.
    ISBN 0–89930–700–0 (alk. paper)
    1. Managerial accounting.   I. Title.
  HF5657.4.B46   1992
  658.15′11—dc20   91–36667

British Library Cataloguing in Publication Data is available.

Library of Congress Catalog Card Number: 91–36667
ISBN: 0–89930–700–0

First published in 1992

Quorum Books, One Madison Avenue, New York, NY 10010
An imprint of Greenwood Publishing Group, Inc.

Printed in the United States of America

The paper used in this book complies with the
Permanent Paper Standard issued by the National
Information Standards Organization (Z39.48–1984).

10 9 8 7 6 5 4 3 2 1

To the Riahi-Belkaouis

CONTENTS

Exhibits   ix

Preface   xi

1. The Accounting Foundations   1

2. The Problem and Decisional Foundations   31

3. The Organizational Foundations   55

4. The Behavioral Foundations   99

5. The Strategic Foundations   139

6. Conclusions   163

Index   167

EXHIBITS

1.1 A Summary of Prior Studies of Cost/Managerial Curriculum Content 17

1.2 Partial Analysis of Overhead Variances 19

1.3 Overhead Variance Analysis—Comparison 20

1.4 Revised Framework for Relating Management Accounting Topics 24

1.5 Tentative Management Accounting Conceptual Framework 25

2.1 Decision Strategies for Reducing Complexity in Problem Diagnosis and Formulation 33

2.2 Theoretical Model of the Problem Recognition Process 35

2.3 Types of Problem Structure 36

2.4 Classification Frameworks of Organizational Problems 37

2.5 Problems Employed in the Sorting Task 38

2.6 Information Requirements by Decision Category 41

2.7 An Expanded Example of the Gorry-Scott Morton Framework 43

2.8 Dearden Framework 47

2.9 The Problem and Decisional Foundations of Management Accounting 49

3.1 A Summary of the Most Frequently Cited Works Using Theoretically Constructed Typologies or Taxonomies 57

3.2 Organizational Chart of a Manufacturing Company 61

3.3 Controllership and Treasurership Functions Defined by
     Financial Executives Institute   68

3.4 The Minimum Necessary Contingency Framework   80

3.5 Categories of Technology   81

3.6 A Comprehensive Contextual Model of Information Systems   82

3.7 Comparison of Major Studies with Simple Linear Model   83

3.8 Characteristics of Organizational Environmental States   87

3.9 Organizational Information Characteristics of the
     Environmental States   88

3.10 Management Accounting: The Organizational Foundations   90

4.1 Proposed Objectives and Concepts for Social Accounting   105

4.2 Functioning of Concrete and Abstract Individuals in Relation
     to Environmental Complexity   116

4.3 2 × 2 Joint Frequency Table   125

4.4 The Behavioral Foundations of Management Accounting   128

5.1 Management Accounting: The Strategic Foundations   140

5.2 Characteristics and Conditions of the Three Modes   146

5.3 Summary of Coping Methods Used by Each Archetype in
     Successful Subsample   150

5.4 Summary of Coping Methods Used by Each Archetype in
     Unsuccessful Subsample   151

PREFACE

This book proposes a theory of management accounting that rests on five foundations: (1) accounting, (2) problem and decisional, (3) organizational, (4) behavioral, (5) and strategic. Each chapter devoted to one of these foundations presents the determinants and elements that should influence the design and conduct of management accounting and best serve the complex needs of management.

Management accounting is designed to supply information to internal decision makers of a given organization, to facilitate their decision making, to motivate their actions and behavior in a desirable direction, and to promote the efficiency of the organization. It is accounting-based and individual-, organization-, strategy-, problem-, and decision-centered. Thus, management accounting requires an accounting, decisional and problem, organizational, behavioral, and strategic grounding. An understanding of each of these foundations may allow the management accountant to design a management accounting system more responsive to the diverse needs and demands emanating from within and without the organization. A recurrent theme of each of these chapters is that a failure to grasp any of these conceptual foundations of management accounting may result in deficiencies in the management accounting systems and inadequacies in the provision of the diverse services required by both the small and the complex organizations of today. The book's five major themes correspond to the five main conceptual foundations underlying a management accounting theory.

The book should be of interest to a variety of reader groups, including researchers in the management accounting area and accounting practitioners interested in the careful design of a management accounting system. The book can also be useful as additional material for a typical undergraduate or graduate course in management accounting. The student in management accounting should be aware not only of the new multidimensional scope of the field but also of the conceptual foundations that justify this extended scope. Most management accounting texts do not introduce and integrate all these foundations and are generally restricted to an exposition of cost accounting techniques. In my judgment, what is needed is to show the student that management accounting theory has a conceptual grounding in various disciplines, justifying the adaptation of their techniques to managerial problem solving. It is to this view of management accounting that this book is addressed.

Many people helped in the development of this book. Eric Valentine and Katie Chase of Greenwood Press are true professionals. They have my best gratitude. I wish also to thank my research assistants at the University of Illinois at Chicago, Kalliopi Karabatsos, Shiela Decena, and Veena Rao, for their cheerful and intelligent assistance. Finally, thanks to the two Riahi-Belkaouis of Chicago, Hedi and Janice, whose sense of humor, affection, and patience made everything possible.

The New Foundations
of Management
Accounting

1

THE ACCOUNTING
FOUNDATIONS

Management accounting is one of the areas in the field and profession of accountancy. As suggested by the 1958 American Accounting Association (AAA) Committee on Management Accounting, it "involves consideration of the ways in which accounting information may be accumulated, synthesized, analyzed, and presented in relation to specific problems, decisions, and day-to-day tasks of business management."[1] An appreciation of management accounting requires a good understanding of the different facets of accounting in organizations. A clarification of each accounting area will help identify the scope of management accounting, the possibility of a management accounting theory, and a taxonomy of management accounting techniques.

The aim of this chapter is to clarify the role of management accounting in the field of accounting per se, and to argue for a management accounting theory as a frame of reference for the justification of present and new management accounting techniques.

NATURE OF ACCOUNTING

The financial community has always regarded the accounting discipline as one of its principal tools in the decision-making process. The primacy of decision has been stressed by both William Paton and the AAA "Statement of Basic Accounting Theory":

The purpose of accounting may be said to be that of interpreting the financial data . . . to provide a sound guide action by management, investor and other interested parties.[2]

The committee defines accounting as the process of identifying, measuring, and communicating economic information to permit informed judgments and decisions by users of the information.[3]

Thus, accounting is perceived as utilitarian in purpose and descriptive in nature. Stated in means-end terms, the end sought is good information and the means employed are descriptions. Accounting provides information for two distinct but closely related purposes: (1) reporting to managers within the organization and (2) reporting to persons outside the organization who have a legitimate interest in its affairs. More precisely the accounting system provides information for three broad objectives:

1. Internal routine reporting to managers to provide information and influence behavior regarding cost management and the planning and controlling of operations.
2. Internal nonroutine, or special, reporting to managers for strategic and tactical decisions on matters such as pricing products or services, choosing which products to emphasize or de-emphasize, investing in equipment, and formulating overall policies and long-range planning.
3. External reporting through financial statements to investors, government authorities, and other outside parties.[4]

The first two areas are those of internal or management accounting, the third is of external or financial accounting. What is the extent of the differences in scope of both financial and management accounting?

FINANCIAL VERSUS MANAGEMENT ACCOUNTING

Financial accounting deals with reporting information that pertains to the financial position, performance, and conduct of a firm for a given period to a set of users and the market in general. Management accounting is more oriented toward internal decision making and purposively channels relevant and timely information to internal managers. Both are production processes of different accounting data for different problem-solving situations.

Financial accounting is the result of applying generally accepted accounting principles (GAAP) to the recording of transactions between different entities. As such, financial accounting statements conform to a set of rules established by the profession. Management accounting, however, reflects the use of techniques from different disciplines, including accounting, for internal problem solving. Therefore, management accounting techniques may differ from GAAP techniques and from one firm to another. They do not conform to any set of prescribed rules, and much may be left to the decision-maker's philosophies.

In short, the frame of reference used in management accounting is much broader than that used in financial accounting. Vergil Boyd and Dale Taylor considered the specific difference to be the following:

1. The managerial approach places the student in the role of a *user* of financial data in decision making. The conventional approach assigns the student the role of *preparer* of financial statements for use by others.

2. The student of managerial accounting is called upon to use his or her entire knowledge of the business world in making business decisions based upon accounting data. Conventional accounting limits itself to accounting techniques, principles, and practices, and rarely deals with decisions other than those required in the preparation of financial statements.

3. An attempt is made to consider the external and internal business environment in managerial accounting. Conventional accounting usually ignores these conditions.

4. The arrangement and emphasis of topical material differs under the two methods because of the differences in objectives.

5. The purpose of managerial accounting is to make a decision related to a business problem. Conventional accounting has as its end the ability to prepare adequate financial statements.[5]

To this list of differences, it may be also added that financial accounting data are required to be objective and verifiable, while management accounting emphasizes relevance and flexibility.

MANAGEMENT VERSUS COST ACCOUNTING

Although the relationship between cost accounting and management accounting has not been explicitly clarified, it is usually believed that it is one point of emphasis. Cost accounting deals mainly with cost accumulation, inventory valuation, and product costing. It emphasizes the cost side. The objective function is implicitly perceived to be cost minimization. Similarly, management accounting deals with the efficient allocation of resources.

The objective function may be perceived to be profit maximization. It is also believed that the cost accountant and the management accountant are performing different activities; cost control is in the domain of the cost accountant, while cost reduction is in the domain of the management accountant.[6] A cursory examination of accounting textbooks shows that, in general, those labeled *cost accounting* emphasize cost control while those labeled *management accounting* or *managerial accounting* emphasize planning, which may have reinforced the belief in a difference between both areas.[7] It is advisable, however, not to stress those differences, but rather to conceive of management accounting as an attempt to bring techniques from other disciplines into the area of cost accounting. In fact, in recent years, the scope of cost accounting has been enlarged in various ways:

1. It emphasizes not only the explanatory but also the predictive ability of accounting data.

2. It develops normative models to be applied in the accounting context with an emphasis on mathematical, statistical, and operations research techniques.
3. It stresses the behavioral impact of accounting information on the users.
4. It uses nonaccounting information—economic, environmental, and qualitative—to improve the relevance of management accounting data.
5. It merges economic and social goals and consequently draws the accountant into program budgets and ''performance'' auditing in not-for-profit organizations.
6. It relies on more frequent and heavier use of computers, leading to a centralization of information and the expected candidature of the management accountant for the job of the ''information manager'' having overall responsibility of this resource.

This enlargement of the scope of cost accounting into management accounting leads to the problem of the modern education of management accountants, which can be resolved by an exposure of students to either a proliferation of courses in the computer, quantitative, and behavioral sciences, or to an integrated multidisciplinary approach as advocated in this book. Following the same line of reasoning, the 1972 AAA Committee on Courses in Managerial Accounting made the following appropriate assumptions:

1. The role of managerial accounting encompasses the entire formalized information function of an organization.
2. The accountant is the best candidate for a manager of this information system.
3. Managerial accounting should be developed around a framework for the information-wide perspective in the analysis and design of the information function.
4. Managerial accounting should integrate material from the computer, the quantitative, and the behavioral sciences areas.
5. Management accounting should continue the traditional emphasis on problems while using more sophisticated approaches to problem solving.[8]

In brief, management accounting should go beyond cost accounting and integrate various material from organization theory, behavioral sciences, information theory, and so on, in a multidisciplinary approach aimed at facilitating the production of information for internal decision making. In spite of these diversifications in the background of management accountants, they remain professionals, as evidenced by the growing popularity of the Certificate in Management Accounting program of the National Association of Accountants (NAA; also NA). The following excerpt from a brochure issued by the NAA highlights the new scope of the management accountant's activities:

More and more people—inside the business world and out—realize the significant changes which have been taking place for years in accounting and the role of the accountant in business. No longer is he simply a recorder of business history. He now plays a dynamic role in making business decisions, in future planning and in almost every aspect of business operations. This new accountant is called a Management Accountant and he sits with top management because his responsibility is developing, producing and analyzing information to help management make sound decisions. Many management accountants make their way to top management positions.

In response to the needs of business and at the request of many in the academic community, the National Association of Accountants has established a program to recognize professional competence in this field—a program leading to the Certificate in Management Accounting [CMA].

The CMA program requires candidates to pass a series of uniform examinations and meet specific educational and professional standards to qualify for and maintain the Certificate in Management Accounting. NA has established the Institute of Management Accounting to administer the program, conduct the examinations and grant certificates to those who qualify.

The objectives of the program are threefold:

1. to establish management accounting as a recognized profession by identifying the role of the management accountant and the underlying body of knowledge, and by outlining a course of study by which such knowledge, can be acquired;

2. to foster higher educational standards in the field of management;

3. to assist employers, educators and students by establishing objective measurement of an individual's knowledge and competence in field of management accounting.

Those management accountants are to occupy important positions in organizations and therefore have to abide by high ethical standards. Accordingly the NAA has promulgated the following ethical standards for management accountants:

Competence

Management accountants have a responsibility to:

- Maintain an appropriate level of professional competence by ongoing development of their knowledge and skills.

- Perform their professional duties in accordance with relevant laws, regulations, and technical standards.

- Prepare complete and clear reports and recommendations after appropriate analyses of relevant and reliable information.

Confidentiality

Management accountants have a responsibility to:

- Refrain from disclosing confidential information acquired in the course of their work except when authorized, unless legally obligated to do so.

- Inform subordinates as appropriate regarding the confidentiality of information acquired in the course of their work and monitor their activities to assure the maintenance of the confidentiality.

- Refrain from using or appearing to use confidential information acquired in the course of their work for unethical or illegal advantage either personally or through third parties.

Integrity

Management accountants have a responsibility to:

- Avoid actual or apparent conflicts of interest and advise all appropriate parties of any potential conflict.
- Refrain from engaging in any activity that would prejudice their ability to carry out their duties ethically.
- Refuse any gift, favor, or hospitality that would influence or would appear to influence their actions.
- Refrain from either actively or passively subverting the attainment of the organization's legitimate and ethical objectives.
- Recognize and communicate professional limitations or other constraints that would preclude responsible judgment or successful performance of an activity.
- Communicate unfavorable as well as favorable information and professional judgments or opinions.
- Refrain from engaging in or supporting any activity that would discredit the profession.

Objectivity

Management accountants have a responsibility to:

- Communicate information fairly and objectively.
- Disclose fully all relevant information that could reasonably be expected to influence an intended user's understanding of the reports, comments, and recommendations presented.[9]

MANAGEMENT ACCOUNTING THEORY

Management accounting is generally understood as a process or as referring to the use of techniques. For example, the 1958 Committee on Management Accounting defines it as "the application of appropriate techniques and concepts in processing the historical and projected economic data of an entity to assist management in establishing a plan for reasonable economic objectives, and in the making of rational decisions with a view towards achieving these objectives."[10] Similarly the emergent conceptual framework of management accounting started by the National Association of Accountants defines it as

the process of identification, measurement, accumulation, analysis, preparation, interpretation and communication of financial information used by management to plan, evaluate, and control within an organization and to assure appropriate use of and accountability for its resources. Management accounting also comprises the preparation of financial reports for nonmanagement groups such as shareholders, creditors, regulatory agencies, and tax authorities.[11]

Those techniques are further explicated as follows:

Identification—the recognition and evaluation of business transactions and other economic events for appropriate accounting action.

Measurement—the quantification, including estimates, of business transactions or other economic events that have occurred or may occur.

Accumulation—the disciplined and consistent approach to recording and classifying appropriate business transactions and other economic events.

Analysis—the determination of the reasons for, and the relationships of, the reported activity with other economic events and circumstances.

Preparation and Interpretation—the meaningful coordination of accounting and/or planning data to satisfy a need for information, presented in a logical format, and, if appropriate, including the conclusions drawn from those data.

Communication—the reporting of pertinent information to management and others for internal and external uses.

Plan—to gain an understanding of expected business transactions and other economic events and their impact on the organization.

Evaluate—to judge the implications of various past and/or future events.

Control—to ensure the integrity of financial information concerning an organization's activities or its resources.

Assure accountability—to implement the system of reporting that is closely aligned to organizational responsibilities and that contributes to the effective measurement of management performance.[12]

A generally accepted definition of a theory, as it could apply to management accounting, is that a theory represents the coherent set of hypothetical, conceptual, and pragmatic principles for a field of inquiry. Accordingly, management accounting theory may be defined as a frame of reference in the form of a set of postulates and/or principles from different disciplines by which management accounting techniques are evaluated. The task of justifying the existence of a management accounting theory lies in the definition of appropriate postulates and principles. Given the differences in the objectives between management accounting and financial accounting, the postulates of financial accounting, with some exceptions, do not hold true for management accounting. In fact, the 1961 AAA Management Accounting Committee, charged with determining the relevance of financial accounting concepts to management accounting, concluded that

1. the concepts underlying internal reporting differ in several important respects from those of external public reporting;
2. these differences are due to differences in the objectives of both areas; and
3. it is justified to develop a separate body of concepts applicable to internal reporting.[13]

There is a need, then, for the accounting profession to develop a conceptual framework in management accounting to guide the development and use of techniques. Similar to financial accounting, such a framework would include the following elements:

1. The *objectives* of management accounting as the first and important step for the development of the elements of the conceptual framework for management accounting.
2. *Qualitative characteristics* to be met as essential attributes of management accounting information.
3. *Management accounting concepts* as the foundation for the body of knowledge contained within the conceptual framework.
4. *Management accounting techniques* and procedures that constitute the internal accounting systems.

Although these elements and the total integrated framework have not yet been formalized through a deductive reasoning process, they do exist in the literature as separate attempts to resolve these issues. Each of the proposed elements of management accounting will be examined next.

Objectives of Management Accounting

The objectives of management accounting are the first and essential step to the formulation of a management accounting theory. Then, the management accounting concepts will be true because they will be based on accepted objectives. In spite of the importance of management accounting objectives, there has never been a formal attempt by the profession to accomplish such a task. One noticeable exception, which may serve as de facto objectives of management accounting, was provided by the 1972 AAA Committee on Courses in Managerial Accounting. Four objectives were presented:

A. Management accounting should be related to the planning functions of the managers. This involves:
    1. Goal identification.
    2. Planning for optimal resource flows and their measurement.
B. Management accounting should be related to organizational problem areas. This includes:
    1. Relating the structure of the firm to its goals.
    2. Installing and maintaining an effective communication and reporting system.
    3. Measuring existing resource uses, discovering exceptional performance, and identifying causal factors of such exceptions.
C. Management accounting should be related to the management control function. This includes:
    1. Determining economic characteristics of appropriate performance areas that are significant in terms of overall goals.

2. Aiding to motivate desirable individual performances through a realistic communication of performance information in relation to goals.

3. Highlighting performance measures indicating goal incongruity within identifiable performance and responsibility areas.

D. Management accounting should be related to operating systems management, by function, product, project, or other segmentation of operations. This involves:

1. Measurement of relevant cost input and/or revenue or statistical measures of outputs.

2. Communication of appropriate data, of essentially economic character, to critical personnel on a timely basis.[14]

The NA's emerging conceptual framework defines the objectives of management accounting as well as management accountants in terms of providing information and participating in the management process. More specifically the true objectives are defined as follows:

Providing Information

Management accountants select and provide, to all levels of management, information needed for:

a. planning, evaluating, and controlling operations;

b. safeguarding the organization's assets; and

c. communicating with interested parties outside the organization, such as shareholders and regulatory bodies.

Participating in the Management Process

Management accountants at appropriate levels are involved actively in the process of managing the entity. This process includes making strategic, tactical, and operating decisions and helping to coordinate the efforts of the entire organization. The management accountant participates, as part of management, in assuring that the organization operates as a unified whole in its long-run, intermediate, and short-run best interests.[15]

While these objectives reflect some of the priorities facing management accounting, they do not necessarily represent all the facets of the environment of management accounting. A formal study for the objectives of accounting is a definite must for the profession.

Qualitative Characteristics of Management Accounting Information

Management accounting information should have certain desirable properties so that benefits are achievable. The 1969 AAA Committee on Managerial Decision Models explored the application to internal reporting of the standards of relevance, verifiability, freedom from bias, and quantifiability.[16] These standards for accounting information were suggested in the AAA Statement of Basic Ac-

counting Theory.[17] This effort was pursued by the 1974 AAA Committee on
Concepts and Standards—Internal Planning and Control.[18] The Committee of-
fered the following closely related properties as representatives of the benefits
information or information systems:

1. Relevance/mutuality of objectives
2. Accuracy/precision/reliability
3. Consistency/comparability/uniformity
4. Verifiability/objectivity/neutrality/traceability
5. Aggregation
6. Flexibility/adaptability
7. Timeliness
8. Understandability/acceptability/motivation/fairness.[19]

The findings of the Committee are discussed next.

1. *Relevance/mutuality of objectives*. Relevant information is that which bears
upon or is useful to "the action it is designed to facilitate or the result it is
desired to produce."[20] For example, given different alternatives, the relevant
costs and revenues are those expected costs and revenues that will be different
for at least one of the alternatives. Historical costs may be only the basis for
estimating expected future costs.

Relevance depends on the structure of the objective function. In other words,
relevant information is the information on any variables in the user's objective
function and must be very close to the definition implicit in the objective function.
Relevance is a qualitative rather than a quantitative characteristic in the sense
that information is either relevant or not.

Finally, relevance depends on the particular user receiving the information
and on his or her particular decision. Some variables may be relevant to one
user and not to others, and to one type of decision and not to others.

Mutuality of objectives refers to the consistency and congruency of the goals
of the information users with those established by top management for the whole
organization. The information provided by the internal reporting system may
contribute to internal goal congruency if the signals of success or failure have
the same meaning for both the total organization and its different segments. The
mutuality of objectives applies also to the management accountants or the "internal information processors." Their goals should be consistent with the organizational goals.

2. *Accuracy/precision/reliability*. These properties are statistically interrelated
in the sense that the notion of accuracy is statistically expressed by the concepts
of precision and reliability. The specification of precision requires the specification of reliability, and vice versa.[21] R. M. Cyert and H. J. Davidson define
these concepts as follows: "reliability is commonly used to describe the chances
that a confidence interval will contain the true value being estimated . . . precision

is often used in describing the interval about a sample estimate.''[22] While it is generally impossible to reach 100 percent accuracy, it is advisable to specify upper and lower bounds within which accuracy may be an effective property of management accounting information.

3. *Consistency/comparability/uniformity*. Consistency refers to the continued use of the same rules and procedures by the same firm over time, leading to comparability of its own statements with each other for one year to another. Uniformity refers to the use of similar rules by different firms. Consistency, uniformity, and the ensuing comparability are considered desirable criteria for financial accounting. Their relevance to management accounting differs between long-term and short-term decisions. A long-range planning decision relies on diverse, unstructered information and nonrepetitive situations, and it may be unduly hampered by an internal accounting system stressing consistency/comparability/uniformity. However, the areas of short-run planning and performance control rely more on carefully structured information and repetitive situations, and lend themselves to an internal accounting system stressing consistency/comparability/uniformity.

4. *Verifiability/objectivity/neutrality/traceability*. Verifiability and objectivity refer to measurements that can be duplicated by independent measurers using the same measurement methods. It is usually operationally measured by the dispersion of the data in terms of the variance of the data. If the measurement rules are well-specified, the verifiability of the measurement may be accomplished through a reconstruction of the initial measurement process and on the basis of evidential documents referred to as the audit trail. Traceability refers to the availability of such an audit trail. Finally, neutrality refers to the impartiality of the data in terms of its impact on different groups. A personal interest of the measurer in the data will not likely lead to neutral measurements. The degree of verifiability/objectivity/traceability of the data generated for management accounting is not as pronounced as when applied to financial accounting. However, neutrality of the information is a desirable objective, especially when the data are used for information evaluation or as a basis for distributing resources or settling claims.

5. *Aggregation*. This refers to the process of reducing the volume of data. A loss of identifiability or information is generally attributed to the process of aggregation, which may be compensated by cost savings in accounting for the information. An optimal level of aggregation is difficult to specify for either financial or management accounting. For financial accounting, the preparation of standard financial statements according to well-defined rules has led to a tendency to aggregate the information at an early stage of information processing. For management accounting, the lack of homogeneity in the reports, the flexibility in the choice of rules for preparing these reports, and the objective to meet a variety of information needs argue in favor of a management accounting system with less aggregated data, but that takes into account the user's limitations in handling voluminous data.

6. *Flexibility/adaptability*. Flexibility refers to the degree to which data may be the basis for several types of information and reports. It depends on both the classification used for the data base into definite categories and the level of aggregation used in each of the categories. For example, purchase data may be classified under the following categories: (1) by individual product or service, (2) by individual purchaser, (3) by supplier, and so on. These data may be aggregated under the following categories: (1) by transaction, (2) by day, (3) by month, and so on.

Adaptability refers to the extent to which information derived from the data base may be tailored to, or harmonized with, the decision processes of the firm. The adaptability of an accounting system requires not only the presence of flexibility, but also an explicit process of harmonizing it with the decision process. The Committee suggested the following procedures for harmonizing:

Such harmonizing is often accomplished iteratively through an understanding of the planning and control process, representing the latter in terms of information parameters and specifying the aggregation rules to be used in going from data base to information and analyzing the impact of such information on the planning processes.[23]

Again, given the lack of homogeneity in the management accounting reports, the large number of these reports and the desire to meet various decision needs, management accounting requires higher levels of flexibility and adaptability than financial accounting.

7. *Timeliness*. Timeliness refers to the age of the information. It has two components: interval and delay. Interval is the period of time elapsing between the preparation of two successive reports. Delay is the period of time necessary to process the data, prepare the reports, and distribute them. Timeliness is also related to the concept of real time. Wayne Boutell provides the following definition: "It [real time] refers to the time in which information is received by the particular decision maker. If the information is received in sufficient time for a decision to be made without a penalty for delay, the information is said to be received in real time."[24] Although timeliness is a uniquely desirable property of management accounting information, it is affected by cost considerations and may conflict with other criteria, such as accuracy.

8. *Understandability/acceptability/motivation/fairness*. This refers to the extent to which the user is able to use the information. Understandability refers to the ability of the user to ascertain the message transmitted. Acceptability is the recognition by the user that the problem specification and measurement criteria have been met. Fairness refers to the neutrality of the information as defined earlier. Finally, motivation refers to the attempt to secure goal congruences between the user and the organization. In brief, management accounting information should be understandable, acceptable, fair to the user, and a motivation to the user to perform in the desired manner.

Management Accounting Concepts

Management accounting concepts based on both the objectives and qualitative characteristics of management accounting would constitute the basic foundation for a management accounting conceptual framework. Although the development and formalization of a management accounting conceptual framework remains to be accomplished, the literature contains references to certain identifiable management accounting concepts. For example, the 1972 AAA Committee on Courses in Managerial Accounting identified measurement, communication, information, system, planning, feedback, control, and cost behavior as some of the management accounting concepts "which represent a necessary, if not minimum, foundation for the body of knowledge contained within the structure."[25] Accordingly, each of these concepts will be explained next.

1. Applied to accounting, *measurement* has been defined as "an assignment of numerals to an entity's past, present, or future economic phenomena, on the basis of past or present observation and according to rules."[26] This concept is very essential to management accounting.

2. As defined by Claude Shannon and Warren Weaver, *communication* encompasses "the procedures by means of which one mechanism affects another mechanism."[27]

3. *Information* represents significant data upon which action is based. It refers to those data that reduce the uncertainty on the part of the user. Thus, data produced by management accounting should be evaluated in terms of their informational content. Although not exhaustive, management accounting information includes the following categories:

a. financial information resulting from the flow of financial resources within the organization,

b. production information resulting from the physical flow of resources within the organization,

c. personnel information resulting from the flow of people within the organization, and

d. marketing information resulting from the interaction with the market for the organization's products.

4. *System* refers to an entity consisting of two or more interacting components or subsystems intended to achieve a goal. Management accounting is generally a subsystem of the accounting information system, which is itself a subsystem of the total management information system within the organization. The interaction of the management accounting system with all the other systems within the organization, and especially the integration of all these systems, is essential for an efficient functioning of the organization. A management accounting system may be defined as *the set of human and capital resources within an organization that is responsible for the production and dissemination of information deemed relevant for internal decision making.*

5. *Planning* refers to the management function of setting objectives, establishing policies, and choosing means of accomplishment. Planning may be practiced at different levels in the organization, from strategic to operational, and may have behavioral implications.

6. *Feedback* refers to the output of a process that returns to become an input to the process in order to initiate control. It is basically a revision of the planning process to accommodate new environmental events.

7. *Control* refers to monitoring and evaluating of performance to determine the degree of conformance of actions to plans. Ideally, planning precedes control, which is followed by a feedback corrective action or a feedforward preventive action.

8. *Cost Behavior:* cost results from the use of an asset for the generation of revenues. The identification, classification, and estimation of costs is essential to any evaluation of courses of action.

Although not exhaustive, this list represents concepts that are representative of those foundation components essential to a grasp of the management accounting process. This is very much in line with the NA's definition of the responsibilities of a management accountant:

1. *Planning.* Quantifying and interpreting the effects on the organization of planned transactions and other economic events. The planning responsibility, which includes strategic, tactical, and operating aspects, requires that the accountant provide quantitative historical and prospective information to facilitate planning. It includes participation in developing the planning system, setting obtainable goals, and choosing appropriate means of monitoring the progress toward the goals.

2. *Evaluating.* Judging implications of historical and expected events and helping to choose the optimum course of action. Evaluating includes translating data into trends and relationships. Management accountants must communicate effectively and promptly the conclusions derived from the analyses.

3. *Controlling.* Assuring the integrity of financial information concerning an organization's activities and resources; monitoring and measuring performance and inducing any corrective actions required to return the activity to its intended course. Management accountants provide information to executives operating in functional areas who can make use of it to achieve desirable performance.

4. *Assuring accountability of resources.* Implementing a system of reporting that is aligned with organizational responsibilities. This reporting system will contribute to the effective use of resources and measurement of management performance. The transmission of management's goals and objectives throughout the organization in the form of assigned responsibilities is a basis for identifying accountability. Management accountants must provide an accounting and reporting system that will accumulate and report appropriate revenues, expenses, assets, liabilities, and related quantitative information to managers. Managers then will have better control over these elements.

5. *External reporting.* Preparing financial reports based on generally accepted accounting principles, or other appropriate bases, for nonmanagement groups such as shareholders, creditors, regulatory agencies, and tax authorities. Management accountants should

participate in the process of developing the accounting principles that underlie external reporting.[28]

Management Accounting Techniques

Management accounting techniques should be derived and supported by the management accounting conceptual framework. Given the absence of such a framework, there is no consensus on a list of management accounting techniques. Most management accounting textbooks include standard cost accounting techniques and only a few attempts at introducing behavioral and/or quantitative considerations in separate chapters. What is needed is a structure that will allow an integration of accounting, organizational, behavioral, quantitative, and other techniques of relevance to internal decision making. The AAA Report of the Committee on Courses in Managerial Accounting proposes such a structure:

Introductory Material

    Systems theory and accounting

    Communications, measurement, and information concepts

    Criteria development

    Feedback and control mechanisms

    Information systems

    Accounting for management planning and control

    Cost concepts and techniques

Cost Determination for Assets

    Job order and process costing

    Standard costing system

    Direct versus absorption costing

    By-product and joint product costing

    Cost allocation practices

    Accounting for human resources

Planning

    Strategic planning

    Continuous planning

    Investment decisions

    Comprehensive budgets

    Cost-volume-profit analysis

    Problems of alternative choice

Management Control

    Responsibility accounting

    Cost centers

      Financial performance centers

      Investment centers

      Centralized versus decentralized structures

      Concern for goal congruence

      Transfer pricing

      Evaluation methods

      Performance reporting

Operational Control

      Internal control

      Project control

      Inventory control[29]

Although not exhaustive, this list represents most of the techniques included in management accounting textbooks, but still fails to incorporate behavioral, organization, and decisional models essential to an adequate performance of a management accounting system of knowledge known as management accounting.

There is, however, no consensus on what the cost/managerial curriculum content should be, as evidenced by Exhibit 1.1. This is particularly due to the absence of a conceptual framework for management accounting. In addition, there is no consensus on what are the appropriate techniques for each of the management accounting topics included. W. B. Pollard used the following overhead variance analysis problem to illustrate the varieties of treatment existing in management accounting:[30]

Problem: The following information is available:

Budgeted production	9,000 units
Actual production	9,450 units
Standard DIRECT LABOR HOURS (DLHs) per unit	3
Actual DLHs (total)	28,000
Standard DLHs (total)　　(9450 * 3)	28,350
Actual FIXED OVERHEAD (FOH)	$56,700
Actual VARIABLE OVERHEAD (VOH)	$54,000
FOH Rate (per DLH)	$2
VOH Rate (per DLH)	$1

The partial analysis of the overhead variance is shown in Exhibit 1.2. The variety of treatments used in the major textbooks of the times is illustrated in Exhibit 1.3.

There is a very useful framework for relating management accounting topics. The framework, proposed by Professor Larry N. Bitner, is shown in Exhibit 1.4.[31] The framework makes three important distinctions (see page 26):

Exhibit 1.1

A Summary of Prior Studies of Cost/Managerial Curriculum Content (ranked lists of topics—maximum of 20 topics displayed)

	Deakin and Summers (1975)	Knight and Zook (1982)	Lander and Reinstein (1987)	Robinson and Barrett (1988)	VanZante (1988)
1.	Performance Evaluation	Preparation of Principal Statements	Internal Control and Accounting Systems	Job Order Costing	Cost Behavior
2.	Responsibility Accounting	CVP Relationships	Operational Budgeting	CVP Relationships	Computer Systems
3.	Internal Control	Current Asset Valuation	Standard Costs	Full Absorption Costing	Forecasting
4.	Tax Factors in Business Decisions	Liabilities Valuation	Capital Budgeting	Variable Costing	Financial Statement Analysis
5.	Profit Planning	Long-term Asset Valuation	Product Costing		Variance Analysis
6.	Cash Management	Equity Valuation	Cost Behavior and Variances	Standard Costs	Working Capital Management
7.	Organization Theory	Other Assets Valuation	Organizational Behavior	Process Costing	Financial Statement Preparation
8.	Information Systems Design	Cost Accumulation Systems	Cost Accumulation, General Accounting, Taxes	Flexible Budgets	Capital Budgeting
9.	Internal Reporting	Cost Control, Flexible Budgets, Standards	Inventories	Direct Costing	Information Content
10.	Forecasting	Short-term Budgeting	Segments and Decentralization	Budgeted Financial Statements	Segment Accounting
				Joint Costs	

Exhibit 1.1 (*continued*)

Deakin and Summers (1975)	Knight and Zook (1982)	Lander and Reinstein (1987)	Robinson and Barrett (1988)	VanZante (1988)
11. Accounting Principles Impact	Ratio Analysis	Economics and Government	Short-term Planning	Valuation Bases
12. Behavioral Implications	Disclosure Standards and Procedures	Quantitative Methods	Spoilage, Waste, Scrap	Ethical Considerations
13. Capital Budgeting	Internal Control	Cost Allocation	Responsibility Accounting	Long-term Financing
14. Systems Implementation	Working Capital Management	(Results summarized in these 13 categories)	Capital Budgeting	Motivation and Perception
15. Internal and Managerial Auditing	Long-term Financing		Return on Investment	Tax Regulations
16. Information Systems Administration	Long-run Forecasting and Planning		Common Costs in Performance Evaluation	Behavioral Implications
17. Divisional Reporting	Capital Budgeting		Overhead Control	Internal Audits
18. Information Economics	Mergers and Acquisitions		Divisional Performance	Microeconomic Theory
19. Computer Use in Decision-Making	Divisional Performance and Transfer Pricing		Transfer Pricing	Regulatory Bodies
20. Nonfinancial Measures of Performance	SEC		Residual Income	Organizational Theory

Source: Reprinted with permission from *Journal of Accounting Education* (Fall): 210–211, A. M. Novin, M. A. Pearson, and S. V. Senge, "Improving the Curriculum for Aspiring Management Accountants: The Practitioner's Point of View," copyright 1990, Pergamon Press plc.

Exhibit 1.2
Partial Analysis of Overhead Variances

VARIABLE OVERHEAD:

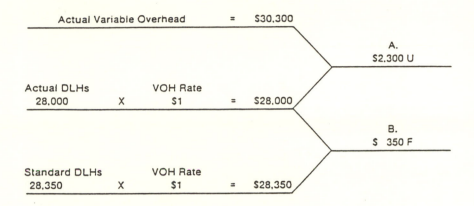

FIXED OVERHEAD:

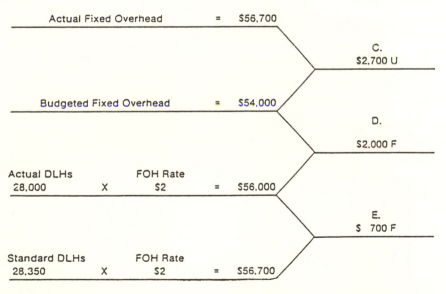

Source: Reprinted with permission from *Journal of Accounting Education* (Spring): 213, W. B. Pollard, "Teaching Standard Costs: A Look at Textbook Differences in Overhead Variance Analysis," Copyright 1986, Pergamon Press plc.

Exhibit 1.3
Overhead Variance Analysis—Comparison

	ASCH [1983]	BELKAOUI [1983] Model A	BELKAOUI [1983] Model B	BROCK and PALMER [1984]	CASHIN and POLIMENI [1981]	CHATFIELD and NEILSON [1983]
TWO-WAY	TWO-WAY	TWO-WAY	TWO-WAY	TWO-WAY	TWO-WAY	TWO-WAY
1.	None	Price A+C+D	Controllable A+B+C	OH Budget A+B+C	Controllable A+B+C	OH Budget A+B+C
2.	None	Efficiency B+E	Uncontrollable D+E	OH Volume D+E	Volume D+E	FOH Volume D+E
THREE-WAY	THREE-WAY	THREE-WAY	THREE-WAY	THREE-WAY	THREE-WAY	THREE-WAY
1.	None	Spending A+C	Spending A+C	Spending A+C	Spending A+C	Combined OH Spending A+C
2.	None	Efficiency B+E	Efficiency B	Efficiency B	Efficiency B+E	VOH Efficiency B
3.	None	Idle Capacity D	Idle Capacity D+E	OH Volume D+E	Idle Capacity D	FOH Volume D+E
FOUR-WAY	FOUR-WAY	FOUR-WAY		FOUR-WAY	FOUR-WAY	FOUR-WAY
1.	VOH Expenditure A	Spending A+C		None	Spending A+C	VOH Spending A
2.	VOH Efficiency B	VOH Efficiency B		None	VOH Efficiency B	VOH Efficiency B
3.	FOH Expenditure C	Idle Capacity D		None	Idle Capacity D	FOH Spending C
4.	FOH Volume D+E	FOH Efficiency E		None	FOH Efficiency E	FOH Volume D+E

20

KILLOUGH and LEININGER [1984]	LOUDERBACK and HIRSCH [1982]	MATZ and USRY [1984]	MORIARITY and ALLEN [1984]	MORSE [1981]
TWO-WAY	**TWO-WAY**	**TWO-WAY**	**TWO-WAY**	**TWO-WAY**
1. Controllable A+B+C	None	Controllable A+B+C	None	OH Budget A+B+C
2. Volume D+E	None	Volume D+E	None	OH Volume D+E
THREE-WAY	**THREE-WAY**	**THREE-WAY**	**THREE-WAY**	**THREE-WAY**
1. Spending A+C	Spending A+C	Spending A+C	Combined Price A+C	OH Spending A+C
2. Efficiency B	Efficiency B	Efficiency B+E	VOH Quantity B	OH Efficiency B
3. Volume D+E	Application D+E	Idle Capacity D	Volume (Denominator) D+E	OH Volume D+E
FOUR-WAY	**FOUR-WAY**	**FOUR-WAY**	**FOUR-WAY**	**FOUR-WAY**
1. VOH Spending A	VOH Price A	Spending A+C	VOH Price A	VOH Spending A
2. Efficiency B	VOH Efficiency B	VOH Efficiency B	VOH Quantity B	VOH Efficiency B
3. FOH Spending C	FOH Budget C	Idle Capacity D	FOH Price C	FOH Budget C
4. Volume D+E	FOH Application D+E	FOH Efficiency E	Volume (Denominator) D+E	FOH Volume D+E

Exhibit 1.3 (continued)

DEAKIN and MAHER [1984]	DOPUCH, BIRNBERG and DEMSKI [1982]	GRAY and RICKETTS [1983]	HARTLEY [1983]	HORNGREN [1982]
TWO-WAY	**TWO-WAY**	**TWO-WAY**	**TWO-WAY**	**TWO-WAY**
1. None	None	Budget $A+B+C$	Controllable $A+B+C$	Flexible Budget $A+B+C$
2. None	None	Volume $D+E$	Noncontrollable $D+E$	Production Volume $D+E$
THREE-WAY	**THREE-WAY**	**THREE-WAY**	**THREE-WAY**	**THREE-WAY**
1. None	Price $A+C$	Spending $A+C$	Spending $A+C$	Price (Spending) $A+C$
2. None	Quantity B	Efficiency B	Efficiency B	Efficiency B
3. None	Volume $D+E$	Volume $D+E$	Noncontrollable $D+E$	Production Volume $D+E$
FOUR-WAY	**FOUR-WAY**	**FOUR-WAY**	**FOUR-WAY**	**FOUR-WAY**
1. VOH Price A	None	None	VOH Spending A	Price (Spending) A
2. Efficiency B	None	None	VOH Efficiency B	Efficiency B
3. FOH Price C	None	None	FOH Spending C	Budget C
4. Production Volume $D+E$	None	None	Noncontrollable $D+E$	Production Volume $D+E$

	MOST and LEWIS [1982]	RAYBURN [1983]	SCHMIEDICKE and NAGY [1983]	SHILLINGLAW [1982]	WALKER [1982]
TWO-WAY					
1.	Spending A+B+C	Controllable A+B+C	Budget A+B+C	Spending A+B+C	None
2.	Volume D+E	Volume D+E	Volume D+E	Volume D+E	None
THREE-WAY					
1.	Spending A+C	OH Spending A+C	Budget (Spending) A+C	Spending A+C	None
2.	Efficiency B+E	VOH Efficiency B	Efficiency B+E	Labor Efficiency B	None
3.	Volume D	Volume D+E	Capacity D	Volume D+E	None
FOUR-WAY					
1.	None	VOH Spending A	None	None	VOH Expenditure A
2.	None	VOH Efficiency B	None	None	VOH Efficiency B
3.	None	FOH Spending C	None	None	FOH Expenditure C
4.	None	Volume D+E	None	None	FOH Volume D+E

Source: Reprinted with permission from *Journal of Accounting Education* (Spring): 214–217, W. B. Pollard, "Teaching Standard Costs: A Look at Textbook Differences in Overhead Variance Analysis," Copyright 1986, Pergamon Press plc.

Exhibit 1.4
Revised Framework for Relating Management Accounting Topics

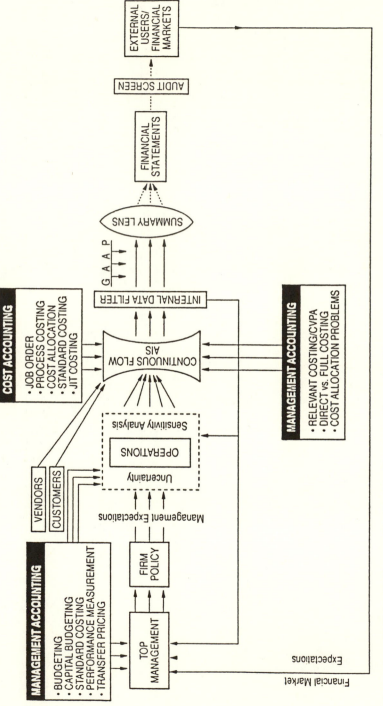

Source: Larry N. Bitner, "A Framework for Teaching Management Accounting," *Issues in Accounting Education* (Spring 1991): 118. Reprinted with permission.

24

Exhibit 1.5
Tentative Management Accounting Conceptual Framework

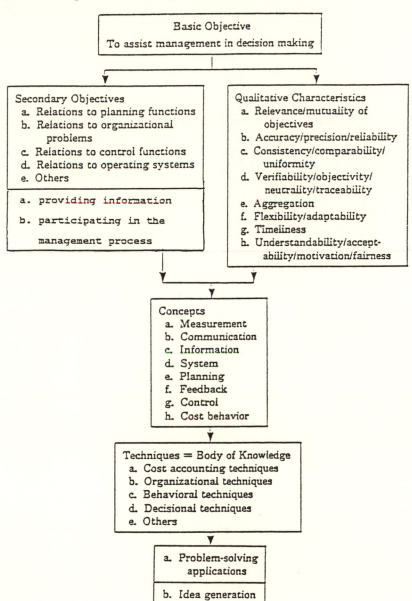

1. Management and cost accounting topics are differentiated following R. N. Anthony's distinctions between the themes of the two subdisciplines: the primary theme of cost accounting is to measure full cost while the pricing theme of management accounting is different purposes.[32]

2. The accounting information system (AIS) pulsator is characterized by continuous flow dimensions, including nonfinancial and external data.

3. The data for internal use are filtered out before any GAAP influences are introduced.

CONCLUSIONS

Management accounting has its foundations in the discipline of accounting, although it recognizes the potential benefits of borrowing relevant techniques from other disciplines. It expanded from its limited scope of cost accounting to a multidisciplined integrated field aimed at assisting management in decision making. Although generally perceived as a set of techniques, management accounting includes most of the components of a *conceptual framework*. Such a management accounting conceptual framework is shown in Exhibit 1.5. From a basic objective that is to assist management in decision making are derived both secondary objectives and qualitative characteristics of management accounting. The management accounting concepts that constitute the foundation components essential to an understanding of the management accounting techniques or body of knowledge rest on their conformance to both the objectives and qualitative characteristics of management accounting. Because of the lack of consensus on these components, the conceptual framework presented in Exhibit 1.5 is only tentative before a formalization by the accounting profession. What must be retained from this exercise is that *management accounting is, first, an accounting subsystem and, second, may be fit in an "emerging" theoretical structure.*

NOTES

1. American Accounting Association (AAA), Committee on Management Accounting, "Report of the 1958 Committee on Management Accounting," *The Accounting Review* (April 1959): 210.

2. William Paton, *Essentials of Accounting* (New York: Macmillan 1949), p. 2.

3. American Accounting Association, *A Statement of Basic Accounting Theory* (Evanston, Ill.: American Accounting Association, 1966), p. 1.

4. C. T. Horngren and G. Foster, *Cost Accounting: A Managerial Emphasis*, 7th ed. (Englewood Cliffs, NJ: Prentice-Hall, 1991).

5. Vergil Boyd and Dale Taylor, "The Magic Words—Managerial Accounting," *The Accounting Review* (January 1961): 210.

6. R. G. Bassett, "Management Accounting Defined," *The Cost Accountant* (October 1962): 386.

7. James S. Earley, "Recent Developments in Cost Accounting and the Marginal Analysis," *The Journal of Political Economy* (June 1955): 299.

8. AAA Committee on Courses in Managerial Accounting, "Report of the Committee on Courses in Managerial Accounting," *The Accounting Review*, Supplement to Vol. 47 (1972): 2.

9. National Association of Accountants; *Standards of Ethical Conduct for Management Accountants* (New York: NA, June 1, 1983), pp. 1–2.

10. AAA Committee on Management Accounting, "Report of the 1958 Committee on Management Accounting," p. 210.

11. National Association of Accountants, *Definition of Management Accounting*, Statement Number 1A (New York: NA, March 18, 1981), p. 4.

12. Ibid, pp. 4–5.

13. AAA 1961 Committee on Management Accounting, "Report of the Management Accounting Committee," *The Accounting Review* (July 1962).

14. AAA Committee on Courses in Managerial Accounting, "Report of the Committee on Courses in Managerial Accounting," pp. 6–7.

15. National Association of Accountants (NAA; NA), *Objectives of Management Accounting, Statement on Management Accounting 1B* (NA, June 17, 1988), p. 2.

16. AAA Committee on Managerial Decision Models, "Report of the Committee on Managerial Decision Models," *The Accounting Review*, Supplement to Vol. 44 (1969): 47–58.

17. AAA, *Accounting Theory*, pp. 51–55.

18. AAA Committee on Concepts and Standards—Internal Planning and Control, "Report of the Committee on Concepts and Standards—Internal Planning and Control," *The Accounting Review*, Supplement to Vol. 49 (1974): 83.

19. Ibid., p. 83.

20. AAA, *Accounting Theory*, p. 9.

21. Richard M. Cyert and H. Justin Davidson, *Statistical Sampling for Accounting Information* (Englewood Cliffs, NJ: Prentice-Hall, 1962), p. 49.

22. Ibid.

23. AAA Committee on Concepts and Standards—Internal Planning and Control, "Report," p. 91.

24. Wayne S. Boutell, *Computer Oriented Business Systems* (New York: Prentice-Hall, 1968), p. 152.

25. AAA Committee on Concepts and Standards—Internal Planning and Control, "Report," p. 91.

26. AAA Committee on Foundations of Accounting Measurement, "Report of the Committee on Foundations of Accounting Measurement," *The Accounting Review*, Supplement to Vol. 46 (1971): 3.

27. Claude E. Shannon and Warren Weaver, *The Mathematical Theory of Communication* (Urbana, Ill.: University of Illinois Press, 1949), p. 95.

28. NAA, *Objectives of Management Accounting*, pp. 3–4.

29. AAA Committee on Courses in Managerial Accounting, "Report on Courses in Managerial Accounting," pp. 9–10.

30. W. B. Pollard, "Teaching Standard Costs: A Look at Textbook Differences in Overhead Variance Analysis," *Journal of Accounting Education* (Spring 1986): 212.

31. Larry N. Bitner, "A Framework for Teaching Management Accounting," *Issues in Accounting Education* (Spring 1991): 112–119.

32. R. N. Anthony, "Reminiscences About Management Accounting," *Journal of Management Accounting Research* (Fall 1989): 1–20.

REFERENCES

American Accounting Association. Committee on Courses in Managerial Accounting. "Report of the Committee on Courses in Managerial Accounting." *The Accounting Review*, Supplement to Vol. 47 (1972): 1–14.

———. Committee on the Future Structure, Content, and Scope of Accounting Education. "Future Accounting Education: Preparing for the Expanding Profession." *Issues in Accounting Education*, (Spring 1986): 168–195.

———. Committee on Management Accounting. "Report of the 1958 Committee on Management Accounting." *The Accounting Review* (April 1959).

———. Committee on Managerial Decision Models. "Report of the Committee on Managerial Decision Models." *The Accounting Review*, Supplement to Vol. 44 (1969): 43–77.

Boyd, Vergil, and Taylor, Dale. "The Magic Words—Managerial Accounting." *The Accounting Review* (January 1961): 105–111.

Bruns, W. J. Jr., and Kaplan, R. S. *Accounting and Management: Field Study Perspectives*. Boston: Harvard Business School Press, 1987.

Corman, E. J. "A Writing Program for Accounting Courses." *Journal of Accounting Education* (Fall 1986): 85–95.

Crossman, Paul T. "The Nature of Management Accounting." *The Accounting Review* (April 1958): 222–227.

Davidson, H. Justin, and Trueblood, Robert M. "Accounting for Decision Making." *The Accounting Review* (October 1961): 577–582.

Deakin, E. B., and Summers, E. J. "A Survey of Curriculum Topics Relevant to the Practice of Management Accounting." *The Accounting Review* (April 1975): 380–383.

DeMaris, E. J., and Copeland, B. R. "The Critical Need for Educational Standards in Management Accounting." *Corporate Accounting* (Winter 1984): 47–53.

Donbrovski, Willis J. "Managerial Accounting: A Frame of Reference." *Management Accounting* (August 1965).

Firmin, Peter A., and Linn, James J. "Information Systems and Managerial Accounting." *The Accounting Review* (January 1968): 75–82.

Godfrey, James T., and Prince, Thomas R. "The Accounting Model from an Information Systems Perspective." *The Accounting Review* (January 1971): 75–89.

Hirsch, M. L., and Collins, J. D. "An Integrated Approach to Communication Skills in an Accounting Curriculum." *Journal of Accounting Education* (Spring 1988): 15–31.

Johnson, H. T., and Kaplan, R. S. *Relevance Lost: The Rise and Fall of Management Accounting*. Boston: Harvard Business School Press, 1987.

Killough, Larry N. "Does Management Accounting Have a Theoretical Structure?" *Management Accounting* (April 1972).

Kircher, Paul. "Theory and Research in Management Accounting." *The Accounting Review* (January 1961): 43–45.

Knight, R. E. and Zook, D. R. "Controllers and CPAs Evaluate the Relevance of Educational Topics." *Management Accounting* (November 1982): 30–34.

Lander, G. R., and Reinstein, A. "Identifying a Common Body of Knowledge for Management Accounting." *Issues in Accounting Education* (Fall 1987): 264–280.

May, G. S., and Arevalo, C. "Integrating Effective Writing Skills in the Accounting Curriculum." *Journal of Accounting Education* (Spring 1983): 119–126.

Parks, S. B. "Bridging the Gap." *Management Accounting* (March 1987): 56.

Pollard, W. B. "Teaching Standard Costs: A Look at Textbook Differences in Overhead Variance Analysis." *Journal of Accounting Education* (Spring 1986): 211–220.

Porter, G. L., and Akers, M. D. "In Defense of Management Accounting." *Management Accounting* (November 1987): 58–62.

Reider, B., and Saunders, G. "Management Accounting Education: A Defense of Criticisms." *Accounting Horizons* (December 1988): 58–62.

Robinson, M. A., and Barrett, M. E. "The Content of Management Accounting Curricula." *The Accounting Educators' Journal* (Spring 1988): 49–60.

Senge, S. V. "The CPA in Industry: Meeting the Relevance Challenge." *The Ohio CPA Journal* (Autumn 1987): 5–10.

Shenkin, William G.; Welsh, A.; and Bear, James A., Jr. "Thomas Jefferson: Management Accountant." *The Journal of Accountancy* (April 1972).

Singer, Frank A. "Management Accounting." *The Accounting Review* (January 1961): 112–118.

2

THE PROBLEM AND
DECISIONAL FOUNDATIONS

A fundamental objective of management accounting is to facilitate and support all the aspects of an organization's decision making. To accomplish this objective, management accountants should be aware of the kinds and levels of problems and decisions involved in order to identify those particular areas where management accounting techniques and information would be most relevant and useful. For this purpose, different conceptual frameworks for viewing problems, decisions, and decision systems have been proposed in the management, accounting, and information systems literature. They provide a good basis for viewing the types of problems, decisions and decision systems, the types of information needed, and the useful role of management accounting.

PROBLEM FOUNDATIONS

It is a fact that executives spend a great proportion of their time defining, formulating, classifying, and solving problems.[1] The concept of a problem in business, management accounting, or any other context lends itself to three major phases—problem definition, problem formulation, and problem classification—which precede the problem solving. The way executives approach each of these phases can substantially affect information processing, decision making, and behavior.[2] A moderating effect on this impact is management accounting playing a crucial role of facilitator by providing the right information needed for the execution of each of the three stages.

Problem Definition

The definition of a problem can be subjective as the way an individual interprets a problem is a direct function of his or her knowledge[3] and the characteristics of the specific context.[4] Yet, a construct characteristic in the definition of a problem is the existence of a discrepancy or gap between an individual's conception of current reality and a desired state of reality.[5] G. P. Agre provided a five-part statement of the conditions implied when a problem is asserted to exist when someone:

1. Is or was conscious of some relevant and detectable situation or object or of something he created, or for plausible reasons believes or believed that it exists or existed;

2. Judged that situation or object to be in some manner undesirable, and undesirable enough that it should be changed into something at least less undesirable, or would have judged it so if he were aware of the situation, or posed some situation with the expectation that it be altered or completed in a desired manner;

3. Judged that it is, was, or would be at least somewhat difficult for himself or for some other person to solve or to define;

4. Believes or believed that the available evidence makes it possible that the situation is solvable, or that it is similar to problems that have been solved in the past; and

5. Believes or believed that it is appropriate to use the concepts of solvability, solving, and solution in considering that situation.[6]

Whether the problem is a discrepancy between conception of reality or a result of the five above conditions, its definition depends on the information role of management accounting. Management accounting is vital to the proper definition of the conceptions of reality and to a signaling of the discrepancy. For example, variance analysis, management by exception, and responsibility accounting are some of the tools that can signal the presence of discrepancies or gaps indicative of a problem.

Problem Foundation

Either to recognize or formulate a problem requires a consideration or a sequential adjustment of the constraints of the problem.[7] W. R. Reitman refers specifically to the "open constraints" (i.e., attributes of a problem that can be specified) and "closed constraints" (specified attributes).[8] As stated by R. N. Taylor, "constraints represent the extent to which the problem is defined or specified and problem reformulation takes place as constraints are adjusted."[9] These constraints are assumed to arise from decision environments characterized by uncertainty, complexity, and conflict.[10] To cope with these types of decision environments, four strategies are suggested:

1. To determine the boundaries of the problem

2. To examine the changes in the decision environment (or decision maker) that may have caused the problem

3. To decompose complex problems into subproblems, and

4. To focus on the controllable components of a decision situation.[11]

Exhibit 2.1
Decision Strategies for Reducing Complexity in Problem Diagnosis and Formulation (using categories suggested by MacCrimmon and Taylor)

a. *Determining Problem Boundaries*
  Explicit Boundary Clarification   Kepner and Tregoe
  Function Expansion   Nadler
  Assumptional Analysis   Mitroff, Emshoff and Kilmann

b. *Examining Changes*
  Focusing on Changes   Kepner and Tregoe

c. *Factoring Into Subproblems*
  Means-Ends Analysis   Newell, Shaw and Simon
  Morphological Analysis   Hall
  Attribute Listing   Rickards
  Input-Output Analysis   Hall

d. *Focusing on the Controllable Components*
  Working Forward, Working Backward   Feldman and Kanter;   Polya
  Planning Process   Bourne *et al.*
  Mixed Scanning   Etzioni
  Selective Focusing   Shull *et al.*

Source: Reprinted by permission of R. J. Volkema, "Problem Formulation in Planning and Design," *Management Science*, 29, no. 6 (June 1983): 643. Copyright 1983 The Institute of Management Sciences.

Exhibit 2.1 identifies some of the decision strategies for reducing complexity in problem diagnosis and formulation. A four-step strategy is also suggested by R. H. Kilmann and I. I. Mitroff as follows:

1. Formulate several, if not many, different definitions of the problem definition.

2. Debate these different definitions in order to examine critically their underlying assumptions, implications, and possible consequences.

3. Develop an integrated or synthesized problem definition by emphasizing the strengths or advantages of each problem definition while minimizing the weaknesses or disadvantages.

4. Include those persons in (1), (2), and (3) who are experiencing the problem, who have the expertise to define problems in various substantive domains, whose commitment to the problem definition and resulting change program will be necessary in order for that program to be implemented successfully, and who are expected to be affected by the outcomes of any change program attempting to solve or manage the felt problem.[12]

This strategy is in fact based on the philosophy of science and inquiring systems that examine the alternative ways of inquiring into the nature of human phenomena. As stated by Kilmann and Mitroff:

These various guidelines are founded on the philosophy of science, inquiring systems which examine the alternative ways of inquiring into the nature of human phenomena. Specifically, (1) above is derived from the Kantian Inquiring System, where the objective is to provide the "decision maker" with at least two different views of the problem situation; (2) is rooted in the Hegelian Inquiring System, emphasizing that a debate among the two most opposing views of a problem is necessary in order to uncover their underlying assumptions, (3) is attempting to foster the Singerian-Churchmanian Inquiring System which seeks to apply a systems approach in synthesizing opposing viewpoints. However, (4) is supported by the literature on participative management, and the need to generate valid information, free of choice, and commitment in order to bring about effective problem solving and change efforts.[13]

All the strategies outlined in Exhibit 2.1 and above require the input of management accounting. The role of management accounting is to provide the information needed for the identification of the constraints of the problem and for the implementation of the strategies outlined.

The above discussion focused on the strategies that may be used for a recognition and formulation of a decision problem but do not provide an overall framework of the recognition process that can be helpful for the conduct of management accounting. Such a framework has been proposed by Cowan[14] and is shown in Exhibit 2.2. It shows that the problem recognition process contains three general stages: gestation/latency, categorization, and diagnosis. Underlying the model are three constructs and six process variables and six process determinants. The process variables are scanning, arousal, classification, clarification, information search, inference, and problem description. The process determinants are cue discrepancy, perceived urgency to respond, persistence or accumulation of discrepancies, familiarity, priority, and information availability. Each of the components of this model—stages, process variables, and determinants—rests on the provision of adequate and timely information by the management accounting system. Accounting information enters the gestation stage to identify the situations where conditions in the environment are changing and building toward recognition. It is then used in the categorization stage to allow the individual to realize that a problem does exist. It serves in the diagnosis stage in creating more certainty about the problem description.

Problem Classification

Problems are generally classified along a continuum going from "well structured" problems on one extreme to "ill-structured" problems on the other extreme.[15] Reitman's view of ill-structured problems includes three classes: an initial stage describing the current state of the decision maker or the resources he has available; the transformation stage, which includes the processes needed to move from the initial state; and the desired stage, which describes the goals the individual hopes to attain.[16] Taylor extended Reitman's classes of ill-structured problems to include the familiarity a decision maker has with each

Exhibit 2.2
Theoretical Model of the Problem Recognition Process (with numbered propositions: boxes represent process variables, and ellipses represent process determinants)

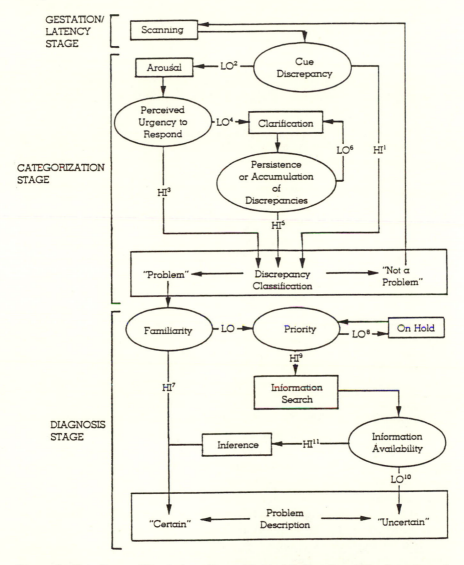

Source: David A. Cowan, ''Developing a Process Model of Problem Recognition,'' *Academy of Management Review*, 11, no. 4 (1986): 265. Reprinted with permission.

Exhibit 2.3
Types of Problem Structure

Problem Type	Initial State	Terminal State	Transformation
Type I, Resource Specification Problems	Unfamiliar	Varies	Varies
Type II, Goal Specification Problems	Varies	Unfamiliar	Varies
Type III, Creative Problems	Varies	Varies	Unfamiliar
Type IV, Well-Structured	Familiar	Familiar	Familiar

Source: R. N. Taylor, "Nature of Problem III-Structuredness: Implications for Problem Formulation and Solution," *Decision Sciences*, 5 (1974): 633. Reprinted with permission of Decision Sciences Institute, Georgia State University.

component.[17] As a result, the influence of a decision maker's familiarity with each of the components of a problem on his or her perception of a problem structure led to a problem classification structure shown in Exhibit 2.3.

The classification goes from one scheme where the individual is unfamiliar with every stage to the well-structured problem where the individual is familiar with all the stages. Taylor gives the following example of a well-structured problem:

For example, in personnel-selection decisions, a battery of predictors may assess potential for job performance and select or classify an applicant. These are repetitive, routine decisions for which we have standard operating procedures. . . . Providing that the problem is correctly identified by the decision maker as well structured, the decision maker would be advised to use the standard response, and no problem reformulation would be needed.[18]

Management accounting can be very useful in the case of the well-formulated problem by providing the standard response from standard operating procedures or established repertoires. It can also assist in the management of ambiguity and uncertainty associated with the unfamiliarity with the three stages of the problem in the case of the ill-structured problems.

In addition to the classification based on the structure of the problem, various other dimensions and classification frameworks of organizational problems have been proposed and can be useful to the conduct of management accounting. A list of these frameworks is provided in Exhibit 2.4. Each of the frameworks included helps understand problems and their relationship and the useful role of management accounting in providing required information. But what is truly needed is an exhaustive list of organizational problems in general and those

Exhibit 2.4
Classification Frameworks of Organizational Problems

Authors	Dimensions of Classification
Acar (1984)	Problem types: outputs of the focal system, transformation process, inputs to the transformation process.
Ackoff and Rivett (1963)	Basic structures: queueing, inventory, allocation, scheduling and routing, replacement and maintenance, search, competition.
Dearborn and Simon (1958)	Problems: sales, marketing, or distribution; clarifying the organization; human relations, employee relations, or teamwork.
Maier and Hoffman (1964)	Problems: type A/Q—high acceptance requirement and low quality; type Q-A—high acceptance requirement and high quality; type Q/A—low acceptance requirement and high quality.
Nadler (1983)	Human purposeful activities: self-preservation, operation and supervision, plan and design, research, evaluation, learning, leisure.
Smith (1988)	Problem types: goal setting, diagnosis, design, description, research, alternative generation, prediction, evaluation, persuasion.
	General problem categories: state change, performance, knowledge, implementation.
Taylor (1974)	Problem types: resource specification, goal specification, creative, well-structured.
Walsh (1988)	Categories: accounting-finance, human relations, marketing, internal-management, external-management.

Source: David A. Cowan, "Developing a Classification Structure of Organizational Problems: An Empirical Investigation," *Academy of Management Journal*, 33, no. 2 (1990): 369.

specifically that require management accounting attention. An interesting list of potential organizational problems is provided in Exhibit 2.5. What is missing in the literature is a similar exhaustive list of those problems requiring management accounting attention and help. Such a list will provide a more solid basis for categorizing and formulating particular management accounting problem categories.

DECISIONAL FOUNDATIONS

Anthony Framework

Although a typology of managerial activities, the Anthony framework may also be conceived as a hierarchy of decision systems, each requiring different planning and control systems. The decision systems are categorized as strategic planning, management control, and operational control.[19]

Strategic planning as defined by R. N. Anthony is "the process of deciding on objectives of the organization, on changes in these objectives, on the resources used to attain these objectives, and on the policies that are to govern the acquisition, use, and disposition of resources."[20] The main concern of the strategic

Exhibit 2.5
Problems Employed in the Sorting Task

1. Uncertainty in determining a company's future staffing needs*
2. "Responsibility" conflicts created by reorganizing staff positions*
3. Difficulty allocating a workforce to different tasks, when understaffed*
4. Difficulty trying to match a company's products with long-term market needs (L)
5. Inability to determine budget costs for a major project*
6. Person assigned to an inappropriate job (poor job match)
7. Difficulty balancing projected staffing needs with budget constraints*
8. Increase in the number of customer complaints (L)*
9. Customer misuse of a new product (L)*
10. Routine audit reveals charges not billed; indicates inaccurate records (N)*
11. Negative cash flow experienced during construction project (N)*
12. Market share eroding because of increasing competition (N)*
13. Adverse economic ramifications from closing a plant*
14. Imbalance of raw materials in manufacturing (L)*
15. Adverse effect on sales from changing social & political attitudes (L)*
16. Deterioration of referral base caused by changing the company location (N)
17. Stockouts occurring too frequently (N)*
18. Useful in-house service is lost because of someone's resignation (N)
19. General management ineffectiveness
20. Difficulty allocating scarce resources
21. Difficulty maintaining business hours during a major construction project*
22. Failing to create cooperative relationship between labor and management
23. Difficulty encountered by changing the basic mission of the organization*
24. Difficulty changing the company's client mix to increase independence
25. Inability to formulate a strategy to rectify company "weaknesses"*
26. Difficulty determining structural changes to meet a changing environment*
27. Difficulty developing working relations with a potential partner firm
28. Raw material resources becoming increasingly scarce*
29. Difficulty trying to balance pricing and service level with related costs*
30. Difficulty choosing outside agencies to help design a new program
31. Not meeting a shipping quota for a particular product*
32. High frequency of absenteeism and tardiness*
33. Deciding who to assign to an undesirable and difficult task
34. "Scheduling" conflicts
35. Lack of communication about a companywide change in operations
36. An important machine continually malfunctions*
37. Difficulty implementing new technology (L)
38. Continually not getting reports finished on time
39. Not keeping production within quality control limits*
40. Inability to develop a workable procedure for a new operation
41. Having to phase out jobs because of budget cutbacks
42. Unable to keep up with the mechanics of data gathering for control*
43. Poor working relations based on personality style conflicts*

Exhibit 2.5 (continued)

44. Inadequate training for newly assigned responsibilities
45. Female employee being discriminated against for promotion
46. Poor performance feedback; too many employees being overrated
47. Declining workgroup morale*
48. Noticeable disinterest in employee involvement (taking commitment for granted)
49. Not putting forth effort (just getting by)*
50. Difficulty communicating with others
51. Difficulty compensating employees effectively
52. Worker bothering coworkers because of a belligerent attitude*
53. Resistance to changes being made regarding working hours
54. A manager's inability to get subordinates to do well
55. Delays resulting from the introduction of new manufacturing technology
56. Difficulty designing and developing a competitive product*
57. Technical differences between departments that need to interact frequently
58. Outdated machinery*
59. Inability to obtain adequate information about customer satisfaction*
60. Confusion over the services expected from the data processing department*
61. Difficulty fulfilling the potential uses of a newly acquired computer (L)*
62. Insufficient reporting procedures for a new project*
63. Difficulty improving the quality of a product
64. Developing an effective network for intra-organizational computer usage*
65. Difficulty encountered when changing accounting methods*
66. Difficulty determining how to comply with new tax legislation (L)*
67. Company image in the marketplace is poor and declining (N)*
68. Complaints of lack of privacy caused by combining workstations (N)
69. Suspicion of theft within the company
70. Complaints of pay dissatisfaction among employees*
71. Complaints arising due to inadequate parking space (N)
72. Difficulty developing a professional atmosphere to support corporate mission*
73. Noticeable space shortages within the company
74. Grievances filed over excessive workload (N)*
75. Expected legislation against particular company activities (L)*
76. Recession likely to decrease customer spending*
77. Violation issued because of delinquency in completing records (N)
78. Difficulty gathering accurate information for data base/record keeping (N)*

Note: Phase one of the data collection for this study generated 57 of these problems; 12 were adapted from Nutt (1984, indicated with ''N''); and 9 were adapted from Lyles and Mitroff (1980, indicated with ''L''). The 45 problems followed by an asterisk loaded most heavily on each end of the six dimensions interpreted in this study.

Source: David A. Cowan, ''Developing a Classification Structure of Organizational Problems: An Empirical Investigation,'' *Academy of Management Journal*, 33, no. 2 (1990): 388–390.

planner is the relationship between the organization and its environment. This concern is expressed in the formulation of a long-range plan that defines the intended future orientation of the firm. Strategic planning is the responsibility of senior managers and analysts who will approach problems on an ad hoc basis as the need for a solution arises.

Management control is "the process by which managers assure that resources are obtained and used effectively and efficiently in the accomplishment of the organization's objectives."[21] The concern is with the conduct of managerial activities within the framework established by strategic planning. These activities require sometimes subjective interpretations and involve personal interactions. Management control involves both top management and the middle managers who will approach problems following a definite pattern and timetable to insure efficient and effective results.

Operational control is "the process of assuring that specific tasks are carried out effectively and efficiently."[22] The concern is with individual tasks or transactions. The performance of these tasks or transactions is accomplished according to rules and procedures derived from management control. These rules and procedures are often expressed in terms of a mathematical model.

Although, as recognized by Anthony, the boundaries between the three categories are often not clear, they are useful for the analysis of the different activities and their information requirements. The decision categories form a continuum and require different information. Exhibit 2.6 summarizes the information requirements by decision category.

Anthony's framework has the advantage of simplicity, and it facilitates communications between individuals in the organization by categorizing different types of decisions and their information requirements. For management accounting, it implies a tailoring of the data produced to the context and category of the particular decision. It also calls for different approaches to planning and control in each of the strategic planning, management control, and operational control areas.

Simon Framework

Similar to Anthony's framework, H. A. Simon's framework presents a taxonomy of decisions.[23] However, while Anthony's framework focuses on the purpose of decision-making activity (strategic planning, management control, and operational control), Simon's framework focuses on the question of problem solving by individuals regardless of their position within an organization.

Simon maintains that all problem solving can be broken down into three distinct phases: intelligence, design, and choice. Intelligence consists of surveying the environment for situations that demand decisions. It implies an identification of the problem(s), the collection of information, and the establishment of goals and evaluative criteria. Design involves delineating and analyzing various courses of action for the problems identified in the intelligence phase. It implies an

Exhibit 2.6
Information Requirements by Decision Category

Information Attribute	Strategic Planning	Management Control	Operational Control
Source	Externally generated	Mostly internally generated	Internally generated
Accuracy	Accurate in magnitude only	Accurate within decision bounds	Very accurate
Scope	Summary data	Moderately detailed data	Detailed data
Frequency	Periodically reported	Regularly reported	Frequently reported
Time span	Long range	Medium range	Short range
Organization	Loose	Structured	Highly structured
Type of information	Qualitative	Mixed	Quantitative
Age of information	Old	Mixed	Current
Characteristic	Unique to problem	Exception reporting	Repetitive
Nature	Relates to establishment of broad policies	Relates to the achievement of organizational objectives	Relates to a specific task

enumeration and combination of feasible alternatives and their evaluation on the basis of the criteria established in the intelligence phase. Choice involves selecting the best alternative. Although not mentioned by Simon, decision making involves a fourth phase, implementation, designed to insure the proper execution of choice.

Simon's framework also makes the distinction between programmed and non-programmed decisions:

Decisions are programmed to the extent that they are repetitive and routine, to the extent that a definite procedure has been worked out for handling them so that they don't have to be treated de novo each time they occur. Decisions are nonprogrammed to the extent that they are novel, unstructured, and consequential. There is no cut-and-dried method of handling the problem because it hasn't arisen before, or because its precise nature and structure are elusive or complex, or because it is so important that it deserves a custom-tailored treatment. . . . By nonprogrammed I mean a response where the system has no specific procedure to deal with situations like the one at hand, but must fall back on whatever general capacity it has for intelligent, adaptive, problem-oriented action.[24]

Because they are repetitive and routine, programmed decisions require little time in the design phase. On the other hand, nonprogrammed decisions require much more time in the design phase. In general, the terms *structured* and *unstructured* are used for *programmed* and *nonprogrammed* to imply less dependence on the computer and to show more dependence on the basic character of the problem-solving activity in question. The two classifications advanced by Simon may be viewed as polar types for a continuum of decision-making activity. For example, "semistructured" decisions may be those for which one or two of the intelligence, design, and choice phases are unstructured.

That decisions may fall on a continuum going from structured to unstructured has implications for management accounting. Structured decisions are solvable by analytic techniques, while unstructured decisions generally are not. The analytic techniques required for the structured decisions may be either based on clerical routine and habit or formalized techniques from operations research and electronic data processing. The decision techniques required for unstructured decisions may be either based on human intuition and judgment or heuristic techniques. While the role of management accounting for structured decisions appears without doubt to be one of providing and assisting in the use of fixed routines, it is not very obvious in the case of unstructured decisions. Users may rely more on their decision style, intuition, or heuristics for the unstructured decisions or tasks.

Gorry-Scott Morton Framework

As mentioned earlier, Anthony's framework is based on the purpose of the decision-making activity, while Simon's framework is based on the methods or techniques of problem solving. The Gorry-Scott Morton framework provides a combination of both frameworks in the form of a matrix that classifies decisions on both a structured-to-unstructured dimension and on an operational-to-strategic dimension.[25] Exhibit 2.7 shows an expanded example of the matrix obtained from the synthesis provided by G. A. Gorry and M. S. Scott Morton.

The implications for management accounting from both the Anthony and Simon frameworks apply to the Gorry-Scott Morton framework. The synthesis, however, presents additional implications. First, different information requirements and different methods of data collection and maintenance are required not

Exhibit 2.7
An Expanded Example of the Gorry-Scott Morton Framework

	Operational Control	Management Control	Strategic Planning
	Accounts receivable	Budgeting	Tanker fleet mix
	Order entry	Short-term forecasting	Warehouse and plant location
Structured	Inventory reordering	Engineered costs	
		Linear programming for manufacturing	
	Inventory control	Variance analysis	Mergers and acquisitions
Semi-Structured	Production scheduling	Overall budget	Capital acquisition analysis
	Bond trading	Budget preparation	New product planning
	Cash management	Hiring personnel	R and D planning
Unstructured	PERT COST systems	Sales and production	

only for the three decision categories borrowed from Anthony, but also for the types of decisions borrowed from Simon. This implies that the design of a management accounting support system is flexible enough to cope with the various complex demands. For example, in the structured case, the goal of management accounting may be to facilitate the processing of information; while in the unstructured case, it may be to improve the organization and presentation of information inputs.[26] Second, different organizational structures, different managerial skills and talents, and different numbers of managers may be required for each decision category. The decision process, the implementation process, and the level of analytic sophistication will differ among the three decision categories and call for different organization structures:

> on strategic problems, a task force reporting to the user and virtually independent of the computer group may make sense. The important issues are problem definition and problem structure; the implementation and computer issues are relatively simple by comparison. In management control, the single user, although still dominant in his application, has problems of interfacing with other users. An organizational design that encourages cross-functional (marketing, production, distribution, etc.) cooperation is probably desirable. In operational control, the organizational design should include the user as a major influence, but he will have to be balanced with operational systems experts, and the whole group can quite possibly stay within functional boundaries.[27]

Finally, the model requirements may be different between the three areas, given the differences in the information requirements, the frequency of decisions in each area, and their relative magnitude. The operational control system calls for frequent decisions, and the models for these decisions need to be "efficient in running time, have ready access to current data, and be structured so as to be easily changed."[28] The models in strategic planning, and to a lesser extent management control, are infrequent, individual, and dependent on the managers involved.

While not referring to management accounting per se, but to a more general information systems concept labeled "Decision Support Systems," P. G. Keen and Scott Morton identified several implications of the framework to the design and implementation of a decision support system:

1. The skills and attitudes of the people involved in building a DSS (decision support system) for semistructured decisions need to differ from those building similar systems for structured decisions.

2. Ill-structured problems require a different technology to support decisions than structured problems.

3. While a well-structured operational control problem may require the use of optimization algorithms, most other problems will rely on different models.

4. The design of a DSS should be accomplished through a continuous evolutionary process to accommodate future needs, learning, and growth.[29]

Because management accounting is a decision support system, the above implications apply also to it. It requires people with different skills and attitudes, different technologies, different models, and different processes to accommodate both structured and unstructured decisions on the one hand and strategic planning, management control, and operational control on the other hand.

Forrester Framework

As developed by Professor Jay Forrester, the essence of industrial dynamics is that social systems such as business organizations can be understood through nonlinear feedback systems concepts.[30] Any system is characterized by its closed-loop (information feedback) structure. He describes the state of the organization by information on the levels of variables in the organization, such as inventory, manpower, open orders, money, sales, and so on. The activity in the organization takes the form of instantaneous flows of the physical values of these variables or rates between the levels in each network. In addition to these physical values, each level produces information representing those values with the result of an information network superimposed on the physical network and controlling it. He expands this notion as follows:

The industrial system . . . is a very complex multi-loop and interconnected system. . . . Decisions are made at multiple points throughout the system. Each resulting action generates information that can be used at several but not all decision points. This structure of cascaded and interconnected information-feedback loops, when taken together, describes the industrial system. Within a company, the decision points extend from the shipping room and the stock clerk to the board of directors.

The interlocking network of information channels emerges at various points to control physical processes such as the hiring of employees, the building of factories, and the production of goods. Every action point in the system is backed up by a local decision point whose information sources reach into other parts of the organization and the surrounding environment.[31]

Forrester viewed management in terms of the sequence information-decision-action, with the decision-making process as a response to the gap between the objectives of the organization and its actual progress toward the accomplishment of these objectives.

Thus, industrial dynamics views organizations from a control perspective. It is intended mostly as a method of designing organizational policies. Nevertheless, industrial dynamics is a useful framework for information systems, management accounting in particular, in several ways:

1. It places information as an explicit and integral part of organizational decision making.
2. The information's function is to represent the physical values of the levels of various activities and entities in the organization.
3. It emphasizes the identification of decision points, objectives, and information requirements.

Dearden Framework

John Dearden observes that the concept of a single information system is "too large and all-encompassing to be a meaningful and useful classification."[32] He suggests instead to break down the systems and data processing activities both horizontally and vertically. Horizontally, systems activities can be classified by the type of work performed; vertically, systems activities can be classified by the kind of information handled.

The horizontal classification includes three stages: systems specification, data processing implementation, and programming. These tasks are assumed to be different and should be treated differently. Systems specification should be decentralized to operating management or users because they have the best knowledge and capabilities required to determine what information should be provided by the system. Data processing implementation can and should be centralized because it improves the economics of integration of the data processing requirements, and should also be controlled by staff specialists because knowledge of equipment and data requirement is the primary requirement. Programming as a process of converting flowcharts to working programs lends itself best to centralization. Dearden gives the following three reasons:

1. Programming is more economically accomplished on a centralized basis.

2. Writing business programs requires a special knowledge of equipment and programming languages, and there is practically no difference in the skills required to program the different systems.

3. Management must delegate the task of programming to someone, and it makes little difference whether it is a staff unit or a department reporting directly to the manager.[33]

The vertical classification is based on the presence of three major information systems in a typical company, and a varying and indefinite number of minor systems.

The major information systems include financial, personnel, and logistics. The basis of the financial system is the flow of dollars through the organization.[34] The personnel system is concerned with the flow of information about people working in the organization. It is assumed to be administered by the industrial relations officer. Finally, the logistics system is concerned with information about the physical flow of goods through an organization covering procurement, production, and distribution. Several separate logistic systems may be found in any one company. Dearden associates the financial system with Anthony's category of management control and the logistics system with operational control.

The minor systems, defined as those confined to a limited part of the organization, include mainly marketing, research and development, strategic planning, and executive observation. Some of these may be integrated to the three major systems or left separate. Dearden finally proposes a generalized organization chart for systems and data processing based on the vertical and horizontal classification just described. Such a structure is illustrated in Exhibit 2.8.

Exhibit 2.8
Dearden Framework

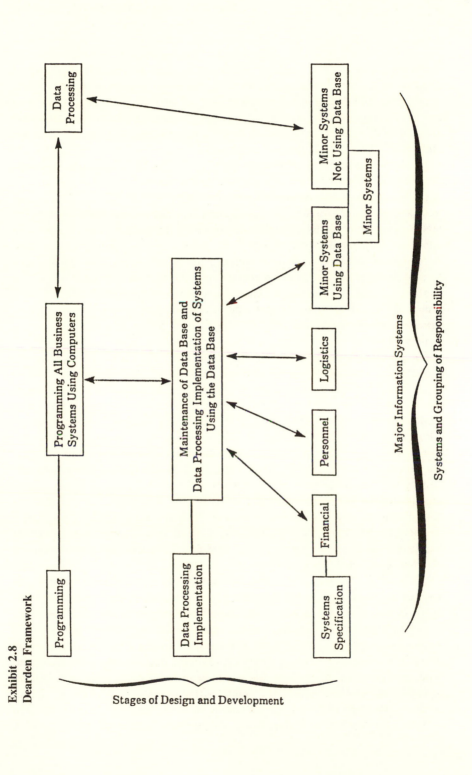

Blumenthal Framework

Sherman Blumenthal presented his framework as a synthesis of the three concepts of information-decision-action suggested by Forrester, programmed and nonprogrammed decisions suggested by Simon, and the hierarchy of planning and control suggested by Anthony.[35] His major concern is the lack of consistent and uniformly applied approaches to the integration of related systems into larger entities of appropriate scope.

He starts with the activity center as being one of the basic organizational units in an organization under the common and direct supervision of a first-line manager. These activity centers are grouped into larger and complex organizational units known as decision centers, functional units, and management control centers. A decision center is defined as one or more management-level people who either prescribe the decision rules or make the decisions for the activity centers. A functional unit is an activity center and its decision center. A management control center is one or more management people together with their supporting staff, which acts as a decision center for a group of functional units or for a group of subordinate management control centers. The actions, carried by the same or different functional units, that regulate the inflow or outflow to or from sequences of levels as a group form an operational function.

Each of these organizational units may constitute groups to execute operational functions as action subsystems, decision subsystems, and information subsystems. The organization subsystems, the operational functions, and various modules constitute the main foundations of a management information system. Hence, a management information system is viewed as an operational function whose functional units are information subsystems of other operational functions. The modules are either operational or management control modules. An operational control module is viewed as that part of an information subsystem supporting the functional units of an operational function. A management control module is that part of an information subsystem supporting the management control centers of an operational function. Blumenthal concludes that a management information system is alternatively definable as an operational function whose parts are the management control modules and operational control modules of other operational functions.[36]

Blumenthal's framework has implications for management accounting. It advocates that the design and planning of any information system, including management accounting, be based on fundamental principles that refer to the effective use of systems resources, efficiency in systems life and performance, and organizational changes. The process advocated to ensure this objective consists of: (1) grouping the most elementary operational activities into identifiable and separate organizational units, (2) linking these activity centers to decision centers to form functional units, and (3) defining different modules (operational control module, management control module) as the basic components of the information system. This implies that both planning and control will take place at two levels:

Exhibit 2.9
The Problem and Decisional Foundations of Management Accounting

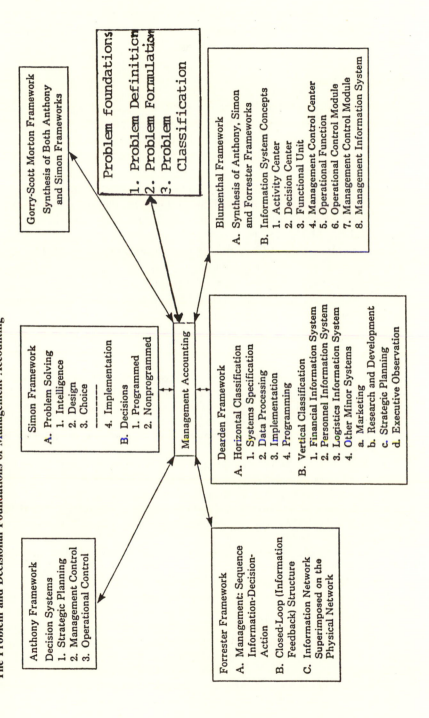

(1) operational planning and control for the operational, repetitive activities of the functional units; and (2) management planning and control for the operational functions.

CONCLUSIONS

A framework is needed in which to position where management accounting is now and the direction in which it can move in terms of determining the types of problems, the needed information, the type of decisions taken and decision centers, and defining the role of management accounting in decision making. Although such a framework has not been explicitly formulated, several conceptual frameworks for viewing information systems in general have been presented in the literature. These are the Anthony framework, the Simon framework, the Gorry-Scott Morton framework, the Dearden framework, the Forrester framework, and the Blumenthal framework. As shown in Exhibit 2.9, these frameworks in addition to the problem foundations constitute the decisional foundations of management accounting by providing the basis for making resource allocation decisions about information systems, in general, and management accounting, in particular. They suggest the types of information needed for different categories of decisions and decision centers.

NOTES

1. H. Mintzberg, D. Raisingharu, and A. Theoret, "The Structure of 'Unstructured' Decision Process," *Administrative Science Quarterly* 21 (1976): 246–275.

2. A. Tversky and D. Kahneman, "The Framing of Decisions and the Psychology of Choice," *Science* 211 (1981): 453–458.

3. W. F. Pounds, "The Process of Problem Finding," *Industrial Management Review* 11 (Fall 1969): 1–15.

4. M. A. Lyles, "Formulating Strategic Problems: Empirical Analysis and Development," *Strategic Management Journal* 2 (1981): 61–75.

5. Pounds, "The Process of Problem Finding," pp. 1–19.

6. G. P. Agre, "The Concept of a Problem," *Educational Studies* 13 (1982): 138.

7. A. Tversky, "Elimination by Aspects: A Theory of Choice," *Psychological Review* (July 1972): 781–799.

8. W. R. Reitman, "Heuristic Decision Procedures, Open Constraints, and the Structure of Ill-Defined Problems," in M. Shelley and G. Bryan (eds.), *Human Judgments and Optimality* (New York: John Wiley, 1964), pp. 282–315.

9. R. N. Taylor, "Perception of Problem Constraints," *Management Science* 22 (September 1975): 22.

10. K. R. MacCrimmon, and R. N. Taylor, "Problem Solving and Decision-Making," in M. D. Dunnette (ed.), *Handbook of Industrial and Organizational Psychology* (Chicago: Rand McNally College Publishing 1976).

11. Ibid.

12. R. H. Kilmann and I. I. Mitroff, "Problem Defining and the Consulting/Intervention Process," *California Management Review* 21 (Spring 1979): 30.

13. Ibid.

14. David A. Cowan, "Developing a Process Model of Problem Recognition," *Academy of Management Review* 11, no. 4 (1986): 763–776.

15. M. Minsky, "Steps Toward Artificial Intelligence," *Proceedings of the I.R.E.* 49 (1961): 8–30.

16. Reitman, "Heuristic Decision Procedures."

17. R. N. Taylor, "Nature of Problem Ill-Structuredness: Implications for Problem Formulation and Solution," *Decision Sciences* 5 (1974): 632–643.

18. Ibid., pp. 633–634.

19. R. N. Anthony, *Planning and Control Systems: A Framework for Analysis* (Cambridge, Mass.: Harvard University Graduate School of Business Administration, Studies in Management Control, 1965).

20. Ibid., p. 24.

21. Ibid., p. 27.

22. Ibid., p. 69.

23. H. A. Simon, *The New Science of Management Decision* (New York: Harper and Row, 1960).

24. Ibid., pp. 5–6.

25. G. A. Gorry and M. S. Scott Morton, "A Framework for Management Information Systems," *Sloan Management Review* (Fall 1971): 55–70.

26. Henry C. Lucas, Jr., Kenneth W. Clowes, and Robert B. Kaplan, "Frameworks for Information Systems," *INFOR* (October 1974): 251.

27. Gorry and Scott Morton, "A Framework for Management Information Systems," p. 67.

28. Ibid., p. 68.

29. P. G. Keen and M. S. Scott Morton, *Decision Support Systems* Addison-Wesley Series on Decision Support (Reading, Mass.: Addison-Wesley, 1978), pp. 92–93.

30. J. W. Forrester, *Industrial Dynamics* (Cambridge, Mass.: MIT Press, 1961).

31. Ibid., p. 94.

32. John Dearden, "How to Organize Information Systems," *Harvard Business Review* (March–April 1965): 66.

33. Ibid., p. 69.

34. It is assumed to be administered by the controller.

35. Sherman C. Blumenthal, *Management Information Systems: A Framework for Planning and Development* (Englewood Cliffs, N.J.: Prentice-Hall, 1969).

36. Ibid., p. 36.

BIBLIOGRAPHY

Acar, W. "What's a Problem?" Paper presented at the Annual Meeting of the American Institute for Decision Sciences, Toronto, 1984.

Ackoff, R. L. *The Art of Problem Solving.* New York: John Wiley, 1978.

——. "Systems, Organizations, and Inter-Disciplinary Research." In F. E. Emery (ed.), *Systems Thinking.* Baltimore: Penguin Books, 1969.

Ackoff, R. L., and Rivett, B.H.P. "The Art and Science of Mess Management." *Interfaces,* 11, no. 1 (1981): 20–26.

——. *A Manager's Guide to Operations Research.* New York: John Wiley, 1963.

Agre, G. P. "The Concept of a Problem." *Educational Studies* 13 (1982): 121–142.

Ansoff, H. I. "Managerial Problem Solving." *Journal of Business Policy* (August 1971): 3–20.

Anthony, R. N. *Planning and Control Systems: A Framework for Analysis*. Cambridge, Mass: Harvard University Graduate School of Business Administration, Studies in Management Control, 1965.

Bass, B. M. 1983. *Organizational Decision Making*. Homewood, Ill.: Richard D. Irwin.

Bateson, G. *Steps to an Ecology of Mind*. New York: Chandler, 1972.

Blumenthal, Sherman C. *Management Information Systems: A Framework for Planning and Development*. Englewood Cliffs, N.J.: Prentice-Hall, 1969.

Bourne, L. E., Jr.; Ekstrand, B. R.; and Dominowski, R. L. *The Psychology of Thinking*. Englewood Cliffs, N.J.: Prentice-Hall, 1971.

Braybrooke, D., and Lindblom, C. E. *A Strategy of Decision*. New York: The Free Press, 1963.

Cowan, D. A. "Developing a Process Model of Problem Recognition." *Academy of Management Review* 11 no. 4 (1986): 763–776.

―――. "Executives' Knowledge of Organizational Problem Types: Applying a Contingency Perspective." *Journal of Management* 14 (1988): 513–527.

Daft, R. L., and Wiginton, J. C. "Language and Organization." *Academy of Management Review* 4 (1979): 179–191.

Davis, Gordon B. *Management Information Systems: Conceptual Foundations, Structure and Development*. New York: McGraw-Hill, 1974.

Dearborn, D. C., and Simon, H. A. "Selective Perception: A Note on the Departmental Indentification of Executives." *Sociometry* 21 (1958): 140–144.

Dearden, John. "How to Organize Information Systems." *Harvard Business Review* (March–April 1965): 65–73.

De Bono, E. *Lateral Thinking: Creativity Step by Step*. New York: Harper and Row, 1970.

Donnellon, A. "Language and Communications in Organizations." In H. P. Sims, Jr., D. A. Gioia, and Associates (eds.), *The Thinking Organizations*. San Francisco: Jossey-Bass, 1986.

Dutton, J. E., and Duncan, R. B. "Strategic Issue Diagnosis and Creation of Momentum for Change." *Strategic Management Journal* 8 (1987): 279–295.

Dutton, J. E., and Jackson, S. E. "Categorizing Strategic Issues: Links to Organizational Action." *Academy of Management Review* 12 (1987): 76–90.

Dutton, J. E.; Walton, E.; and Abrahamson, E. "Important Dimensions of Strategic Issues: Separating the Wheat From the Chaff." *Journal of Management Studies* 14 (1989): 379–396.

EinDor, Phillip, and Segev, Eli. *Managing Management Information Systems*. Lexington, Mass.: Lexington Books, 1978.

Etzioni, A. "Mixed Scanning: A 'Third' Approach to Decision Making." *Public Administration Review* 27 (1967): 385–392.

Feldman, J., and Kanter, H. E. "Organizational Decision Making." In J. G. March (ed.), *Handbook of Organizations*. Chicago: Rand McNally, 1965.

Forrester, J. W. *Industrial Dynamics*. Cambridge, Mass.: MIT Press, 1961.

Gorry, G. A., and Scott Morton, M. S. "A Framework for Management Information Systems." *Sloan Management Review* (Fall 1971): 55–70.

Hall, A. D. *A Methodology for Systems Engineering*. New York: Litton Educational Publishing, 1962.

Herden, R. P., and Lyles, M. A. "Individual Attributes and the Problem Conceptualization Process." *Human Systems Management* 2 (1981): 275–284.

Hurtubise, Rolland. "La Conception des Systemes d' Information: Un Cadre Conceptuel Global." *INFOR* (October 1978): 253–275.

Janis, I. L., and Mann, L. *Decision Making: A Psychological Analysis of Conflict, Choice, and Commitment* New York: The Free Press, 1977.

Keen, P. G., and Scott Morton, M. S. *Decision Support Systems: An Organizational Perspective* Addison-Wesley Series on Decision Support. Reading, Mass.: Addison-Wesley, 1978.

Kepner, C. H., and Tregoe, B. B. *The Rational Manager*. New York: McGraw-Hill, 1965.

Kilmann, R. H., and Mitroff, I. I. "Problem Defining and the Consulting/Intervention Process." *California Management Review* 21 (Spring 1979): 26–33.

Lucas, Henry C. Jr.; Clowes, Kenneth W.; and Kaplan, Robert B. "Frameworks for Information Systems." *INFOR* (October 1974): 245–260.

Lyles, M. A. "Defining Strategic Problems: Subjective Criteria of Executives." *Organization Studies*, 8 (1987): 263–280.

———. "Formulating Strategic Problems: Empirical Analysis and Development." *Strategic Management Journal* 2 (1981): 61–75.

Lyles, M. A., and Mitroff, I. I. "Organizational Problem Formulation: An Empirical Study." *Administrative Science Quarterly* 25 (1980): 61–75.

MacCrimmon, K. R., and Taylor, R. N. Problem Solving and Decision Making." In M. D. Dunnette (ed.), *Handbook of Industrial and Organizational Psychology* Chicago: Rand McNally College Publishing, 1976.

Maier, N.R.F., and Hoffman, L. R. "Types of Problems Confronting Managers." *Personnel Psychology* 17 (1964): 261–269.

March, J. G. and Simon, H. A. *Organizations*. New York: John Wiley, 1958.

Mintzberg, H.; Raisinghani, D.; and Theoret, A. "The Structure of 'Unstructered' Decision Processes." *Administrative Science Quarterly* 21 (April 1976): 246–275.

Mitroff, I. I., and Betz, F. "Dialectical Decision Theory: A Meta Theory of Decision Making." *Management Science* 19, no. 1 (1972): 11–24.

Mitroff, I. I., and Featheringham, T. A. "On Systematic Problem Solving and the Error of the Third Kind." *Behavioral Science* 19 (1974): 383–393.

Mitroff, I. I.; Emshoff, J. R.; and Kilmann, R. H. "Assumptional Analysis: A Methodology for Strategic Problem Solving," *Management Science* 25, no. 6 (1979): 583–593.

Mitroff, I. I., and Kilmann, R. H. *Methodological Approaches to the Social Science*. San Francisco: Jossey-Bass, 1978.

Nadler, G. "Human Purposeful Activities for Classifying Management Problems." *Omega* 11 (1983): 15–26.

———. *The Planning and Design Approach*. New York: John Wiley, 1981.

———. "A Timeline Theory of Planning and Design." *Design Studies* 1, no. 5 (1980): 299–307.

———. *Work Design: A Systems Concept*. Homewood, Ill.: Richard D. Irwin, 1967.

———. *Work Systems Design: The IDEALS Concept*. Homewood, Ill.: Richard D. Irwin, 1967.

Newell, A.; Shaw, J. C.; and Simon H. A. "Report on a General Problem-Solving

Program for a Computer." *Information Processing: Proceedings of the International Conference on Information Processing*, 1960, pp. 256–264.

Newell, A., and Simon, H. A. *Human Problem Solving*. Englewood Cliffs, N.J., Prentice-Hall, 1972.

Nutt, P. C. "An Experimental Comparison of the Effectiveness of Three Planning Methods." *Management Science* 23, no. 5 (1977): 499–511.

———. "Types of Organizational Decision Processes." *Administrative Science Quarterly* 29 (1984): 414–450.

Polya, G. *How to Solve It*. Princeton, N.J.: Princeton University Press, 1973.

Pounds, W. F. "The Process of Problem Finding." *Industrial Management Review* 11 (Fall 1969): 1–15.

Reitman, W. R. "Heuristic Decision Procedures, Open Constraints, and the Structure of Ill-Defined Problems." In M. Shelley and G. Bryan (eds.), *Human Judgments and Optimality*, New York: John Wiley, 1964.

Rickards, T. *Problem Solving Through Creative Analysis*. Epping, Essex: Gower Press, 1975.

Shull, F. A., Jr.; Delbecq, A. L.; and Cummings, L. L. *Organizational Design Making*, New York: McGraw-Hill, 1970.

Simon, H. A. *The New Science of Management Decision*. New York: Harper and Row, 1960.

———. "The Structure of Ill-structured Problems." *Artificial Intelligence* 4 (1973): 181–201.

Smith, G. F. "Towards a Heuristic Theory of Problem Structuring." *Management Science* 34 (1988): 1489–1506.

Taylor, R. N. "Nature of Problem Ill-Structuredness: Implications for Problem Formulation and Solution." *Decision Sciences* 5 (1974): 632–643.

———. "Perception of Problem Constraints." *Management Science* 22 (September 1975): 22–29.

Tversky, B., and Hemenway, K. "Categories of Environmental Scenes." *Cognitive Psychology* 15 (1983): 121–149.

Tversky, A., and Kahneman, D. "The Framing of Decisions and the Psychology of Choice." *Science* 211 (1981): 453–458.

Volkema, R. J. "Problem Formulation in Planning and Design." *Management Science* (June 1983): 639–652.

———. "Problem Formulation as a Purposive Activity." *Strategic Management Journal* 7 (1986): 267–279.

Walsh, J. P. "Selectivity and Selective Perception: An Investigation of Managers' Belief Structures and Information Processing." *Academy of Management Journal* 31 (1988): 873–896.

Walsh, J. P., and Fahey, L. "The Role of Negotiated Belief Structures in Strategy Making." *Journal of Management* 5 (1986): 188–200.

Walsh, J. P.; Henderson, C. M.; and Deighton, J. "Negotiated Belief Structures and Decision Performance: An Empirical Investigation." *Organizational Behavior & Human Decision Processes* 42 (1988): 194–216.

3

THE ORGANIZATIONAL
FOUNDATIONS

Management accounting is built on organizational foundations. First, elements of organizational structure shape its techniques, approaches, and role in the firm. Second, it is a function of the theories of organization to describe and explain organizational behavior. Robert Golembiewski was among the first authors to point to the problem of adapting accounting to organization theory and vice versa:

... it seems appropriate that organization theory receive considerable attention by members of the accounting profession, which is presently in the throes of rethinking its scope and methods. For an inappropriate organization structure can frustrate the most worthy of intentions and, in any case, any fundamental changes in accountancy will require changes in the traditional theory of organization.[1]

Thus, management accounting requires a good grasp of the elements of organizational structure and theories of organization. Identifying the elements of an organization structure most prevalent and essential to a proper functioning of a management accounting system allows the tailoring of the internal reporting system to that structure or the suggestion of a more appropriate organization structure. Similarly, the theories of organization point to significant elements that approximate the patterning and order inherent in organizations. Determination of these characteristics guides management accounting to more effective ways of providing its services. This chapter will introduce elements of organizational structure and theories of organization most relevant to a proper functioning of management accounting.

ELEMENTS OF ORGANIZATIONAL STRUCTURE

Formal organizational structure is the aspect of the organization that management often seeks to change in order to improve the functioning of the organization. The elements of this structure affect the ways the management accounting function will be exercised and they need to be fully understood by a management accountant. Before presenting the elements or organizational structure most relevant to a proper functioning of management accounting, the nature of an organization will be examined.

Nature of an Organization

Organizations can be viewed for various perspectives, and the choice of a perspective leads to different organizational topologies or taxonomies as shown in Exhibit 3.1. Each typology calls for different management accounting systems to accommodate the informational needs of each type of organization included.

A more general depiction of an organization is that of a "relatively permanent and relatively complex discernible interaction system."[2] In other words, the organization is an observable result of the interaction rather than the group of actors. The three components of the definition deserve more clarification.

First, the organization is a *going concern* in the sense that the interaction system is relatively stable. Second, the organization is an *exclusive entity*. It is different from a group or a society in terms of structural complexity. Structural complexity refers to both horizontal and vertical integration. Finally, the organization is an *interaction system*. It assumes the existence of two or more persons who have independent relationships. With these in view, three problems appear: (1) organizational membership; (2) organizational boundaries; and (3) organizational environments.

George Homans chose to associate organizational membership with the frequency of interaction.[3] If members interact more with each other than with subject E, then E is not considered a member of the group. To this definition, Eugene Hass and Thomas Drabeck added two criteria for organizational membership: the frequency of interaction and the content of interaction. In brief, "those interaction units that are perceived high in frequency and similar in content constitute the interaction system."[4]

The organizational boundaries depend on the analyst (for example, the management accountant) and the questions asked by the analyst. Assembling the interaction units in a system on the basis of their frequency and content leads to a delimitation of the boundaries of the organization. The predominant school of thought is that boundaries ought to be viewed as flexible rather than rigid. In recent works of Donald Katz and Robert Kahn[5] and James Thompson,[6] organizations are perceived as "open systems."

The functioning of the organization is affected by a multitude of environments.

Exhibit 3.1

A Summary of the Most Frequently Cited Works Using Theoretically Constructed Typologies or Taxonomies

Author (Data)	Organization Studied	Criterion Variables	No. of Types	Typologies Specified
Weber (1947)	Social and Economic	Rationality	1	Bureaucracy as an ideal type
Woodward (1958, 1965)	British Industrial Firms	Production Technology	3	Unit/small batch Large batch/mass Continuous process
Gordon and Babchuk (1959)	Voluntary Associations	Accessibility of membership; status-defining capacity; the function of the assoc. for the members	12	The only typology of voluntary associations reported to date
Parsons (1956, 1960)		The goals or functions of the organization	4	Economic Political Integrative pattern Maintenance
Burns and Stalker (1961)	Industrial Firms in Great Britain	Patterns of adaptation to technological and commercial change	2	Mechanistic Organic

Exhibit 3.1 (continued)

Author (Data)	Organization Studied	Criterion Variables	No. of Types	Typologies Specified
Etzioni (1961, 1975)		Compliance relationship	3*	Coercive Utilitarian Normative
Blau and Scott (1962)		Who benefits	4	Mutual benefit Business concerns Service organizations Commonwealth organizations
Emery and Trist (1965)	British Canning Firm and Farmer's Union	Environments	4	Placid random Placid clustered Disturbed reactive Turbulent fields
Katz and Kahn (1966)		Genotypic functions and second-order factors	4	Productive Maintenance Adaptive Managerial or political Cf. Parsons (1956, 1960)
Van Ripper (1966)		The amount of power those at the top of an organization have over those below	6	Control organizations Production organizations Bargaining Representative organizations Research organizations Communal organizations Cf. Etzioni (1961, 1975)

Perrow (1967, 1970)	Technology, number of exceptional cases, and type of search process	4	Craft Routine Nonroutine Engineering Cf. Woodward (1958, 1965)
Thompson (1967)	Core technologies	3	Long-linked Mediating Intensive Cf. Woodward (1958, 1965) & Perrow (1967, 1970)
Rice and Bishoprick (1971)	The rights of members to determine the goals of the organization	4	Directive or entrepreneurial Consensual Democratic Collegial
Meyer (1977)	The salience of organization goals and the environment	5	Insular Oligopolies Competitive Administrative Composite

*Although Etzioni's matrix created 9 types, only 3 were termed viable and hence are reported here.

Source: W. B. Carper and W. E. Snizek, "The Nature and Types of Organizational Taxonomies: An Overview," *Academy of Management Review 5*, no.1 (1980): 68–69. Reprinted with permission.

They define the major constraints within which the organization is called to function. The idea is stated well in the following passage from Sherman Krupp:

The range of behavior which the business firm's internal variables will have depends, among other things, on the structure of the market. Under conditions of oligopoly (let us assume the firm is large), phenomena that might appear external and compelling to the small competitive firm become themselves internal and susceptible of manipulation. Thus, the large firm in oligopoly is much more independent of external constraints than is the firm under competition. In a competitive market, on the other hand, the behavior of the firm is largely determined by environmental conditions. The firm in a world of oligopoly is a more self-contained empirical structure than the firm in competition. The independence of the firm from external factors is an empirical matter; empirical structure defines the bounded units of the world of observables.[7]

These environments are characterized by their instability and exclusivity. The nature of an organization as a relatively complex and relatively permanent interaction system places management accounting in the role of an organizational process intended for strengthening these interactions. More specifically, the management accountant will provide essential services that will concretize the interaction between individuals and their membership in the organization, define the boundaries of the organization to include all the interaction units, and structure all analyses, taking into account the constraints imposed by the organizational environments. In brief, interaction units, organizational membership, boundaries, and environment are important organizational concepts that define the scope and nature of the management accountant's activities.

Organizational Structure

Organizational structure is the system of relationships existing among the position holders of an organization. It results from a deliberate and conscious planning of the areas of responsibility, specialization, and authority for each of the organizational members. In general, it takes a hierarchical form where authority and responsibility are differentiated along a vertical dimension, and units, such as departments or divisions, along a horizontal dimension. What results is a pyramid-shaped organization, usually referred to as an organization chart, shown in Exhibit 3.2. Each vertical level in the hierarchy depicts different levels of authority. For example, each of the manufacturing centers is responsible to the manufacturing superintendent. In turn, the latter, with all the other organizational units on the same horizontal line, is responsible to the manufacturing vice president. Finally, the latter, with all the other vice presidents, is responsible to the board of directors. Let us note again that each horizontal dimension is differentiated by specialization rather than by authority. This process is termed *departmentalization*, whereby employees are grouped into organizational units on the basis of similar skills and specialization. Growth and environmental change are usually the main determinants for departmentalization. In general, the de-

Exhibit 3.2
Organizational Chart of a Manufacturing Company

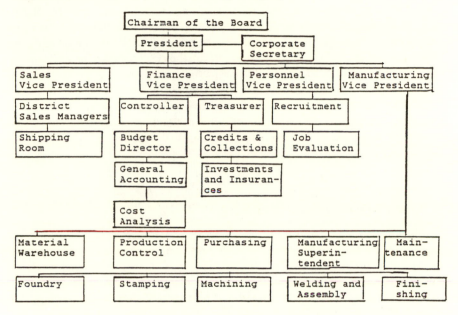

partmentalization in organizations takes four major forms: by function, by location, by process, and by product. A firm may departmentalize or differentiate horizontally according to one of several of these forms.

First, firms may departmentalize by function. For example, a typical manufacturing firm may include sales, production, accounting, finance, personnel, research and development, and purchasing as necessary functions to be departmentalized.

Second, firms may departmentalize by process. Most production activities include different technological processes that require different organizational units. In the example presented in Exhibit 3.2, the finishing, foundry, stamping, machining, welding and assembly are "housed" in different organizational units.

Third, firms may departmentalize by location. A large corporation may be differentiated on the basis of territories, districts, regions, and such. The relatively independent units are referred to as divisions. Hence a multinational corporation may divisionalize by location to adapt to different legal, taxation, and market environments.

Finally, firms may departmentalize by product. This is beneficial to those firms producing different products for different markets.

Vertical differentiation by authority and responsibility and horizontal differentiation through departmentalization or divisionalization lead to the creation of periodic planning and control. This need is met only by the management accounting system in general and responsibility accounting in particular. Management accounting will produce accounting reports of performance and budgets that will serve as the means of communication between these units. Similarly, by making the smallest areas of responsibility the main foundations of the management accounting system, responsibility accounting allows definition and consolidation of the decisions and the nature of the responsibility of each of the organizational units, and may facilitate effective communication.[8] In brief, while organizational structure is concerned with authority, responsibility, and specialization relations aimed at assuring effective and efficient performance, management accounting, through responsibility accounting, represents the design and implementation of the accounting system for the purpose of better defining and consolidating these relations.

Types of Organizational Structure

Most theorists believe that organizational structure is developed as a response to the problem of control. Basically, control can be achieved by the type of organizational structure adopted. Those aspects of the organizational structure most effective as tools of control have been identified as the span of control, the functional specialization, vertical and horizontal differentiation, centralization, and formalization and standardization. The same structural dimensions can be combined in various ways to constitute an organizational structure. Henry Mintzberg argued that most organizational structures can be classified as belonging to one of five ideals of "pure" structural types, which he called "simple structure, machine bureaucracy, professional bureaucracy, divisionalized form, and adhocracy."[9] Other hybrids are possible. Mintzberg argued, however, that "there are times when we need to caricature, or stereotype, reality in order to sharpen differences and so to better understand it."[10]

The Simple Structure. According to Mintzberg, the basic simple structure can be summarized as follows. It has little or no technostructure, few support staffers, a loose division of labor, minimal differentiation among its units, and a small managerial hierarchy. Little of its behavior is formalized, and it makes minimal use of planning, training, and the liaison devices. It is above all organic.[11]

Basically, the simple structure is a nonstructure where a strong entrepreneur-manager holds all of the decision powers, including planning and control. Most organizations, especially small and young organizations, pass through the simple structure in their formative years. The entrepreneurial firm fits best in the simple-structure category. It depends on the health and whims of one individual and generally has a sense of its mission. The simple structure, although ideal for the small and entrepreneurial firms, may be criticized for being paternalistic, unfashionable in contemporary society, and sometimes autocratic.

The Machine Bureaucracy. According to Mintzberg, the basic structure of a machine bureaucracy can be summarized as follows. It has highly specialized, routine operating tasks, very formalized procedures in the operating core, a proliferation of rules, regulations, and formalized communications throughout the organization, large-sized units at the reoperating level, reliance on the functional basis for grouping tasks, relatively centralized power for decision making, and an elaborate administrative structure with a sharp distinction between line and staff.[12]

The machine bureaucracy is ideal when an integrated set of simple repetitive tasks must be performed well by human beings. It requires direct supervision by first-line managers and standardization of work processes. It depends on strict sets of rules and regulations governing every aspect of the enterprise's life. In fact, the machine bureaucracy is obsessed with control to contain all possible conflicts created by the structure. In fact, decision making in general and planning and control in particular are a top-down affair.

The machine bureaucracy is generally found to prosper in a mature organization, large enough to have been able to settle on the standards it is going to use.[13] It is the second stage of structural development following the aging and growing of simple structures. Mass-production firms are the best-known machine bureaucracies. The main problem of the machine bureaucracy lies in its treatment of people as means or categories of status and function rather than as individuals. A machine bureaucracy also has to deal with the conflict between engineering and efficiency and individual satisfaction. To solve these problems it relies heavily on control and direct supervision.

The Professional Bureaucracy. The professional bureaucracy is an organization that is bureaucratic without being centralized. It calls for standardization and decentralization at the same time. According to Mintzberg, it "relies for coordination on the standardization of skills and its associated design parameters, training and indoctrination. It hires only trained and indoctrinated specialists—professionals—for the operating core, and then gives them considerable control over their own work."[14] The professional bureaucracy structure fits best the personal service organizations, like universities and accounting, law, and consulting firms. The structure of these firms is essentially bureaucratic, in that its coordination—like that of machine bureaucracy—is achieved by design or standards that determine what is to be done.[15] The standards came from the external self-governing organizations that regulate all aspects of the given profession.

The professional bureaucracy is composed of an operating core of professionals serving and backed by a support staff to aid them and do whatever routine work can be formalized. This calls for parallel administrative and control hierarchies, one democratic and bottom-up for the professionals and another bureaucratic and top-down for the support staff.[16]

The professional bureaucracy is not without its problems and limitations. It has no mechanisms for correcting deficiencies that have been ignored by the profession. It cannot easily deal with incompetent or unconscious professionals. As Mintzberg put it, "discretion not only enables some professionals to ignore the needs of their clients; it also encourages many of them to ignore needs of the organization.''[17]

The only way to bring effective changes in the professional bureaucracy is by causing effective changes in the professional organizations themselves, the professional schools that educated the professionals, and the oversight bodies that regulate them.

The Divisionalized Form. According to Mintzberg, the basic structure of a divisionalized concern can be summarized as follows:

like the Professional Bureaucracy, the Divisionalized Form is not so much an integrated organization as a set of quasiautonomous entities coupled together by a central administrative structure. But whereas those ''loosely coupled'' entities in the Professional Bureaucracy are individuals—professionals in the bureaucratic core—in the Divisionalized Form, they are units in the middle line. These units are generally called *divisions*, and the central administration, the *headquarters*. And here the flow of power is not bottom-up, but top-down.[18]

The divisionalized concern is the most widely used structure by the large corporations in the United States and the world. It is basically a structure superimposed on others, where each division has its own structure and where the focus is on the structural relationship between the headquarters and divisions. In general the divisionalized form uses the markets for products as a basis for grouping units or divisions that will have full control of the operating functions to serve these markets. These divisions have practically full autonomy to make their own decisions and then monitor the results of these decisions. They have their own set of goals and work most of the time as machine bureaucracies, characterized by their own technical systems. They work best in environments that are neither very complex nor very dynamic—the same type of environment that leads to the machine bureaucracy.[19] In fact, the structural response to machine bureaucracies that started out working in a simple, stable environment moved to the divisionalized form when the companies diversified into new product or service lines horizontally or when older age and/or large sizes led to diversification.

The Adhocracy. According to Mintzberg, the basic structure of an adhocracy can be summarized as follows: It has a

highly organic structure, with little formalization of behavior; high horizontal job specialization based on formal training; a tendency to group the specialists functional units for housekeeping purposes but to deploy them in small, marketbased project teams to do their work; a reliance on the liaison devices to encourage mutual adjustment, the key coordination mechanism, within and between these teams; and selective decentralization to and within these teams, which are located at various places in the organization and involve various mixtures of line managers and staff and operating experts.[20]

Adhocracy is essential to sophisticated innovation because it allows experts from various disciplines to work mostly together on ad hoc project teams. It tends to use the functional and market basis for grouping concurrently in a matrix structure.[21] Coordination is possible by the mutual adjustment of one team member to another. Adhocracy is ideal for an environment that is both dynamic and complex. The dynamism for the environment calls for the need to decentralize selectivity to differentiated work constellations. In short, it calls for "emphasis on expertise, organic structure, project teams and task forces, decentralization without a single concentration of power, matrix structure, sophisticated and automated technical systems, youth, and environments that are complex and dynamic."[22] It is generally considered the structure of the future.

Line and Staff Relationships

In the organization chart of Exhibit 3.2, the nature of the relationships implied by the lines connecting the organization unit boxes has not been explicitly defined. These relationships may be either line or staff. Line implies a basic hierarchical subordinate-superior relationship as defined by the line of authority or chain of command. Line managers are directly responsible for the particular tasks entrusted to them. Staff implies that a part of the managerial task has been assigned by an executive to someone outside the chain of command. Thus, staff managers facilitate the work of the line managers, providing them with essential services. The authority relationships between the staff member and employees of the line at the same or lower levels may be of four types: staff advice, compulsory advice, concurring authority, or limited company authority.[23] Let us examine each type.

1. The "staff advice" is purely advisory. In general, people are inclined to accept the advice of staff managers when they are regarded as technical experts, when they have impressive titles, when they are skilled in presenting ideas, when they have potential backing by a senior operating executive, and when their views may influence the reward and penalty system. In short, "even though a staff man may have no command authority whatsoever, he may still get his recommendations accepted if he is smart, persuasive, impressive, and influential."[24]

2. Staff managers may have a "compulsory advice" relationship in the sense that they must always be consulted before action is taken.

3. Staff managers may have a "concurring authority" relationship in the sense that no action can be taken until a designated staff manager agrees to it.

4. Finally, staff managers may have a "functional authority" or "limited company authority" relationship in the sense that they are authorized to personally give direct orders to operating personnel rather than merely making recommendations to line managers. For example, the financial accounting department may decide that certain production statistics ought to be disclosed in the annual reports, forcing the production department to produce them periodically.

The concepts of line and staff are another element of organizational structure of relevance to management accounting. First, management accounting is a process that provides services and assistance to other units in the organization. Its role is supportive by nature. It is basically a staff function. Second, as a staff manager the management accountant's authority may range from purely advisory to limited company authority. Third, because of the great need for the specialized knowledge provided by the management accounting department, it is likely to be positioned rather highly in the organization. In any case, management accounting is a decision support system.

The Controllers in the Organization

The managers in charge of accounting departments are known as controllers. They are staff members of the top management team and are line managers in their own departments. As a member of the staff, they advise management in the areas of corporate reporting, planning, and control. Controllers' activities include mainly the following:

1. They are responsible for the supervision of all facets of financial accounting leading to the publication of annual reports.
2. They coordinate all the activities leading to the establishment of the master budget and long-term plan of the firm.
3. They promote maintenance of a system of control through proper circulation of performance reports.
4. As designers and activators of the basic organizational communication system, the electronic data processing system, controllers act as the essential persons for proper collection, diffusion, and channeling of relevant and timely information.

The role of controllers varies, however, from one firm to another, covering the total continuum of staff work. In other words, their role may be a purely advisory relationship, a "compulsory advice" relationship, a "concurring authority" relationship, or an effective "functional authority" relationship.

Because of their position in the top management team, controllers are overseers of the work of others. They initiate and direct the preparation of specific reports for internal or external reporting, and they advise top management on key issues.

Generally reporting to controllers are the staff departments of electronic data processing, taxes, financial analysis and budgeting, financial services, corporate accounting, management services, and payroll. This shows that corporate controllers have moved to the important and central stage. Consider the following quotation:

As the controller's job has changed so have the tools of the trade. In the old days, the controller simply worked up the profit and loss statement and the balance sheet. Today the job involves elaborate monitoring and cross checking of scads of financial data from profits and expenses to return on investment and the cost of capital. Instead of the adding machine and ledger books, the controller works with increasingly complex, sophisticated computer programs that keep him in almost daily touch with almost every facet of the business. [25]

The increase in the size and complexity of business entities, the growth in the use of the planning and control technique, and the new enlarged scope of management accounting activities are the reasons for this new controller concept. It is a top-level function with a primary responsibility for the detailed analysis and interpretation of operating results, policies, procedures, and proposals of major importance. The job of controllers is difficult to define and depends on the particular organizational structure of the firm and the role and scope of the accounting activities. In any case, the job is a complex one. The large list of activities implies that controllers must have personal, educational, and experience qualifications in order to handle all these duties properly. These requirements are very important, given the new expanded role of management accounting in the organization as the "director of management information." Controllers are also essential to the acceptance of the new nature and uses of management accounting. Some of their tasks may involve teaching and convincing the rest of the organization about the new scope of management accounting.

The Role of the Controller in the Design and Operation of the Control System

The controller plays the most important role in the design and operation of the control system, which raises fundamental questions and suggests various solutions. There are misconceptions about the respective roles of the controller and the treasurer, to the point where in many firms the jobs described as falling under the responsibility of one of them belongs in fact under the responsibility of the other. In general, the treasurer is responsible for money-management activities, and the controller acts as chief accountant and financial planner. To clear up this dichotomy, the Financial Executives Institute approved a formal official statement of the controllership and treasurership functions, which is depicted in Exhibit 3.3.

There are also misconceptions about the staff function of the controller. The authority relationship between the staff member and employees of the line at the same or lower levels may be of four types: staff advice, compulsory advice, concurring authority, and limited company authority.

The controller functions best when he or she has a "functional authority," meaning a form of direct involvement in business decisions. The determinants of the degree of involvement of controllers in business decisions remains an empirical question. Vijay Sathe's empirical study of the control function in large ($300 million plus), multidivisional U.S. corporations revealed seven determinants of the degree of involvement of the typical controller in business decisions. [26] They are, by degree of significance, the following:

Exhibit 3.3
Controllership and Treasurership Functions Defined by Financial Executives Institute

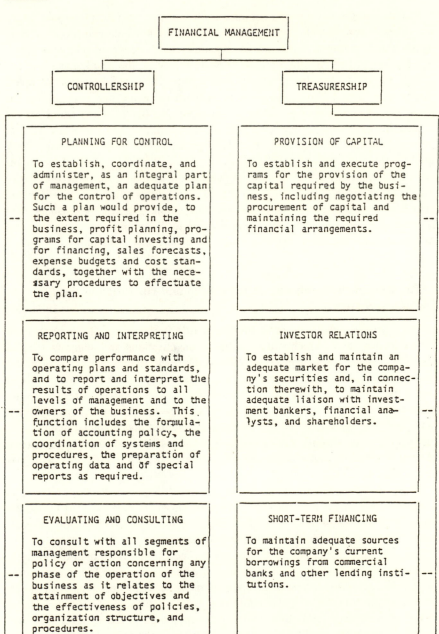

FINANCIAL MANAGEMENT

CONTROLLERSHIP

TREASURERSHIP

PLANNING FOR CONTROL

To establish, coordinate, and administer, as an integral part of management, an adequate plan for the control of operations. Such a plan would provide, to the extent required in the business, profit planning, programs for capital investing and for financing, sales forecasts, expense budgets and cost standards, together with the necessary procedures to effectuate the plan.

PROVISION OF CAPITAL

To establish and execute programs for the provision of the capital required by the business, including negotiating the procurement of capital and maintaining the required financial arrangements.

REPORTING AND INTERPRETING

To compare performance with operating plans and standards, and to report and interpret the results of operations to all levels of management and to the owners of the business. This function includes the formulation of accounting policy, the coordination of systems and procedures, the preparation of operating data and of special reports as required.

INVESTOR RELATIONS

To establish and maintain an adequate market for the company's securities and, in connection therewith, to maintain adequate liaison with investment bankers, financial analysts, and shareholders.

EVALUATING AND CONSULTING

To consult with all segments of management responsible for policy or action concerning any phase of the operation of the business as it relates to the attainment of objectives and the effectiveness of policies, organization structure, and procedures.

SHORT-TERM FINANCING

To maintain adequate sources for the company's current borrowings from commercial banks and other lending institutions.

Exhibit 3.3 (continued)

TAX ADMINISTRATION	BANKING AND CUSTODY
To establish and administer tax policies and procedures.	To maintain banking arrangements; to receive, have custody of, and disburse the company's monies and securities, and to be responsible for the financial aspects of real estate transactions.

GOVERNMENT REPORTING	CREDITS AND COLLECTIONS
To supervise or coordinate the preparation of reports to government agencies.	To direct the granting of credit and the collection of accounts due the company, including the supervision of required special arrangements for financing sales such as time payment and leasing plans.

PROTECTION OF ASSETS	INVESTMENT
To assure protection for the assets of the business through internal control, internal auditing, and assuring proper insurance coverage.	To invest the company's funds as required, and to establish and coordinate policies for investment in pension and other similar trusts.

ECONOMIC APPRAISAL	INSURANCE
To continuously appraise economic and social forces and government influences, and to interpret their effect upon the business.	To provide insurance coverage as required.

Note: The first formal official statement of the responsibilities of the corporate-treasurership function was approved by the Board of Directors of Financial Executives Institute (established in 1931 as Controllers Institute of America) at its meeting in French Lick Springs, Indiana, on May 17. For many years the institute and its predecessor body had published an established list of functions of controllership. The newly approved list of treasurership functions was developed coincident with the change of scope and name of the Institute from Controllers Institute to Financial Executives Institute. (See "CIA Becomes FEI," *The Controller* [May 1962], p. 228.)

Source: Reprinted by permission from *The Controller*, June 1962, copyright 1962 by Financial Executives Institute.

1. The degree of corporate management's financial orientation, with its emphasis on financial goals and on a "portfolio approach" type of management

2. The degree of corporate management's emphasis on the company's financial planning, budgeting, and capital-expenditure-review system

3. The duration of sustained emphasis on development of controllership personnel, in terms of career planning, job rotation, or other programs concerned specifically with the development of personnel in the controllership function

4. The working capital intensity of a business (inventories plus receivables divided by net sales)

5. Corporate management's expectations regarding controller involvement in business decisions

6. The emphasis that the corporation places upon transfers from the line organization to the controller function as part of the management development strategy

7. The emphasis the corporate controller organization places on the advisory role

To be effective at being involved in business decisions and at exercising "functional authority," it is important for the controller to be a "strong controller."[27]

The definition of the controller role differs generally from the traditional definition of a functional role. An empirical study by Dale Henning and Roger Moseley indicates that controllers do not have the same authority in all of their functions or in the various decisions within those functions.[28] They concluded as follows:

The role of the controller appears to be much more complex than the literature suggests. He is assigned certain functional responsibilities, yet as he attempts to fulfill those responsibilities, he finds himself with different degrees of authority as he moves from one function to another and from one decision to another. His superior, who has considerable say about his destiny, and his executive peers, with whom he must establish good relationships if he is to successfully fulfill his responsibilities, observe his behavior with different expectations about his authority. The controller might be looked upon in one instance by his superior as being too aggressive, and, at the same time, as not aggressive enough by his peers, or just the reverse. The profile of the controller is that of an executive with substantial authority in some functions and more limited authority in others: with varying degrees of authority in different decisions within a function, many times as making unilateral decisions and often sharing in the making of decisions; perceiving himself as having more authority than he is seen to have by his superior and his peers. He occupies a role with great opportunity, yet is both ill-defined and fraught with potential conflict.[29]

While still in its infancy, research findings point to a number of significant relationships between the nature of the controller's department and characteristics of the overall organization. For example, K. Rosenzweig found size and unionization to be important considerations in the design of a controller's department structure.[30]

Although the case for active involvement of the controller in management may be easily made and defended, it raises, however, the question of controller independence. The issue is important to both society and the corporation. Inaccurate reporting will undermine public confidence and distinct internal resource allocation. Can the controller wear two hats, one for being actively involved and one for keeping his or her sense of objectivity and independence? Most people would argue that the answer is no. One solution lies in using the internal audit function in general and internal and external compliance auditing to ensure overall organizational control, including the controller's department.

Another unresolved organization design question is whether the division controller should report directly to the decision manager or to the corporate controller. If the division controller reports to the division manager, one may question his or her "independence." In fact, M. Schiff and A. Y. Lewin reported that in those cases, the division controller appears to have undertaken the task of creating and managing division slack and is most influential in the internal allocation of this slack.[31] The solution seems to lie again on the role of the internal audit function. J. G. San Miguel and V. Govindarajan found a contingent relationship between the division controller's independence from the division manager and the duties and responsibilities assigned to the internal audit function.[32] Basically,

in firms where the division controller was less independent, the internal audit functions were employed to perform a significantly greater amount of financial, compliance auditing than firms with more independent division controllers. This contingent relationship appears to have evolved quite naturally because of top management's concern for maintaining effective organizational control to satisfy the firm's and their own objectives.[33]

THEORIES OF ORGANIZATION

The theories of organization represent different attempts in the literature to describe and explain organizational behavior. Each of these theories attempts to determine the significant elements that may approximate the patterning or order existing in organizations. Because these elements comprise the key organizational variables or the ways they are related, they define the ways management accounting will better provide its services to the organization. Although not exhaustive, the theories examined comprise those that currently reflect organizational literature: the rational perspective, the classical perspective, the human relations perspective, and the natural system perspective. Management accounting is thought to rest on elements provided by each of these formulations, rather than on any single one, because none provides an entirely adequate theory organization on its own.

The Rational Perspective

Max Weber argued that the social behavior and social interaction of individuals depend on their "ideas" of the existence of a *legitimate authority*.[34] He distinguished between three pure types of legitimate authority, each dependent on a different source of legitimation:

1. *Traditional authority*, legitimated by time and resting "on established belief in the sanctity of immemorial traditions and the legitimacy of the status of those exercising authority under them."[35]
2. *Charismatic authority*, legitimated by the appealing personality of the leader and resting on the "devotion to the specific and exceptional sanctity, heroism or exemplary character of an individual person, and of the normative patterns or order revealed or ordained by him."[36]
3. *Bureaucratic or rational-legal authority*, legitimated by rules and resting "on a belief in the 'legality' of patterns of normative rules and the right of those elevated to authority under such rules to issue commands."[37]

The last type of authority was viewed by Weber as an ideal characteristic of modern organizations. He drew attention to the fact that in modern society the bureaucratic type has become dominant because of its alleged greater efficiency. The bureaucratic organization is composed of a bureaucratic administrative staff. The position occupied by the chief of such an organization is by virtue of appropriation, election, or succession. The individuals comprising the organization conform to the following ten criteria:

1. They are personally free and subject to authority only with respect to their impersonal official obligations.
2. They are organized in a clearly defined hierarchy of offices.
3. Each office has a clearly defined sphere of competence in the legal sense.
4. The office is filled by a free contractual relationship. Thus, in principle, there is free selection.
5. The candidates are selected on the basis of technical qualifications. In the most rational case, this is tested by examination or guaranteed by diplomas certifying technical training, or both. They are appointed, not elected.
6. They are remunerated by fixed salaries in money, for the most part with a right to pensions. Only under certain circumstances does the employing authority, especially in private organizations, have a right to terminate the appointment, but the official is always free to resign. The salary scale is primarily graded according to rank in the hierarchy; but in addition to this criterion, the responsibility of the position and the requirements of the incumbent's social status may be taken into account.
7. The office is treated as the sole, or at least the primary, occupation of the incumbent.
8. It constitutes a career. There is a system of promotion according to seniority or achievement, or both. Promotion is dependent on the judgment of superiors.
9. The official works entirely separated from ownership of the means of administration and without appropriation of his position.
10. He is subject to strict and systematic discipline and control in the conduct of his office.[38]

The organization under a rational perspective is viewed as a highly efficient machine where members strive together in an orderly fashion to complete a given objective. Empirical evidence related to the organizational effectiveness of the Weberian type of organization was provided by James Price.[39]

The rational perspective stresses both goal specificity and formalization. As A. W. Gouldner notes,

fundamentally, the rational model implies a "mechanical" model, in that it views the organization as a structure of manipulable parts, each of which is separately modifiable with a view to enhancing the efficiency of the whole. Individual organizational elements are seen as subject to successful and planned modification, enactable by deliberate decision.[40]

Robert Merton also appropriately notes that "formality facilitates the interaction of the occupants of offices despite their (possibly hostile) private attitudes toward one another."[41]

Different points of criticism appear in the literature against the rational perspective in organizational structure and behavior. Organizations tend to change from bureaucratic to charismatic during crisis situations. Weber uniquely assumed a formal behavior existing in the organization. People within the organization were assumed to behave rigidly and mechanistically according to established rules. Thus, informal behavior, group norms, environmental changes, and internal conflict are not discussed by Weber, who provided the first of the original studies designed to examine the nature and functioning of bureaucracy and organization in general. Weber in fact was confused between two analytically distinguishable bases of authority by once arguing that authority is based on incumbency in a legally defined office and later arguing that it is based on technical competence. Gouldner, again, notes:

Weber, then, thought of bureaucracy as a Janus-faced organization, looking two ways at once. On the one side, it was administration based on discipline. In the first emphasis, obedience is invoked as a means to an end; an individual obeys because the rule or order is felt to be the best known method of realizing some goals.

In his second conception, Weber held that bureaucracy was a mode of administration in which obedience was an end in itself. The individual obeys the order, setting aside judgment either of its rationality or morality, primarily because of the position occupied by the person commanding. The conduct of the order is not examinable.[42]

Despite its apparent limitations, the rational perspective designates significant elements approximating the patterning or order inherent in organizations and of relevance to management accounting. Organizations may be seen as a deliberate, rational arrangement of means to accomplish a desired end. Rules are established in order to regulate the organization's structure and processes. Finally, legal authority is used to coordinate all the elements of an organization in order to allow their efficient functioning. In response to these patterns, management

accounting will focus on the legally prescribed structures and the mechanisms
by which they are maintained. For example, control will focus on whether persons
comply with organizational rules given that each person's actions are essential
to the accomplishment of the organizational goals. Similarly, management accounting as a form of organizational behavior will be consciously and rationally
administered with the organizational goals in mind.

The Classical Perspective

The classical school originated with Frederick Taylor and his "Principles of
Scientific Management."[43] The concern was with insuring the most efficient
utilization of the physical resources of the organization. Taylor's aim was to
replace the arbitrary and capricious work of managers with analytical, scientific
procedures:

Under scientific management arbitrary power, arbitrary dictation, ceases and every single
subject, large and small, becomes the question for scientific investigation, for reduction
to law. . . .
   The man at the head of the business under scientific management is governed by rules
and laws which have been developed through hundreds of experiments just as much as
the workman is, and the standards which have been developed are equitable.[44]

Scientific management was based on four main principles:

1. The development of an ideal or best method primarily through time and motion study.
2. The selection and development of workers.
3. The combination between the best method and the best selected and trained workers.
4. The close cooperation of managers and workers.

Taylor's approach led to major advances in industrial efficiency and influenced
the works of Henry Gantt[45] and Frank Gilbreth.[46]
   The main goal of scientific management is to use scientific methods to establish
a standard for completing a job in the best manner. The productive processes
are concerned with the ratio of output to input, *the criterion of efficiency*. To
accomplish these objectives, the work force is to be organized so that each person
is assigned a standard for his or her highly specialized job, based on the most
efficient method of completing the work and rewarded on the basis of task
accomplishment. From these objectives stem two basic characteristics of the
organization. It is *work centered* and *authoritarian*. The central characteristic
of an organization is work and, given that work is considered distasteful by
some, authority is necessary for insuring the accomplishment of organizational
objectives. Authority is centralized and flows from the owners to the board of
directors to the workers. The authority of the president lies in POSDCORB.[47]
The acronym stands for Planning, Organizing, Staffing, Directing, Coordinating,

Reporting, and Budgeting. Work is specialized in units, leading to what is known as the departmentalized approach to the problem of management. These units are coordinated in a hierarchical structure. The authority in each unit is defined by the "span of control" of each manager. All these characteristics reflect a facet of the traditional school known as "the principles of management" or "administrative management theory." Henri Fayol, in particular, viewed the principles of management as follows:

1. Division of work
2. Authority
3. Discipline
4. Unity of command
5. Unity of direction
6. Subordination of individual interests to the general interests
7. Remuneration
8. Centralization
9. Scalar chain (line of authority)
10. Order
11. Equity
12. Stability of tenure of personnel
13. Initiative
14. Esprit de corps[48]

The classical school has also had its share of criticism. It has been labeled as normative rather than analytical. Like the Weberian model, it has ignored the impact of the external environment, the existence of internal conflict, and the behavioral idiosyncrasies resulting from the different cognitive make-up of organization members.

Like the Weberian perspective, the classical perspective identifies elements approximating the patterning or order inherent in organizations and of relevance to management accounting. Organizations are viewed only as means in the pursuit of a specific end, defined as optimal organizational efficiency. The accomplishment of this objective lies in the arrangement of the employees and machines. This arrangement relies on scientific means of associating the best person and/or machine to the ideal job. It requires developing scientific standards rather than rules of thumb for each individual and each task.

The work of every workman is fully planned out by the management at least one day in advance, and each man received in most cases complete written instructions, describing in detail the task which he is to accomplish, as well as the means to be used in doing the work.[49]

Briefly, the classical perspective rests on management accounting by calling for both planning and control: planning by the setting of rigid scientific standards for each job, and control by insuring the realization of *optimal organizational efficiency*. Let us note, however, that the classical perspective calls for planning and control primarily at the operative or worker level and is essentially short-range and specific. What may then be learned and extrapolated from the classical perspective is the requirement of planning and control at all levels of management, short-term and long-term, toward the realization of the optimal organizational efficiency.

The Human Relations Perspective

As a counterpoint against the impersonality of classical theory, the human relations perspective emphasizes the human dimension of management. The major thrust of this perspective is that

the dominant focus of organization was transformed from a rational model, free from the friction of man's emotions, to a model which appears to be less determined and unfathomable. That is, the new look in organizational theory took cognizance of the unanticipated consequences of organizations: workers' feelings, beliefs, perceptions, ideas, and sentiments—exactly those elements of passion Weber believed escaped calculation. Administrators began to take seriously—in part through the seminal work of several social scientists—not only their formal organizational chart, but workers' feelings about the structure and hierarchy. This model of organization . . . took as its major assumption that man could be motivated to work more productively on the basis of fulfilling certain psychological needs. This "new look" of organization was no less rational than the earlier machine model, except that man's motivation was a tricker and more elusive concept than the machine.[50]

The essence is to distinguish between the formal organization and the informal organization. F. J. Roethlisberger and W. J. Dickson, the founders of the human relations school, proposed that

the patterns of human interrelations, as defined by the systems, rules, policies, and regulations of the company, constitute the formal organization. . . . It includes the systems, policies, rules, and regulations of the plant which express what the relations of one person to another are supposed to be in order to achieve effectively the task of technical production.[51]

By contrast, the informal organization is described as follows:

Many of the actually existing patterns of human interaction have no representation in the formal organization at all, and others are inadequately represented by the formal organization. . . . Too often it is assumed that the organization of a company corresponds to a blueprint plan or organization chart. Actually, it never does.[52]

This perspective started when Elton May and other Harvard University professors were invited to study new ways to increase plant productivity at the Hawthorne plant of the Western Electric Company. Known as the Hawthorne Studies, they showed that workers are complex social creatures with feelings, desires, and fears, and they react to change in terms of the meaning change has for them. What change meant to workers depended on their social conditioning (feelings, fears, hope, etc.) and their social situation at work where group pressures determined attitudes and sentiments. Other similar findings were included in *Management and the Worker*, the publication resulting from the Hawthorne experiment.[53] This line of research was pursued through the empirical works of such theorists as Rensis Likert,[54] Chris Argyris,[55] and Douglas McGregor.[56]

What stems from the human relations perspective is that workers as social creatures are motivated by attitudes formed through interactions in the formal group rather than uniquely by economic factors. Group norms act as a major regulatory tool, affecting member behavior given that persons desire group acceptance. Thus, the organizations become essentially sets of interlocked functioning groups. Likert suggests that these groups may be linked together to create a working organization where each individual will increase a sense of participation because each individual is more aware of the congruence between personal goals and the company's objectives.[57] In fact, Likert advocated the use of the participative group type of management system as the most effective, rather than the exploitive-authoritative, benevolent-authoritative, and consultative systems.[58] These characteristics of the human relations perspectives have great implications for management accounting. First, management accounting concepts and techniques, in general, and planning and control, in particular, have to take into account the individuals and what motivates them. "Each of us wants appreciation, recognition, influence, a feeling of accomplishment, and a feeling that people who are important to us believe in us and respects us."[59] Second, it implies that workers should be involved in some participatory ways in the setting of standards. Preferably group norms should be considered in the setting of standards with an emphasis on cooperation rather than competition among group members.

The best performance, lower costs, and the highest level of earnings and of employee satisfaction occur when the drive for a sense of personal worth is used to create strong motivational forces to *cooperate* rather than *compete* with one's peers and colleagues. The use of this motive in ways which yield cooperative rather than competitive relationships appears to yield stronger motivational forces oriented toward achieving the organizations' objectives and is accompanied by positive rather than negative side effects. Subordinates aid each other and share leadership tasks rather than putting immediate self-interest ahead of long-range self-interest and organizational success.[60]

Third, performance reports used for control should not be limited to financial data and should be expanded to include a measure of the "organizational atmosphere" or climate that determines workers' productivity.

The Natural System Perspective

The natural system perspective views organizations as continually adapting to a changing environment in order to maintain equilibrium. Once created, the organizations acquire a life of their own and behave in unplanned and spontaneous or "natural" ways. This perspective is best illustrated in the works of three sociologists: Robert Michels,[61] Talcott Parsons,[62] and Philip Selznick.[63] For example, Selznick emphasizes "coaptation" as a predominant adaptive process of organization; that is, "the process of absorbing new elements in the leadership or policy-determining structure of an organization as one means of averting threats to its stability or existence."[64] These continuous attempts at adapting to their environments lead the organizations to modify their basic structures and create a character or personality. The structure of an organization, therefore, is inseparable from the functioning of the organization.[65]

Viewed as a system, the organization stresses the interdependence of parts or subsystems. These are:

1. the productive subsystem responsible for the technical processes,
2. the supportive subsystems responsible for the efficient flow of inputs in the organization and output of the organization,
3. the maintenance subsystem responsible for the maintenance of the organization by recruiting and rewarding the members,
4. the adaptive subsystem responsible for responding to the environmental changes, and
5. the managerial subsystem responsible for directing and controlling all other subsystems.

The natural system perspective, like the other perspectives, identifies elements and characteristics of importance to management accounting. First, each organization acquires a given personality that will require specific management techniques different from those adopted by other organizations. "Every structure has a set of basic needs and develops systematic means of self-defense."[66] Second, because the organization faces a given changing environment, it must change and adapt to the new environmental conditions requiring management accounting to be dynamic in the sense of continuously absorbing new elements and information into its reporting function, adapting old techniques, and adapting new techniques to avert threats to the stability or existence of the organization. Third, the control process should rely on feedforward techniques that precipitate internal changes. Fourth, because the organization is a collection of systems, each trying to maintain its own equilibrium, management accounting should be designed to serve the subsystems and to maintain their autonomy. Deliberate changes can be made without affecting other subsystems, because each subsystem is part of an organic whole. Under the natural system perspective, management accounting adopts a structural-functional model of analysis that assumes that the organization, as a social unit, has needs and requirements to be met if it is to survive.

Accordingly, information about salient changes in the environment of the firm must be produced and communicated by the management accounting system. Given that the structural elements of the firm are mutually interdependent, management accounting information should play the crucial role for these systems to tend toward a state of equilibrium.

ORGANIZATIONAL DESIGN

Toward a Contingency Model for the Design of Management Accounting

The contingency approach to the design of accounting systems assumes that a general strategy applicable to all organizations does not exist. On the contrary, it assumes that the design of various components of accounting systems depends on the specific contingencies that can create a perfect match. It is then the perfect link or match between the design of accounting systems and the specific contingencies that is the scope of contingency theory. To date, the contingency formulations have considered the effects of technology, organizational structure and theory, and the environment in attempting to explain how accounting systems differ in various situations. All of these formulations point to the accepted thesis that there is no universal "best design" for a management accounting information system, and that "it all depends upon situational factors."[67]

These formulations adopt a general framework depicted in Exhibit 3.4, which links

1. some contingent variables (that is, variables that cannot be influenced by the organization) to
2. any components of an organizational control package (consisting of accounting information design, other management information design, organizational design, or organizational control arrangements), and then through
3. some interviewing variables provide a link to
4. a measure or organizational effectiveness.[68]

The formulations are either empirical or theoretical. The literature includes various theoretical speculations about the nature of a contingency theory of accounting-information systems and/or control systems. L. A. Gordon and D. A. Miller identified environment, organizational characteristics, and decision-making styles as the main classes of contingent variables,[69] similarly, J. H. Waterhouse and P. A. Tiessen proposed environment and technology.[70] A more elaborate contextual model of information system, provided by N. B. Macintosh, combines both personal decision style and organizational technology to derive four distinct information-system styles—concise, cursory, diffuse, and elabo-

Exhibit 3.4
The Minimum Necessary Contingency Framework

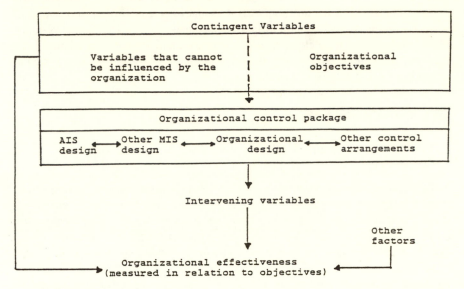

Source: David T. Otley, ''The Contingency Theory of Management Accounting: Achievement and Prognosis,'' *Accounting, Organizations and Society* (December 1980): 421. Reprinted with permission.

rate—each of which is suited to a particular technology.[71] The model is illustrated in Exhibits 3.5 and 3.6. The four distinct information-system styles are defined as follows:

The concise information system. Small to moderate amounts of information that is precise and unambiguous, and is used in a quick and decisive way.

The elaborate information system. Large amounts of information, frequently in the form of data bases or stimulation models, which tend to be detailed or precise; recipients normally use such information in a slow and deliberate manner.

The cursory information system. Small amounts of information, neither precise nor detailed and frequently superficial, that is used in a casual yet decisive way.

The diffuse information system. Moderate to large amounts of information, covering a wide range of material, frequently ill-defined and imprecise, that typically is used in a slow, deliberate manner.[72]

All of these attempts at formulating a contingency theory of accounting information systems and/or control systems fail to provide a more exhaustive list of the main classes of contingent variables.

A summary of the structural features affecting accounting system design is shown in Exhibit 3.7. A wide range of potentially influential factors is shown

Exhibit 3.5
Categories of Technology

		Low	High
Task Knowledge	**Unanalyzable**	Craft technology	Research technology
	Analyzable	Routine technology	Technical-professional technology
		Low	High

Task Variety

in these empirical studies. The most significant factors are technology, environment, size, strategy, and culture.[73] The two most important factors of technology and the environment are reviewed next.

Impact of Technology

Technology includes not only machines and equipment but also all of the techniques used to transform materials in a prescribed manner. Harold Leavitt defined *technology* as direct problem-solving inventions like work-measurement techniques or computers or drill presses.[74] However, Charles Perrow defined technology as the "actions that an individual performs upon an object, with or without the aid of tools or mechanical devices, in order to make some change in that object."[75] He saw as dimensions of technology both *variability*, which is the number of exceptional cases that must be handled in work, and *analyzability*, which is the nature of the search process that must be used when exceptions occur.

Various ways of classifying organizations in terms of their technology have been used. Most theories disagree with the Standard Industrial Classification System, which classifies firms on the basis of their primary function, and argue for a classification that conforms to the technical systems. For example, Joan Woodward suggested the following three groupings:

1. *unit production*—units or small batches produced to customer specifications
2. *mass production*—making large batches of the product at one time
3. *continuous process*—a steady flow of inputs into a continuous process.[76]

She also identified three aspects of organizational design affected by technology: structure, control mechanisms, and management systems. With respect

Exhibit 3.6
A Comprehensive Contextual Model of Information Systems

Organizational situation					Information system			
Search procedures available for task completion	Perceived nature of tasks	Technology type	Organizational structure	Personal decision style	Amount	Ambiguity	Use	Style
Analyzable search	Uniform and stable	Routine	Classical bureaucratic	Decisive	Minimal	Single focus	Quick and decisive	Concise
Analyzable search	Nonuniform and unstable	Technical professional	Functional bureaucratic	Hierarchic	Large	Single focus	Careful and deliberate	Elaborate
Unanalyzable search	Uniform and stable	Craft	Decentralized autonomous	Flexible	Minimal	Multiple focus	Intuitive reaction	Cursory
Unanalyzable search	Nonuniform and unstable	Research	Organic matrix	Integrative	Large	Multiple focus	Slow and creative	Diffuse

Source: Norman B. MacIntosh, "A Contextual Model of Information Systems," *Accounting, Organizations and Society* (February 1981). Reprinted with permission.

Exhibit 3.7
Comparison of Major Studies with Simple Linear Model

Study	Contingent variables	Organizational design	Type of accounting Information system	Organizational effectiveness
Bruns & Waterhouse	Organizational context (origin, size, technology, dependence)	Structuring of activities Concentration of authority	Control system complexity and perceived control leading to budget-related behavior, interpersonal and administrative control strategies	
Draft & MacIntosh	Technology (task variety; search procedures)		I.S. style (amount, focus and use of data)	
Dermer	Organizational objectives Technology Managerial style	Decentralization Differentiation	Choice of A.I.S. or M.C.S. techniques	
Gordon & Miller	Environment (dynamism heterogeneity and hostility)	Decentralization Bureaucratization Resource availability	Technical characteristics of accounting I.S.	

83

Exhibit 3.7 (continued)

Study	Contingent variables	Organizational design	Type of accounting information system	Organizational effectiveness
Hayes	Environmental factors Interdependency factors Internal factors		Appropriate performance evaluation techniques	Departmental effectiveness
Khandwalla	Type of competition faced		Sophistication of accounting controls	
Piper	Task complexity (product range and diversity variability between units)	Decentralization of decision-making	Financial control structure (e.g. use of financial planning models; frequency of reports)	
Waterhouse and Tiessen	Environmental predictability Technological routineness	Nature of sub-units operational or managerial	Management accounting system design	

Source: D. T. Otley, "The Contingency Theory of Management Accounting: Achievement and Prognosis," *Accounting, Organizations and Society* (December 1980): 420. Reprinted with permission.

to structure, the findings indicated that structural characteristics of firms tended to vary from group to group. More explicitly, successful large-batch or mass-production firms tended to be organized along classical lines, with duties and responsibilities clearly delineated, a unity of command, a clear distinction between line and staff, and a narrow span of control. With respect to control mechanisms, the type of control found in the technical subsystem of an organization is directly related to the type of technology employed. Although unit technology puts an emphasis on personal controls, continuous-process technology focuses on impersonal controls, and mass-production technology relies on a mix of personal and impersonal controls.[77] With respect to information systems, the findings indicate that the impact of technology extends to the production tools that can alter the flow of material through the system. Of new interest to this book is the finding that technology plays a major role in dictating the type of control system that is feasible or practical. More explicitly, it states that with routine and repetitive production recesses, task uncertainty is relatively low, and organizational coordination requires only programmed interactions; also, impersonal controls in the form of budgeting and accounting-performance measures are easier to use.[78] In fact, Kenneth Merchant provided significant results supporting the expectation that automation of processes and standardization of output, both indicators of the repetitiveness of technology, have a positive relationship with the reliance placed on budgeting for purpose of communication of intentions to coordinate organizational activities and for evaluation of managerial performance.[79]

Impact of the Environment

The type of control system is generally developed as a response to the environment. In effect, the external environment is the societal context for the organization and its members. D. Silverman, for example, perceived it as the source of meaning, providing the stock of knowledge in guiding the behavior of the organization and its members.[80]

The impact of the environment on control has been examined by various researchers. E. G. Flamholtz identified three broad classes of environmental factors likely to be potential mechanisms of control on the behavior of organizational members: the dominant work values in the temporal social setting, the level of professionalism, and direct demands from clients and customers.[81] Hence there is an emerging need for active involvement and increased responsibility, professionalism is growing in many occupations, and the demand for quality service or products from customers and clients may act as potential mechanisms of control.

Organizations are "hiring purposeful" or "adaptively rational" systems whose survival depends on their ability to interact successfully, on a continuous basis, with the surrounding environment. Based on that assumption Kweka Ewusi-Mensah identified three states of the external organizational environ-

ment—controllable, partially controllable, and uncontrollable—and discussed
the information characteristics of each state.[82] The environments are characterized
by mostly homogeneous factors in the controllable state, both homogeneous and
heterogeneous factors in the partially controllable state, and uncertainties with
respect to events and changes in the environment in the uncontrollable state.

The external organizational environment may also be classified as static or
dynamic. This last classification depends on the degree of stability in the environmental factors. The static environment can be characterized by a high level
of stability, calling for the use of formalized procedures for dealing with environmental factors or elements. The dynamic environment can be characterized
by "an increasing rate of interconnection and/or interaction among environmental
factors, resulting in a higher degree of uncertainty and complexity" and calling
for the use of sophisticated strategies for monitoring the environment to collect
pertinent data.[83]

Both classifications of the external environment (static or dynamic; controllable, partially controllable, or uncontrollable) may be combined to describe the
total external organizational environment, as illustrated in Exhibit 3.8, with the
relevant characteristics identified in each cell. Each of the cells calls for an
appropriate control system and different information characteristics. Exhibit 3.9
shows the proposed organizational information characteristics of the environmental states.

Different types of competition may lead to a different use of management
controls. Basically, the greater the competition, the greater the need to control
costs and to evaluate production, marketing, finance, and so on as operating
according to expectations. This argument was empirically verified by P. N.
Khandwalla.[84] He examined the effects of different types of competition on the
use of management controls and showed a positive association between competition and the use of sophisticated management controls. One of the implications follows:

This implies that as competition intensifies, the expected benefits from the application of
these controls tend to outweigh their costs. Thus, for those entrusted with the planning
of control systems, it is important to know the degree of competition faced by the firm.
Other things being equal, an elaborate control system for a firm not facing serious
competition can produce net benefits, but a sophisticated control system in a firm which
does not face intense competition may do more harm than good.[85]

Models of sectorial economic differentiation derived from theories of economic
dualism include various perspectives such as theories of dual economy, dual
labor markets, and labor-force segmentation.[86] Common to all of these perspectives is the proposal of a division of the industrial structure of the economy
into two distinct sectors (at least in the two-sector model), consisting of the core
and periphery sectors.

Theories of dual economy suggest that these sectoral differences have im-

Exhibit 3.8
Characteristics of Organizational Environmental States

| Org. env. | Environmental state | | |
	Controllable	Partially controllable	Uncontrollable
Static	Environmental factors remain basically same over a period Mostly homogeneous, but they can be heterogeneous with relatively homogeneous segments Environmental state relatively comprehensible Formal procedures for data gathering can be developed Examples — customers and suppliers	Some environmental factors both homogeneous and heterogeneous remain basically same over a period Other environmental factors may be continually changing Interaction of stable and turbulent factors produce fluid environment which may be partially comprehensible Some formal procedures for data gathering may be possible Examples — Customers and suppliers, Competitors of customers and/or suppliers, Regulatory agencies, Trade Unions, etc.	Relatively heterogeneous factors but level of complexity defies clear comprehension Monitoring best left to decentralized units or segments of organization Some formal procedures for data gathering feasible on regional or decentralized basis Business intelligence activities can be encouraged
Dynamic	Relatively homogeneous factors and heterogeneous with relatively homogeneous segments with predictable changes Monitoring can be undertaken on differentiated basis to meet organization capacity for data gathering Business intelligence activities may be unnecessary	Business intelligence activities encouraged	Environmental factors continually interacting with each other and changing to produce unstable environmental state Environmental state relatively incomprehensible due to turbulence and level of complexity Examples — Political upheavals, social/cultural factors, Demographic changes Some systematic approaches to data gathering may be feasible on highly decentralized or localized basis Business intelligence activities needed

Source: K. Ewusi-Mensah, ''The External Organizational Environment and Its Impact on Management Information Systems,'' *Accounting, Organizations and Society* (December 1981): 306. Reprinted with permission.

portant implications for the opportunity structures and environment faced by individual firms. Firms in the periphery sector face a more restricted opportunity structure and a higher degree of environmental uncertainty than firms in the core sector. Therefore, firms in the periphery sector may need a more complex and exhaustive management accounting system than firms in the core sector.

CONCLUSIONS

Management accounting rests on organizational foundations. The elements of organizational structure and the theories of organization define its role and scope in the organization and the techniques, approaches, and philosophies it may espouse in order to provide adequate services to the organization. The elements of organizational structure—the nature of organizations, organizational struc-

Exhibit 3.9
Organizational Information Characteristics of the Environmental States

Org. infor. variable	Controllable	Partially Controllable	Uncontrollable
Information quality	High with low risk	Medium with low-medium risk	Low with high risk
Information availability	Good	Fair	Poor
Information value	Relatively high	Medium	Relatively low
Impact on decision-making	Relatively high	Medium	Relatively low
Organizational interaction	Active interaction	Active-reactive	Mainly reactive
Organizational search	Mostly opportunistic	Both opportunistic and problemistic	Mostly problemistic
Organizational response time	Either prompt or slow	Slow to fast	Relatively prompt
Organizational time frame	Present to future oriented	Present to future oriented	Mainly future oriented
Source of Information	Some internal but mostly externally based	Mostly externally based	Externally based
Type of information	Both quantitative and qualitative	Some quantitative but mostly qualitative	Mostly qualitative

Source: K. Ewusi-Mensah, "The External Organizational Environment and Its Impact on Management Information Systems," *Accounting, Organizations and Society.* (December 1981): 306. Reprinted with permission.

tures, the implications of the line/staff relationships, and the new role of controllers—provide management accounting with different organizational concepts that define and shape some of its techniques and approaches. The organization theories—the rational, classical, human relations, and natural system perspectives—point to the significant elements that approximate the patterning and order inherent in organizations, and that may direct management accounting to more effective ways of providing its services. These relationships between management accounting and the elements of organization structure and organization theories are illustrated in Exhibit 3.10.

NOTES

1. Robert T. Golembiewski, "Accountancy as a Function of Organizational Theory," *The Accounting Review* (April 1964): 341.

2. Eugene J. Hass and Thomas E. Drabeck, *Complex Large Organizations: A Sociological Perspective* (New York: Macmillan, 1973), p. 8.

3. George Homans, *The Human Group* (New York: Harcourt, Brace, 1950), pp. 82–86.

4. Hass and Drabeck, *Complex Large Organizations*, p. 14.

5. Donald Katz and Robert L. Kahn, *The Social Psychology of Organizations* (New York: John Wiley, 1966), p. 172.

6. James D. Thompson, *Organizations in Action* (New York: McGraw-Hill, 1967).

7. Sherman Krupp, *Pattern in Organizational Analysis* (New York: Holt, Rinehart & Winston, 1961), p. 60.

8. George J. Benston, "The Role of the Firm's Accounting System for Motivation," *The Accounting Review* (April 1963): 348.

9. Henry Mintzberg, *Structures in Files: Designing Effective Organizations* (Englewood Cliffs, N.J.: Prentice-Hall, 1983).

10. Ibid., p. 156.

11. Ibid., pp. 157–158.

12. Ibid., p. 164.

13. Ibid., p. 171.

14. Ibid., p. 190.

15. Ibid., p. 191.

16. Ibid., p. 198.

17. Ibid., p. 208.

18. Ibid., p. 215.

19. Ibid., p. 217.

20. Ibid., p. 219.

21. Ibid., p. 254.

22. Ibid., p. 256.

23. Don Hellriegel and John W. Slocum, Jr., *Management: A Contingency Approach*, 2nd ed. (Reading, Mass.: Addison-Wesley, 1979).

24. William H. Newman, Charles E. Summer, and Warren E. Kirby, *The Process of Management—Concepts, Behavior and Practice*, 2nd ed. (Englewood Cliffs, N.J.: Prentice-Hall, 1962), p. 110.

Exhibit 3.10
Management Accounting: The Organizational Foundations

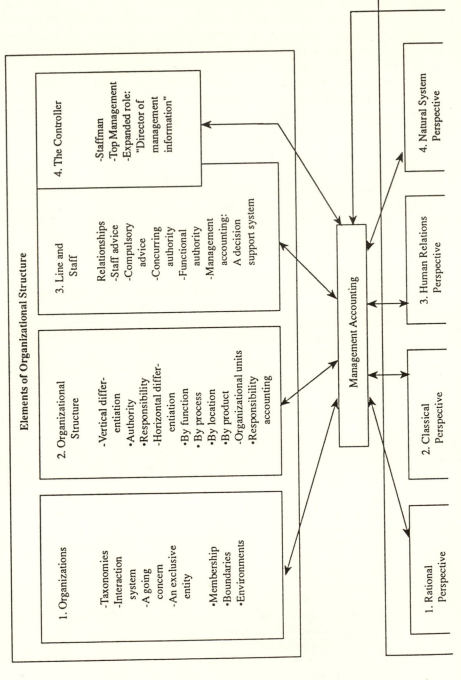

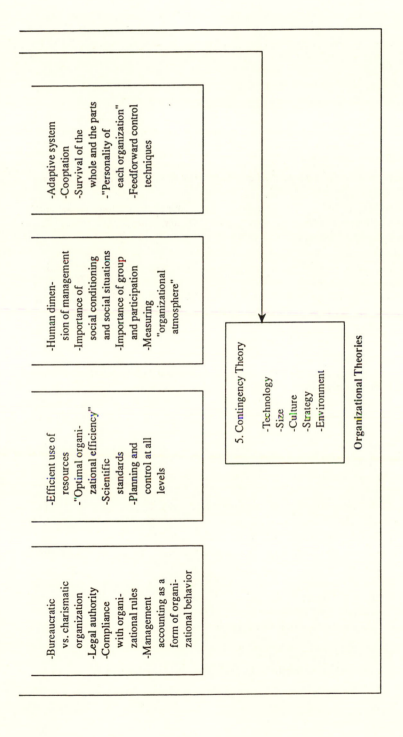

Organizational Theories

- Bureaucratic vs. charismatic organization
- Legal authority
- Compliance with organizational rules
- Management accounting as a form of organizational behavior

- Efficient use of resources
- "Optimal organizational efficiency"
- Scientific standards
- Planning and control at all levels

- Human dimension of management
- Importance of social conditioning and social situations
- Importance of group and participation
- Measuring "organizational atmosphere"

- Adaptive system
- Cooptation
- Survival of the whole and the parts
- "Personality of each organization"
- Feedforward control techniques

5. Contingency Theory
- Technology
- Size
- Culture
- Strategy
- Environment

25. "The Controller: Inflation Gives More Power with Management," *Business Week* (August 5, 1977): 85.

26. Vijay Sathe, *Controller Involvement in Management* (Englewood Cliffs, N.J.: Prentice-Hall, 1982), p. 110.

27. Ibid., p. 140.

28. Dale A. Henning, and Roger L. Moseley, "Authority Role of a Functional Manager: The Controller," *Administrative Science Quarterly* 15 (1970): 482–489.

29. Ibid., p. 488.

30. K. Rosenzweig, "An Exploratory Field Study of the Relationship Between the Controller's Department and Overall Organizational Characteristics," *Accounting, Organizations and Society* (December 1981): 339–354.

31. M. Schiff and A. Y. Lewin, "Where Traditional Budgeting Fails," *Financial Executive* 36, no. 5 (May 1968): 51–62.

32. J. G. San Miguel and V. Govindarajan, "The Contingent Relationship Between the Controller and Internal Audit Functions in Large Organizations," *Accounting, Organizations and Society* (February 1984): 179–188.

33. Ibid., p. 184.

34. Max Weber, *Basic Concepts in Sociology*, trans. H. P. Secher (New York: Citadel, 1962).

35. Max Weber, *The Theory of Social and Economic Organization*, trans. Alexander M. Henderson and Talcott Parsons (New York: The Free Press, 1947), p. 328.

36. Ibid.

37. Ibid.

38. Ibid., pp. 404–405.

39. James L. Price, *Organizational Effectiveness: An Inventory of Propositions* (Homewood, Ill.: Richard D. Irwin, 1968).

40. A. W. Gouldner, "Organizational Analysis," in Robert K. Merton, Leonard Broom, and Leonard S. Cottnell, Jr. (eds.), *Sociology Today* (New York: Basic Books, 1959), p. 405.

41. R. K. Merton, *Social Theory and Social Structure*, 2nd ed. (Glencoe, Ill: The Free Press, 1957), p. 195.

42. A. W. Gouldner, *Patterns of Industrial Bureaucracy* (Glencoe, Ill: The Free Press, 1954), pp. 22–23.

43. Frederick W. Taylor, *Scientific Management* (New York: Harper and Row, 1947).

44. Ibid., pp. 211, 189.

45. Henry L. Gantt, *Work Wages and Profits* (Easton, Pa.: Hive, 1973).

46. Frank B. Gilbreth, *Bricklaying System* (Easton, Pa.: Hive, 1972); see also *Motion Study* (Easton, Pa.: Hive, 1972).

47. Luther Gulick, "Notes on the Theory of Organizations," in Luther Gulick and Lyndall F. Urwick (eds.), *Papers on the Science of Administration* (New York: Institute of Public Administration, Columbia University, 1937).

48. H. Fayol, *General Principles of Management* (New York: Pitman, 1949), Chapter 4, p. 19.

49. Taylor, *Scientific Management*, p. 40.

50. W. G. Bennis, "Some Problems in Organization and Administration," *Hospital Administration* 6 (1959).

51. F. J. Roethlisberger and W. J. Dickson, *Management and the Workers* (Cambridge, Mass.: Harvard University Press, 1939), p. 558.

52. Ibid., p. 559.

53. Ibid.

54. Rensis Likert, *New Patterns of Management* (New York: McGraw-Hill, 1961).

55. Chris Argyris, *Integrating the Individual and the Organization* (New York: John Wiley, 1964); and *Understanding Organizational Behavior* (Homewood, Ill: Dorsey Press, 1960).

56. Douglas McGregor, *The Human Side of Enterprise* (New York: McGraw-Hill, 1960); and Caroline McGregor and Warren G. Bennis (eds.), *The Professional Manager* (New York: McGraw-Hill, 1967).

57. Likert, *New Patterns of Management*, p. 240.

58. Ibid., pp. 223–233.

59. Ibid., p. 98.

60. Rensis Likert, *The Human Organization* (New York: McGraw-Hill, 1967), p. 75.

61. Robert Michels, *Political Parties*, trans. Eden Paul and Cedar Paul (New York: The Free Press, 1949; first published in 1915).

62. Talcott Parsons, *The Social System* (New York: The Free Press, 1951); and "Suggestions for a Sociological Approach to Theory of Organizations," *Administrative Science Quarterly* (June 1956): 63–85.

63. Philip Selznick, *TVA and the Grass Rotts* (Berkeley: University of California Press, 1949).

64. Ibid., p. 13.

65. Katz and Kahn, *The Social Psychology of Organizations*.

66. Selznick, *TVA and the Grass Roots*, p. 252.

67. D. T. Otley, "The Contingency Theory of Management Accounting: Achievement and Prognosis," *Accounting, Organizations and Society* (December 1980): 413–428.

68. Ibid., pp. 420–421.

69. L. A. Gordon and D. A. Miller, "A Contingency Framework for the Design of Accounting Information Systems," *Accounting, Organizations and Society* (January 1976): pp. 59–69.

70. J. H. Waterhouse and P. A. Tiessen, "A Contingency Framework for Management Accounting Systems Research," *Accounting, Organizations and Society* (March 1978): 65–76.

71. Norman B. MacIntosh, "A Contextual Model of Information Systems," *Accounting, Organizations and Society* (February 1981): 39–52.

72. Ibid., p. 47.

73. Clive Emmanuel, D. Otley, and K. Merchant, *Accounting For Management Control* (London: Chapman and Hall, 1980), pp. 60–66.

74. Harold J. Leavitt, "Applied Organizational Change in Industry: Structural, Technological, and Humanistic Approaches," in James G. March (ed.), *The Handbook of Organizations* (Chicago: Rand McNally, 1965), pp. 1144–1146.

75. Charles Perrow, "A Framework for the Comparative Analysis of Organizations," *American Sociological Review* 32 (April 1967): 195–208.

76. Joan Woodward, *Industrial Organization: Theory and Practice* (London: Oxford University Press, 1965).

77. Joan Woodward, *Industrial Organization: Behavior and Control* (New York: Oxford University Press, 1970).

78. J. Hage and M. Aiken, "Relationship of Centralization to Other Structural Properties," *Administrative Science Quarterly* (June 1967): 72–92.

79. Kenneth A. Merchant, "Influences on Departmental Budgeting: An Empirical Examination of a Contingency Model," *Accounting, Organizatons and Society* (June 1984): 291–307.

80. D. Silverman, *The Theory of Organizations: A Sociological Framework* (London: Heineman Educational Books, 1970).

81. E. G. Flamholtz and T. K. Das, "Toward an Integrative Framework of Organizational Control," *Accounting, Organizations and Society* (January 1985): 35–50.

82. Kweka Ewusi-Mensah, "The External Organizational Environment and Its Impact on Management Information Systems," *Accounting, Organizations and Society* (December 1981): 301–316.

83. Ibid., p. 306.

84. P. N. Khandwalla, "The Effects of Different Types of Competition in the Use of Management Control," *Journal of Accounting Research* (Autumn 1972): 275–285.

85. Ibid., p. 282.

86. G. G. Cain, "The Challenge of Segmented Labor Market Theories to Orthodox Theory," *Journal of Economic Literature* 14 (1976): 1215–1257.

BIBLIOGRAPHY

Amigoni, F. "Planning Management Control Systems." *Journal of Business Finance and Accounting* (Fall 1978): 279–291.

Ansari, S. L. "An Integrated Approach to Control System Design." *Accounting, Organizations and Society* (April 1977): 101–112.

Anthony, R. N. *Planning and Control Systems: A Framework for Analysis*. Cambridge, Mass.: Harvard University Press, 1965.

Argyris, C. "Organizational Learning and Effective Management Information Systems: A Prospectus for Research." Harvard University, Program on Information Technologies and Public Policy, Working Paper 76–4 (1976).

———, and Schon, D. *Organizational Learning: A Theory of Action Perspective*. Reading, Mass.: Addison-Wesley, 1978.

Armstrong, J. C. "Derivation of Theory by Means of Factor Analysis or Tom Swift and his Electric Factor Analysis Machine." *The American Statistician* (December 1967): 17–21.

Banbury, J., and Nahapiet, J. E. "Towards a Framework for the Study of the Antecedents and Consequences of Information Systems in Organizations." *Accounting, Organizations and Society* (February 1979): 163–177.

Baumler, J. V. "Defined Criteria of Performance and Organizational Control." *Administrative Science Quarterly* (September 1971): 340–349.

Belkaoui, Ahmed. *Behavioral Accounting*. Westport, Conn.: Quorum Books, 1989.

Benston, George J. "The Role of the Firm's Accounting System for Motivation," *The Accounting Review* (April 1963): 347–354.

Blau, P. M., and Scott, W. R. *Formal Organizations*. San Francisco: Chandler, 1962.

Bruns, W. J., and Waterhouse, J. H. "Budgetary Control and Organizational Structure." *Journal of Accounting Research* (Autumn 1975): 177–203.

Burchell, S.; Clubb, C.; Hopwood, A. G.; Hughes, T.; and Nahapiet, J. "The Roles of

Accounting in Organizations and Society." *Accounting, Organizations and Society* (April 1980).

Burns, T., and Stalker, G. M. *The Management of Innovation*. London: Tavistock, 1961.

Campbell, J. P. "Contributions Research Can Make in Understanding Organizations Effectiveness." In S. L. Spray (ed.), *Organizational Effectiveness: Theory-Research Utilization*. Comparative Administration Research Institute, Graduate School of Business Administration, Kent State University, 1976.

Caplan, E. H. "Behavioral Assumptions of Management Accounting." *Accounting Review* (July 1966): 496–509.

Carper, W. B., and Snizek, W. E. "The Nature and Types of Organizational Taxonomies: An Overview," *Academy of Management Review* 5, no. 1 (1980): 65–75.

Chandler, A. *Strategy and Structure*. Cambridge, Mass.: MIT Press, 1962.

————, and Daems, H. "Administrative Co-ordination, Allocation and Monitoring: A Comparative Analysis of the Emergence of Accounting and Organizations in the U.S.A. and Europe." *Accounting, Organizations and Society* (January 1979): 3–20.

Child, J. *Organization: A Guide to Problems and Practice*. New York: Harper and Row, 1977.

————. "Organization Structure, Environment and Performance—The Role of Strategic Choice." *Sociology* (January 1972): 1–22.

Cooper, D. "A Social and Organizational View of Management Accounting." In M. Bromwich and A. G. Hopwood (eds.), *Essays on British Accounting Research*. London: Pitman, 1980.

Crowson, R. A. *Classification and Biology*. New York: Atherton Press, 1970.

Cyert, R., and March, J. G. *A Behavioral Theory of the Firm*. Englewood Cliffs, N.J.: Prentice-Hall, 1963.

Draft, R. L., and MacIntosh, N. B. "A New Approach to Design and Use of Management Information." *California Management Review* (Fall 1978): 82–92.

Dermer, J. *Management Planning and Control Systems*. Homewood, Ill.: Richard D. Irwin, 1977.

Emery, F. E., and Trist, E. L. "The Causal Texture of Organizational Environments." *Human Relations* 18 (1965): 21–32.

Etzioni, A. *A Comparative Analysis of Complex Organizations*, rev. and enlarged ed. New York: The Free Press, 1975. (Originally published in 1961.)

Evan, W. M. "Organization Theory and Organizational Effectiveness: An Exploratory Analysis." In S. L. Spray (ed.), *Organizational Effectiveness: Theory-Research Utilization*. Comparative Administration Research Institute, Graduate School of Business Administration, Kent State University, 1976.

Gordon, C. W., and Babchuck, N. "A Typology of Voluntary Organizations." *American Sociological Review* 24 (1959): 22–29.

Gordon, L. A., and Miller, D. "A Contingency Framework for the Design of Accounting Information Systems." *Accounting, Organizations and Society* (January 1976): 59–70.

Goronzy, F. "A Numerical Taxonomy of Business Enterprises." In A. J. Cole (ed.), *Numerical Taxonomy*. London: Academic Press, 1969.

Haag, I., and Hedlund, G. "Case Studies in Accounting Research." *Accounting, Organizations and Society* (March 1979): 135–143.

Haas, J. E.; Hall, R. H.; and Johnson, N. J. "Toward an Empirically Derived Taxonomy of Organizations.'' In R. V. Bowers (ed.), *Studies on Behavior in Organizations: A Research Symposium*. Athens: University of Georgia Press, 1966.

Hall, R. H.; Haas, J. E.; and Johnston, N. J. ''An Examination of the Blau-Scott and Etzioni Typologies.'' *Administrative Science Quarterly* 12 (1967): 118–139.

Hayes, D. ''The Contingency Theory of Management Accounting.'' *Accounting Review* (January 1977): 22–39.

————. ''The Contingency Theory of Management Accounting: A Reply.'' *Accounting Review* (April 1978): 530–533.

Hofstede, G. *The Game of Budget Control*. London: Tavistock, 1968.

Hopwood, A. G. ''An Empirical Study of the Role of Accounting Data in Performance Evaluation.'' *Empirical Research in Accounting, Supplement to Journal of Accounting Research* (Fall 1972): 156–182.

————. ''Towards an Organizational Perspective for the Study of Accounting and Information Systems.'' *Accounting, Organizations and Society* (March 1978): 3–14.

Jackson, J. H., and Morgan, C. P. *Organization Theory: A Macro Perspective for Management*. Englewood Cliffs, N.J.: Prentice-Hall, 1978.

Jelinek, M. ''Technology, Organizations, and Contingency.'' *Academy of Management Review* 2 (1977): 17–26.

Johnson, N. J. ''Toward a Taxonomy of Organizations.'' Unpublished doctoral dissertation, Ohio State University, 1963.

Karpik, L. (ed.). *Organization and Environment: Theory, Issues and Reality*. Los Angeles: Sage, 1978.

Katz, D., and Kahn, R. L. *The Social Psychology of Organizations*. New York: John Wiley, 1966.

Khandwalla, P. N. ''The Effect of Different Types of Competition on the Use of Management Controls.'' *Journal of Accounting Research* (Autumn 1972): 275–285.

Koonitz, H. ''The Management Theory Jungle.'' *Journal of the Academy of Management* 4 (1961): 174–188.

Lawler, E. E. III. ''Control Systems in Organizations.'' In M. D. Dunnette (ed.), *Handbook of Industrial and Organizational Psychology*. Chicago: Rand McNally, 1976.

McKelvey, B. ''Guidelines for the Empirical Classification of Organizations.'' *Administrative Science Quarterly* 20 (1975): 509–525.

Meyer, M. W. *Theory of Organizational Structure*. Indianapolis: Bobbs-Merrill, 1977.

Mitroff, I. I., and Kilman, R. H. *Methodological Approaches to the Social Sciences*. San Francisco: Jossey-Bass, 1978.

Murray, W. *Management Controls in Action*. Irish National Productivity Committee, 1970.

Otley, D. T. ''Budget Use and Managerial Performance.'' *Journal of Accounting Research* (March 1978): 122–149.

————. ''The Role of Management Accounting in Organizational Control.'' In M. Bromwich and A. G. Hopwood (eds.), *Essays in British Accounting Research*. London: Pitman, 1980.

————, and Berry, A. J. ''Control, Organization and Accounting.'' *Accounting, Organizations and Society* (April 1980).

Ouchi, W. G. ''The Relationship Between Organizational Structure and Organizational Control.'' *Administrative Science Quarterly* (May 1977): 95–113.

————, and Maguire, M. A. "Organizational Control: Two Functions." *Administrative Science Quarterly* (June 1975): 559–569.

Parsons, T. *Structure and Process in Modern Societies*. New York: The Free Press, 1960.

————. "Suggestions for a Sociological Approach to the Theory of Organizations." *Administrative Science Quarterly* (June 1956): 63–85, 225–239.

Pennings, J. M. "The Relevance of the Structural Contingency Model for Organizational Effectivness." *Administrative Science Quarterly* (October 1975): 393–410.

Perrow, C. "A Framework for the Comparative Analysis of Organizations." *American Sociological Review* 32 (April 1967): 194–208.

————. *Complex Organizations: A Critical Essay*. Glenview, Ill: Scott, Foresman, 1972.

————. *Organizational Analysis: A Sociological View*. Belmont, Calif.: Brooks/Cole, 1970.

Pfeffer, J., and Salancik, G. R. *The External Control of Organizations: A Resource Dependence Perspective*. New York: Harper and Row, 1978.

Piper, J. "Determinants of Financial Control Systems for Multiple Retailers—Some Case Study Evidence." Unpublished paper, University of Loughborough, 1978.

Price, J. L. *Organizational Effectiveness: An Inventory of Propositions*. Homewood, Ill.: Richard D. Irwin, 1968.

Pugh, D. S., and Hickson, D. J. (eds.). *Organizational Structure in its Context (The Aston Programme 1)*. London: Saxon House, 1976.

Pugh, D. S.; Hickson, D. J.; and Hinings, C. R. "A Conceptual Scheme for Organizational Analysis." *Administrative Science Quarterly* 8 (1963): 289–315.

————. An Empirical Taxonomy of Work Organizations. *Administrative Science Quarterly* 14 (1969): 115–126.

Pugh, D. S.; Hickson, D. J.; Hinings, C. R.; and Turner, C. "Dimensions of Organizational Structure." *Administrative Science Quarterly* 13 (1968): 65–105.

Pugh, D. S., and Hinings, C. R. (eds.). *Organizational Studies: Extensions and Replications (The Aston Programme 2)*. London: Saxon House, 1976.

Pugh, D. S., and Payne, R. L. (eds.), *Organizational Behavior in its Context (The Aston Programme 3)*. London: Saxon House, 1977.

Rice, G. H., Jr., and Bishoprick, D. W. *Conceptual Models of Organizations*. New York: Appleton-Century-Crofts, 1971.

Salaman, G. *Work Organizations: Resistance and Control*. New York: Longman, 1979.

Samuel, Y., and Mannheim, B. F. "A Multidimensional Approach Toward a Typology of Bureaucracy." *Administrative Science Quarterly* 15 (1970): 216–228.

Sathe, V. "Contingency Theories of Organizational Structure." In J. L. Livingstone (ed.), *Managerial Accounting: The Behavioral Foundations*. Columbus, Ohio: Grid, 1975.

————. "The Relevance of Modern Organization Theory for Managerial Accounting." *Accounting, Organizations and Society* (1978): 89–92.

Silverman, D. *The Theory of Organizations: A Sociological Framework*. London: Heineman Educational Books, 1970.

Steers, R. M. *Organizational Effectiveness: A Behavioral View*. New York: Goodyear, 1977.

Thompson, J. D. *Organizations in Action*. New York: McGraw-Hill, 1967.

Tiessen, P., and Waterhouse, J. H. "The Contingency Theory of Management Accounting: A Comment." *Accounting Review* (April 1978): 523–529.

Tomkins, C.; Rosenberg, D.; and Colville, I. "The Social Process of Research: Some

Reflections on Developing a Multi-Disciplinary Accounting Project.'' *Accounting, Organizations and Society* (1980).

Van Ripper, P. P. "Organizations: Basic Issues and Proposed Typology." In R. V. Bowers (ed.), *Studies on Behavior in Organizations*. Athens: University of Georgia Press, 1966.

Waterhouse, J. H., and Tiessen, P. A. "A Contingency Framework for Management Accounting Systems Research." *Accounting, Organizations and Society* (March 1978): 65–76.

Watson, D.J.H. "Contingency Formulation of Organizational Structure: Implications for Managerial Accounting." In J. L. Livingstone (ed.), *Managerial Accounting: The Behavioral Foundations*. (Columbus, Ohio: Grid, 1975).

Weber, M. *Essays in Sociology*, trans. H. H. Gerth and C. W. Mills. New York: Oxford University Press, 1946.

————. *The Theory of Social and Economic Organizations*, trans. A. Henderson and T. Parsons. New York: The Free Press, 1947.

Weldon, P. D. "An Examination of the Blau-Scott and Etzioni Typologies: A Critique." *Administrative Science Quarterly* 17 (1972): 76–78.

Westerlund, G., and Sjostrand, S. *Organizational Myths*. New York: Harper and Row, 1979.

Wood, S. "A Reappraisal of the Contingency Approach to Organization. "*Journal of Management Studies* (October 1979), pp. 334–354.

Woodward, J. *Industrial Organization: Theory and Practice*. London: Oxford University Press, 1965.

————. *Management and Technology*. London: Her Majesty's Stationery Office, 1958.

4

THE BEHAVIORAL
FOUNDATIONS

Management accounting is built on behavioral foundations. Its explicit aim is
to affect the behavior of individuals in a desirable direction. To accomplish this
purpose, management accounting has to be adapted to the different characteristics
that shape the "cognitive make-up" of individuals within an organization and
affect their performance. In general, these characteristics pertain to three factors:
(1) the perception by the individual of what should be the objective function or
goals in the firm; (2) the various factors likely to motivate the individual to
perform; and (3) the decision-making model most relevant to particular contexts
and most preferred by the individual. Although these factors do not constitute
an exhaustive list of the behavioral concepts likely to affect the performance of
an individual within an organization, they have been identified in the literature
of various disciplines as essential factors to be considered for an understanding
of an individual behavior within an organization and the design of any information
system.

Thus, management accounting requires a good grasp of the behavioral concepts; namely, the objective function in management accounting, motivation
theories, and models of decision making. Each of these concepts identifies factors
and situations that influence the individual behavior and indicates avenues for
management accounting to adapt its services.

THE OBJECTIVE FUNCTION IN MANAGEMENT
ACCOUNTING

Many authors in the field of complex organizations define an organization as
a social system that is created to achieve certain specific goals or objectives.
For example, Amitai Etzioni defines organizations as "social units (or human

groupings) deliberately constructed and reconstructed to seek specific goals."[1]
Richard Hall states:

An organization is a collectivity with a relatively identifiable boundary, a normative order,
authority ranks, community systems, and membership coordinating systems; this collectivity exists on a relatively continuous basis in an environment and engages in activities
that are usually related to a goal or a set of goals.[2]

The concept of organizational goal and/or objective has not, however, been
clearly defined in the literature. The general goals refer to the intentions or
wishes espoused by those persons who develop them. For example, V. Buck
gives the following operational definition of organizational goals:

It is the decision to commit resources for certain activities and to withhold them from
certain others that operationally defines the organization's goals. Verbal pronouncements
are insufficient for defining goals; the speaker must put his resources where his mouth
is if something is to be considered a goal.[3]

Different typologies of goals have also been proposed. First, J. D. Thompson
differentiated between goals held for an organization and goals of an organization.[4] The former are held by persons who are not members of the organization
but have a given interest in the activities of the firm, such as clientele, investors,
action groups, and so on. The latter are held by persons who are part of the
"dominant coalition" in terms of holding enough control to commit the organization to a given direction.

C. Perrow made a distinction between "official goals" and "operative
goals."[5] Official goals refer to those objectives or general purposes stated either
orally or in writing by key members. Operative goals refer to the designated
objectives based on the actual operating policies of the organization. Etzioni
refers to such goals as real goals. They constitute "the future states toward which
a majority of the organizational means and major organizational commitments
. . . are directed, and which, in cases of conflict with goals which are stated but
command few resources, have clear priority."[6]

Each discipline conceives a different goal or objective in its examination of
profit-oriented organizations. The discipline of economics, for example, in its
neoclassical approach views profit maximization as the single determinant of
behavior. As seen in a previous chapter, organizational and management theories
have provided various behavioral theories of the firm. In management accounting,
as in corporate finance, neither the economic model nor the behavioral model
appears entirely suitable. In fact, both models have influenced three held views
of business behavior applicable to management accounting: the shareholder
wealth maximization model, the managerial welfare maximization model, and
the social welfare maximization model.[7] Each of these models constitutes an
acceptable objective of profit-oriented organizations in the field of management

accounting. Because the scope and practice of management accounting is heavily influenced by these assumptions, each of them will be examined next.

The Shareholder Wealth Maximization Model

In most textbooks in the field of corporate finance and specifically in management accounting, authors operate on the assumption that management's primary goal is to maximize the wealth of its stockholders. This view is referred to as the shareholder wealth maximization (SWM) model. According to this model, the firm accepts all projects yielding more than the cost of capital, and in equity financing prefers retaining earnings to issuing new stocks. It also assumes that earnings are objectively determined to show the true financial position of the firm to its owners and other users. In fact, the SWM model translates into maximizing the price of the common stock. Management is assumed to use decision rules and techniques that are in the best interests of the stockholders. In a management accounting context, SWM implies an acceptance by management of budgeting and control standards, a rejection of slack budgeting, any suboptimizing behavior, and an adoption of management accounting techniques that are in the best interests of the owners of the firm. If management behaves otherwise, its right to manage may be either questioned or revoked, given that stockholders own the firm and elect the management team. E. Solomon made a similar suggestion as follows:

But what if management has other motives, such as maximizing sales or size, growth or market share, or their own survival, or peace of mind? These operating goals do not necessarily conflict with the operating goal of wealth maximization. Indeed, a good case could be made for the thesis that wealth maximization also maximizes the achievement of these other objectives. But the point of issue is what if there is a conflict? What, for example, if management's quest for its own peace of mind or for some other goal consistently leads it to reject operating decisions that should be accepted by the wealth-maximizing criterion? The traditional answer is that such a management will be replaced sooner or later, and this is the only answer possible. Legally, management governs only as the appointed representatives of the owners. It may reject over-all goals so long as it substitutes goals which are designed to promote that of society as a whole. But if it rejects owner-oriented goals and socially-oriented goals in favor of goals that are solely management-oriented and which lead to substantially different courses of action, its right to govern is open to question.[8]

The Managerial Welfare Maximization Model

Another school of thought maintains that a different objective function other than shareholder wealth maximization exists for the firm—namely, that managers run firms for their own benefits. It is maintained that because the stock of most large firms is widely held, the managers of such firms have a great deal of freedom. This being the case, they may be tempted for personal benefits to pursue an objective other than shareholder welfare maximization. This school of thought is generally referred to as the managerial welfare maximization (MWM) model. So rather than maximizing profits, the managers may maximize sales or assets,[9] the rate of growth,[10] or managerial utility[11]. As a consequence, managers may engage in suboptimization schemes as long as they contribute to their own welfare. For example, an entrenched management may avoid risky ventures even though the returns to stockholders would be high enough to justify the endeavor. In a management accounting context, MWM implies a lesser acceptance by management of budgeting and control standards, a recourse to slack budgeting and any suboptimization behavior, a manipulation or avoidance within legality of full disclosure in order to present the firm's operation favorably (i.e., income smoothing), and, finally, adoption of management accounting techniques that are in the best interest of managers. In a recent survey, B. Branch concludes as follows:

The evidence to date may be summarized as follows. Many managers have considerable discretion to substitute their own interests for that of the stockholders. Stockholder and manager interests can conflict or be independent in significant respects. The extent to which firms are managed in stockholder interests vary considerably. Most of the empirical work suggests that firms managed in stockholders' interests tend in some sense to outperform management-oriented firms.[12]

That managers may elect to substitute their own different interests raises the question of how goals within MWM are "determined" or "set" in decisions to commit the organization to a particular course of action. Three distinct models have been identified to represent the goal-setting processes: the bargaining model, the problem-solving model, and the coalition model.[13] Because they present good conceptualizations of the goal determination process under MWM, they are briefly presented next.[14]

The Bargaining Model. The bargaining model depicts goal determination as the result of an open-minded negotiation process among all interested parties leading to a series of trade-offs and compromises. It is based on three important assumptions:

1. There is an active group of participants (internal or external) who impose demands on the organization.
2. These demands are conflicting; they cannot be accommodated simultaneously.
3. The individuals or groups are interdependent.[15]

The Problem-Solving Model. The problem-solving model describes goal determination as the result of successive decisions made by high level administrators. It is based on three important assumptions:

1. Policy commitments are made within a set of constraints or requirements that are known to decision makers.

2. These constraints can be ranked and a preferred set accommodated.

3. The goals of different individuals or groups can be simultaneously satisfied.[16]

The Dominant Coalition Model. Given the existence of controlling interests in the firm, the dominant coalition model describes goal determination as the result of decisions made by those who control the ends to which policies and resources are committed. It is based on two assumptions:

1. There are many persons or groups who hold goals for an organization. These goals are frequently in conflict and cannot all be accommodated.

2. One individual or group does not have sufficient power alone to act unilaterally. Power is dispersed. Collective behavior is required to secure support for goals.[17]

The Social Welfare Maximization Model

The climate in which businesses operate is changing with pressures on organizations to be more sensitive to the impact of behavior on society. In adopting a more socially responsible attitude and responding to the pressures of new dimensions—social, human, and environmental—organizations may have to alter their main objective, whether SWM or MWM, to include as an additional constraint the welfare of society at large. This view may be referred to as the social welfare maximization (SOWM) model. Under SOWM, the firm undertakes all projects that, in addition to the usual profitability objective, minimize the social costs and maximize social benefits created by the productive operations of the firm. Thus, under SOWM the firm is not only liable to the shareholders and managers, but also to the society at large. Given the different interest groups in the society at large, the organization may have to develop different corporate purposes. For example, it was reported that one group has defined eight corporate purposes: "profit, sensitivity to natural and human environment, growth, responsiveness to consumer needs, equitable distributions of benefits, dynamic business structure, fair treatment of employees, and legal and ethical behavior."[18]

In a management accounting context, SOWM implies the developing of a social reporting system oriented toward the measurement of social performance, including not only social costs but also social benefits. It suggests the development of a new concept of organization performance that will be more indicative of the firm's social responsibility than is provided by conventional accounting. For example, the AAA Committee on Measurement of Social Cost suggested a total organization performance, which is a function of "five outputs":

1. Net income, which benefits stockholders and provides resources for further business growth

2. Human resource contribution, which assists the individual in the organization to develop new knowledge or skills

3. Public contribution, which helps the organization's community to function and provides services for its constituency

4. Environmental contribution (closely allied with public contribution), which affects "quality of life" for society

5. Product or service contribution, which affects customer well-being and satisfaction[19]

While a theory of social accounting is still emerging in the new public interest accounting paradigm, the proposed objectives and concepts for social accounting shown in Exhibit 4.1 offer an interesting beginning.

However, regardless of the objective function adopted by managers, social reporting and particularly social reports are needed by management for relevant decision making and to comply with both social pressures and legal requirements.

MOTIVATION THEORIES

Motivation is related to the intrinsic forces within the individual—namely, the motives and unsatisfied needs of the individual. More explicitly, motivation is concerned with "how behavior gets started, is energized, is sustained, is directed, is stopped, and what kind of subjective reaction is presented in the organization while all this is going on."[20] For this reason, motivation is important for an organization and for management accounting. It basically refers to an individual's needs or motives that make that individual act in a specific manner. It relates all aspects of individual behavior where a deliberate and conscious action is initiated in the organization to direct individuals so that they can satisfy their needs as much as possible while they strive to accomplish the objectives of the organization. These actions may be initiated either directly by the managers' actions or through the adoption of appropriate management accounting techniques. Thus, management accounting techniques necessitate a good grasp of motivation in organizations. The identification of the factors and situations that may influence and coordinate employee action allows the management accountant to adapt the services to offer to the realities of human behavior. The literature on motivation identifies five theories of motivation: the need theory, the two-factor theory, the value/expectancy theory, the achievement theory, and the inequity theory. Each of these theories identifies what factors within the individual and his or her environment activate high performance, or attempts to explain and describe the process of how behavior is activated, what directs it, and how it is controlled and stopped. Let us examine each of these theories of motivation and their implications for management accounting.

Need Theory

Originally advanced by Abraham Maslow, need theory holds that people are motivated to satisfy a "hierarchy" of needs.[21] These needs are as follows (in ascending order of prepotency):

Exhibit 4.1
Proposed Objectives and Concepts for Social Accounting

Objective 1
An objective of corporate social accounting is to identify and measure the periodic net social contribution of an individual firm, which includes not only the costs and benefits internalized to the firm, but also those arising from externalities affecting different social segments.

Objective 2
An objective of corporate social accounting is to help determine whether an individual firm's strategies and practices which directly affect the relative resource and power status of individuals, communities, social segments and generations are consistent with widely shared social priorities, on the one hand, and individuals' legitimate aspirations, on the other.

Objective 3
An objective of corporate social accounting is to make available in an optimal manner, to all social constituents, relevant information on a firm's goals, policies, programs, performance and contributions to social goals. Relevant information is that which provides for public accountability and also facilitates public decision making regarding social choices and social resource allocation. Optimality implies a cost/benefit-effective reporting strategy which also optimally balances potential information conflicts among the various social constituents of a firm.

Concept 1
A *social transaction* represents a firm's utilization or delivery of a socioenvironmental resource which affects the absolute or relative interests of the firm's various social constituents and which is not processed through the market place.

Concept 2
Social overheads (returns) represent the sacrifice (benefit) to society from those resources consumed (added) by a firm as a result of its social transactions. In other words, social overheads is the measured value of a firm's negative externalities, and social returns is the measured value of its positive externalities.

Concept 3
Social income represents the periodic net social contribution of a firm. It is computed as the algebraic sum of the firm's traditionally measured net income, its aggregate social overheads and its aggregate social returns.

Concept 4
Social constituents are the different distinct social groups (implied in the second objective and expressed in the third objective of social accounting) with whom a firm is presumed to have a social contract.

Concept 5
Social equity is a measure of the aggregate changes in the claims which each social constituent is presumed to have in the firm.

Concept 6
Net social asset of a firm is a measure of its aggregate nonmarket contribution to the society's well being less its nonmarket depletion of the society's resources during the life of the firm.

Source: Kavasseri V. Ramanathan, "Towards a Theory of Corporate Social Accounting," *The Accounting Review* (July 1976): 527. Reprinted with permission.

1. The physiological needs: food, shelter, warmth, and other bodily wants.
2. The safety needs: security and protection.
3. The need for love and belongingness: desire to both give and receive love and friendship.
4. The need for esteem: self-respect and the respect of others.
5. The self-actualization need: "What a man can be, he must be."

Thus, individuals strive to satisfy these needs in a sequential fashion, starting with the physiological needs. The process of deprivation-domination-gratification-activation continues until the self-actualization need has been activated. This suggests that once the basic physiological and safety needs are satisfied, individuals will respond better to rewards leading to self-respect and self-actualization than to economic rewards, which are primarily related to the satisfaction of lower-level needs. What this implies for management accounting is that assuming individuals in the organization are well paid, the emphasis should be on the introduction of management accounting techniques, in general, and control techniques, in particular, that are consistent with the satisfaction of higher-level needs. This view is also shared by E. H. Caplan when he states that "it may be more important to concentrate on the development of organizational structures, leadership practices, and control systems which are consistent with satisfaction of the higher level needs."[22]

Two-Factor Theory

In a series of studies, F. Herzberg and his associates developed the "motivation hygiene" theory.[23] Briefly, they found two factors affecting a job situation, which they labeled *satisfiers* and *dissatisfiers*. The satisfiers were related to the nature of the work itself and to rewards that flowed directly from the performance of that work: (1) perceived opportunity for achievement on the job, (2) recognition, (3) a sense of performing interesting and important work, (4) responsibility, and (5) advancement. The dissatisfiers were related to the context rather than the content of the job: (1) company policies that foster ineffectiveness, (2) incompetent supervision, (3) interpersonal relations, (4) working conditions, (5) salaries, (6) status, and (7) job security. The satisfiers were classified as "motivators" and the dissatisfiers as "hygiene" factors.

According to Herzberg, the satisfiers contribute very little to job dissatisfaction; and conversely, the dissatisfiers contribute very little to job satisfaction. Similarly, motivation to work is created by the satisfaction of the individual's needs for the satisfiers and not from an elimination of the dissatisfiers. The implications of Herzberg's theory for management accounting are twofold. First, to contribute to the motivation of employees, management accounting techniques should focus on better measurement and reporting of achievement, recognition, work, responsibility, and advancement. Second, given that the key to motivation is to make jobs more meaningful, management accounting techniques should focus on job enrichment. Job enrichment is the attempt by managers to design tasks in such a way as to affect employees' positive feelings about their job and to build in the opportunity for personal achievement, recognition, challenge, and personal growth. It gives the employees a greater amount of responsibility in carrying out complete tasks and insures a timely feedback on their performance.[24] Martin Evans suggests several steps to insure job enrichment of relevance to management accounting:[25]

1. Eliminating controls from the job while keeping accountability.
2. Increasing the individual's accountability for his or her job.
3. Providing each individual with a complete and natural work module (or elements of work).
4. Allowing greater job freedom for an individual's own work.
5. Providing timely feedbacks on performance to the employee instead of the supervisor.
6. Improving old tasks and introducing new tasks.
7. Assigning specific tasks so the employee can develop expertise in performing them.

Value/Expectancy Theory

The theories of Maslow, McClelland, and Herzberg are content theories in the sense that they attempt to identify what factors within the individual and the individual's environment induce high performance. The value/expectancy theory is a process theory in the sense that it attempts to explain and describe the process of how behavior is initiated, maintained, and terminated.

Originally developed by K. Lewin,[26] and later specially applied to motivation to work by V. H. Vroom,[27] the basic tenet of the value/expectancy theory is that an individual chooses personal behavior on the basis of: (1) expectations that such behavior will result in a specific outcome, and (2) the sum of the valences—that is, personal utilities or rewards, derived from the outcome. Vroom advances the following theoretical proposition:

The force on a person (motive) to perform a given act is based on the weighted value (or utility) of all the possible outcomes of the act multiplied by the perceived usefulness of the given act in the attainment of these outcomes. Whenever an individual chooses between alternatives that involve certain outcomes, it seems clear that his behavior is affected not only by his preferences among outcomes, but also by the degree to which he believes these outcomes to be probable.[28]

Hence, an individual's motivation may be expressed as:

$$M = \Sigma \left[(E \rightarrow O)\,(V) \right]$$

where

E = Effort

O = Outcome

V = Values placed on the outcome

The above expression may be reformulated to include both an effort-performance linkage and a performance-reward linkage. The new model will include two expectancies. The first one refers to the probability that the effort will lead to a task accomplishment or performance. The second one refers to the probability that the task accomplishment will result in the desired outcomes. Hence, the individual's motivation may also be expressed as:

$$M = (E \to P)\Sigma[(P \to O)\ (V)]$$

where

P = Performance

L. W. Porter and E. E. Lawler have extended the value/expectancy theory by arguing that poor performance may result if abilities are lacking and the individual's role perceptions are erroneous.[29] Thus, for preferences and expectations to affect performance, adequate ability and accurate role perceptions are necessary.

R. J. House's formulation of the model can be expressed as follows:[30]

$$M = IV_b + P_i \left(IV_a + \sum_{i=1}^{n} P_{2i}EV_i \right),$$

where

i = 1, 2, . . . , n

M = Motivation to work

IV_a = Intrinsic valence associated with successful performance of the task

IV_b = Intrinsic valence associated with goal-directed behavior

EV_i = Extrinsic valences associated with the ith extrinsic reward contingent on work-goal accomplishment

P_i = The expectancy that goal-directed behavior will accomplish the work goal (a given level of specified performance); the measure's range is $(-1, +1)$

P_{2i} = The expectancy that work-goal accomplishment will lead to the ith extrinsic reward; the measure's range is $(-1, +1)$

This formulation shows some of the implications of expectancy theory for management accounting. Appropriate management accounting techniques may be chosen to affect the independent variables of the model in the following ways:

1. By determining what extrinsic rewards (EV_i) follow work-goal accomplishment.

2. By increasing through timely reports the individual's expectancy (P_2) that work-goal accomplishment leads to extrinsic rewards.

3. By increasing the intrinsic valence associated with work-goal accomplishment (IV_a) through a greater role of the individual in goal-setting and task-directed effort.

4. By recognizing and supporting the individual's effort thereby influencing P_i.

5. By increasing the net intrinsic valences associated with goal-directed behavior (IV_b).

Achievement Theory

The concept of "achievement motive" was first introduced by McClelland, Atkinson, and their associates.[31] It is based on the desire of people to be challenged and to be innovative and adopt an "achievement-oriented behavior"— that is, a behavior directed toward meeting a standard of excellence. McClelland viewed the motive to achieve as distinct from acquisitiveness for money, except insofar as money is considered a symbol of achievement. Using the Thematic Apperception Test (TAT) to measure three distinct needs (need for achievement, need for power, and need for affiliation), he found the achievement level to be correlated with personality and cultural variables.

The achievement-oriented individual likes to assume responsibility for individual achievement, seeks challenging tasks, and takes calculated risks depending on the probabilities of success. Therefore,

he will take small risks for tasks serving as stepping stones for future rewards, take intermediate risks for tasks offering opportunities for achievement, and will attempt to find situations falling somewhere between the two extremes, providing the highest probability of success, and hence maximizing his sense of personal achievement.

According to the theory, the individuals will particularly behave in an achievement-oriented way in situations that enable them to strive for a standard of excellence, require the use of skills, present a challenge, and allow the individuals to appraise their performance. Accordingly, Atkinson stated that the strength of one's tendency to succeed at a task (T_s)

is a multiplicative function of three variables: motive to achieve success (M_s) which is conceived as a relatively general and stable disposition of personality and measured in terms of need for achievement; and two other variables which represent the effect of the intermediate environment—the strength of expectancy (or subjective probability) that performance of a task will be followed by success (P_s) and the relative attractiveness of success of that particular activity, which is called the incentive of success (I_s). I_s assumed to be greater the more difficult the task.[32]

Another important contention of the theory is that all motives are learned, including the achievement motive. As a result, the high achiever is experienced in making maximizing decisions, is less affected by anxiety, and proceeds in an efficient way in any endeavor.

What these contentions imply for management accounting is: (1) the necessity of constructing ways of developing the achievement motive at all managerial levels, and (2) the need to introduce management accounting techniques and to report management accounting information that encourages and facilitates the performance of high achievers.

Inequity Theory

Elaine Walster, Stacey Adams, and their colleagues have advanced that individuals in a relationship have two motives: to maximize their own gains and to maintain equity in the relationship.[33] Inequity results when a person's rewards from a relationship are not proportional to what that person has put in the relationship. More explicitly, inequity theory is based on the premise that when individuals compare their own situations with other situations and have a feeling of inequity, in terms of feeling either underrewarded or overrewarded for their contributions, they experience increased tension and strive to reduce it. Hence, overpaid workers will increase their efforts by producing more as a way of reducing inequity, while underpaid workers will produce less to achieve a contribution-reward balance. Other methods of restoring equity may be used also. Walster et al. state that individuals can restore actual equity by altering either their own payoffs or those of other participants. Similarly, a psychological equity can be restored when individuals change their perceptions of either rewards or contributions so that their contributions appear greater or lower than originally thought. They may also restore equity by quitting their jobs, severing relationships with comparison persons, or by forcing comparison persons to leave the field.

The inequity theory suggests, then, that rewards must appear to the employees to be fair or equitable. An appeal to equity norms can be used to reduce conflict. The role of management accounting in restoring equity is in insuring correct and accurate measurement and reporting of performance and the corresponding rewards. To avoid creating feelings of inequity, the methods of measuring performance and rewards should be made public to the employees.

MODELS OF DECISION MAKING

Management accounting necessitates a good grasp of decision making in organizations. The identification of the decision-making models most relevant to particular contexts and most preferred by particular individuals allows the management accountant to adapt the services to offer to the realities of the decision situation. The literature on decision making identifies five main perspectives: the "rational" manager view, the "satisficing" process-oriented view, the organizational procedures view, the political view, and the individual differences perspective.[34]

Before analyzing each of these models, it is appropriate to mention the excellent analysis of the Cuban missile crisis by G. T. Allison using three of these models: the rational actor view, the organizational procedures view, and the political view.[35] Addressing the central issues of the crisis from one of the three perspectives "lead[s] one to see, emphasize, and worry about quite different aspects of events."[36] By analogy, addressing management issues from any of the five perspectives leads one to have different perceptions and understanding of events and place on the management accountant different demands for services. Let us examine each of these models and its importance to management accounting.

The Rational View

The rational view of decision making is a normative model that refers to a consistent value-maximizing choice process in the presence of specific constraints. This process may be summarized as follows:

1. Individuals assume that there is a set of alternative acts or courses of action displayed before them in a particular situation.
2. They associate a set of possible outcomes or consequences with the set of possible acts.
3. They have a preference ordering over the consequences or payoff function that allows them to rank the consequences and select that act which ranks highest in their payoff function.

This view is used and relied upon as the model of the "economic man" in neoclassical economic theory and as the model of the "rational man" in game theory and statistical decision theory. Both make optimal choices in the presence of well-defined specific constraints.

As a defense of the rational view of decision making, one of the two assumptions has been made. On the one hand, there is the assumption of comprehensive rationality where individuals have perfect knowledge of all alternative acts, all the consequences, and the corresponding payoff function. On the other hand, there is the assumption of limited rationality with its inherent restricted claim on "optimal choice." Whatever the assumptions, the rational view of decision making requires the management accountant to define all the possibilities in terms of acts, consequences, and payoff function, and to evaluate the costs and benefits associated with rational decision making.

The rational view of decision making, although normative and rigorous, has been criticized as being descriptively unrealistic. H. A. Simon, in particular, advanced the principle of bounded rationality of the human decision maker:

When the limits to rationality are viewed from the individual's standpoint, they fall into three categories: he is limited by his values and conceptions of purpose, which may diverge from the organizational goals; he is limited by the extent of his knowledge and information. The individual can be rational in terms of the organization's goals only to the extent that he is able to pursue a particular course of action, he has a correct conception of the goal of the action, and he is correctly informed about the conditions surrounding his action. Within the boundaries laid down by these factors, his choices are rational-goal oriented.[37]

In replacement of the "economic man," Simon suggests the notion of the "administrative" or "satisficing" man as more representative of what is in decision making.

The Satisficing and Process-Oriented View

The satisficing and process-oriented view of decision making is a descriptive model that maintains that the administrative individual satisfices rather than optimizes when making most decisions. Thus, rather than searching the haystack for the sharpest needle, the objective of the administrative man is to find one sharp enough to sew with.[38] Simon summarizes the assumptions of the satisficer's theory as follows:

In actual organizational practice, no one attempts to find an optimal solution for the whole problem. Instead, various particular decisions, or groups of decisions, within the whole complex are made by specialized members or units of the organization. In making these particular decisions, the specialized units do not solve the whole problem but find a "satisfactory" solution for one or more subproblems, where some of the effects of the solution on other parts of the system are incorporated in the definition of "satisfactory."[39]

Thus, the satisficing man makes a decision-making choice in the context of a simplified view of the real situation. Simon introduces a concept of "subjective rationality" as a challenge to the concept of "objective rationality" advocated by the rational view of decision making. Subjective rationality depends on the individual's personal values. Thus, an objectively rational decision calls for a maximizing behavior given values in a specific situation, while a subjectively rational decision calls for maximizing attainment relative to the actual knowledge of the individual.[40] To be able to satisfice, the individual's strategies will consist essentially of heuristics or rules of thumb that meet a subjective minimum standard with respect to the things being sought.

That managers satisfice rather than optimize, refer to subjective rather than objective rationality, and rely on their heuristics places distinctive demands on the management accountant. To be able to service managers and facilitate their decision-making process, an understanding of their heuristics is essential. It is not an insurmountable task, given the general evidence suggesting how simple and how few are the heuristics used by managers. It also implies a good working relationship between managers and management accountants.

The Organizational Procedures View

The organizational procedures view of decision making is a descriptive model that maintains that individuals comply with an act according to a fixed set of standard operating procedures and programs. They make their choice in terms of goals and on the basis of expectations. R. M. Cyert and J. G. March perceive the organization as a coalition of individuals with different demands, priorities, goals, focus of attention, and competencies.[41] Decision making within the organization requires bargaining among the coalition members, resulting in de facto agreements and standard procedures for dealing with problematic situations.

Thus, individuals will act according to standard patterns of behavior established in their particular organizational unit to achieve its stated goals. What results in the organization is: (1) a permanent goal conflict between the units with possibly the dominant coalition imposing its independent constraints, (2) a quasi resolution of conflict marked by a sequential attention to problems, (3) uncertainty avoidance, (4) problematic search where the search is triggered by a specific problem and motivated to finding a solution to the problem, and (5) organizational learning leading to changes in goals, expectations, and standard procedures.

This process-oriented view of decision making has been applied with some success to simulate the working of a retail department store by Cyert and March,[42] the trust investment process used by officers in a bank by G. E. Clarkson,[43] the behavior of government units in municipal budgeting by John Crecine,[44] and the foreign investment decision process of businesses by Lair Aharoni.[45]

That managers may belong to coalitions that rely on programs and standard procedures places distinctive demands on management accountants. These coalitions and their standard procedures should be identified by management accountants to be able to service managers and facilitate their decision making. This implies that management accountants must be careful not to be identified with any of these coalitions, but as support agents providing the necessary information for an efficient resolution of problems. Following P. R. Lawrence and J. W. Lorsch's[46] appeal for a balance between integration and differentiation within complex organizations, management accountants may act as integrating agents between the subunits of the organization.

The Political View

The political view of decision making is a descriptive model that maintains that decisions are due partly to political processes. In this process, different groups committed to different courses of action interact and arrive at decisions through the "pulling and hauling that is politics."[47] The differences between this view and the rational and process views are summarized by Allison as follows: "what moves the chess pieces is not simply the reasons that support a course of action or the routines of organizations that enact an alternative but the power and skill of proponents and opponents of the action in itself."[48] Thus, each individual in the firm is a player in a competitive game called politics, where persuasion, accommodation, bargaining, and the constant search for support are the determinants of decision making. This may be justified because

managers [government leaders] have competitive, not homogeneous interests; priorities and perceptions are shaped by positions; problems are much more varied than straight-forward strategic issues; management of piecemeal streams of decisions is more important than steady-state choices; making sure that management [the government] does what is decided is more difficult than selecting the preferred solution. [49] (Allison's original words are shown in brackets.)

This political view resulted in the concept of incremental change advanced mainly by C. W. Lindblom.[50] According to this view, labeled as "the art of the possible," managers attack rather than solve problems incrementally through "successive limited comparisons."

That managers may be motivated by political positions and disagree with other political positions in the firm, that they may favor managing through incremental muddling rather than comprehensive, satisfactory, or procedural choice is very relevant for the management accountant and should not be ignored. The acceptance and use of either management accounting techniques or information suggested by the management accountant is very much a function of the political dimensions existing in the firm.

The Individual Differences View

The individual differences view maintains that individuals have specific decision-making styles appropriate for some cases and less so for others. This view emerged from the recognition in psychology of the concept of cognitive style as a hypothetical construct to explain the mediation process between stimuli and responses. Five approaches have been reported for the study of cognitive style: authoritarianism, dogmatism, cognitive complexity, integrative complexity, and field dependence.[51]

1. Authoritarianism arose from the focus by T. W. Adorno et al. on the relationship between personality, antidemocratic attitudes, and behavior.[52] They were primarily interested in individuals whose way of thinking made them susceptible to antidemocratic propaganda. Two of the behavioral correlates of authoritarianism—rigidity and intolerance of ambiguity—were reflections of an underlying cognitive style. For example, J. Dermer investigated the relationship between intolerance of ambiguity and subjective cue usage.[53] His result showed a significant positive correlation between intolerance of ambiguity and the amount of information perceived to be important.

2. Dogmatism arose from M. Rokeach's efforts to develop a structurally based measure of authoritarianism to replace the content-based measure developed by Adorno and his colleagues.[54] His interest was in developing a measure of cognitive style that would be independent of the content of thought.

3. Cognitive complexity as introduced by G. A. Kelly[55] and J. Bieri et al.[56] focuses on the psychological dimensions that individuals use to structure their environments and to differentiate the behavior of others. The more cognitively complex individuals are assumed to have a greater number of dimensions available with which to construe the behavior of others than the less cognitively complex persons. Another clarification of decision makers in the literature is made in terms of two cognitive styles: heuristic and analytic. Based on terms and meanings used by Jan Huysmans,[57] they may be defined as follows: Analytic decision makers reduce problem situations to a more or less explicit, often quantitative, model as a basis for their decision. Heuristic decision makers refer instead to common sense, intuition, and unquantified feelings about future development as they apply to the totality of the situation as an organic whole rather than as built from clearly identifiable parts. Huysmans's findings show particularly that cognitive style may operate as an effective constraint on the implementation of operations research recommendations, and that operations researchers perceive their own analytic style as self-evident and tend to ignore the impact of cognitive style on the acceptance and use of analytic techniques. Similarly, in an experimental study of the relationship between different information structures, decision approaches, and learning patterns, T. Mock, T. Estrin, and M. Vasarhelyi[58] found that analytics significantly outperformed heuristics in terms of profit and decision time.

4. Integrative complexity as presented by O. J. Harvey et al.,[59] and later expanded by H. M. Schroder et al.,[60] results from the view that people engage in two activities in processing sensory input: differentiation and integration. Differentiation refers to the individual's ability to place stimuli along dimensions. Integration refers to the individual's ability to employ complex rules to combine these dimensions. Then a person low on both activities is said to be concrete, while a person high on both activities is said to be abstract. The continuum from concrete to abstract is referred to as an integrative or conceptual complexity. To the concept of integrative complexity is usually added the concept of environmental complexity and the level of information processing. It is expressed by the "U-Curve Hypothesis" as depicted in Exhibit 4.2. As the level of information processing increases and reaches a maximum level at an optimal level of environmental complexity beyond which it begins to decrease.[61] H. M. Schroder et al. extended the concept of the inverted U-shaped curve to the study of integrative complexity. The differences between the concrete and the abstract individual are also shown in Exhibit 4.2. The more abstract the individual, the higher the maximum level of information processing.

5. Finally, field dependence as presented by H. A. Witkin and his associates is a measure of the extent of differentiation in the area of perception.[62] Field-

Exhibit 4.2
Functioning of Concrete and Abstract Individuals in Relation to Environmental Complexity

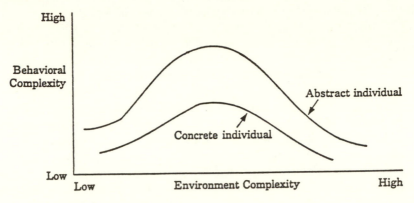

dependent individuals tend to perceive the overall organization of a field and are relatively unable to perceive parts of the field as discrete. Field-independent individuals, however, tend to perceive parts of the field as discrete from organized parts rather than fused with it.

That managers have specific cognitive styles in terms of authoritarianism, dogmatism, cognitive complexity, integrative complexity, and field dependence, which give them specific styles of decision making, has strong implications for management accounting. First, management accounting reports should be compatible with the cognitive structures of its users. They should be designed on the basis of realistic assumptions about the users' decision styles. Second, the utilization and the acceptance of management accounting techniques and information depend on their suitability to the cognitive style of the users. Thus, management accountants should be aware of the cognitive style constraint in the implementation of management accounting. Quantitative-based management accounting techniques may be more attractive to the analytic rather than the heuristic decision makers. Finally, the analytic management accountants should not assume that all users are and should be like themselves.

HEURISTICS AND BIASES

Research in behavioral decision theory suggests that individuals seem to employ heuristics and biases in order to reduce complete cognitive processes to simpler judgmental obligations that are more manageable. Research in behavioral accounting has tried to verify the existence of these heuristics and biases in judgments in an accounting setting. To date, this type of research has examined the following heuristics: representativeness, availability, confirmation bias, anchoring and adjustment, the conjunction fallacy, hindsight bias, illusory correlation, and the Weber-Fechner law. That managers resort to these heuristics in making professional and business judgments also has strong implications for management accounting. Management accountants have to take these heuristics into account when devising the content and format of management accounting reports. To understand the differences in information needs, the various types of heuristics are explicated.

Representativeness

A frequent heuristic in probability assessment appears to be representativeness. "A person who follows this heuristic evaluates the probability of an uncertain event, or a sample, by the degree to which it is: (i) similar in essential properties to its parent population; and (ii) reflects the salient features of the process by which it is generated."[63] According to this heuristic, a person will estimate the probability that subject A belongs to class B by the extent to which A resembles B. This heuristic, where class membership is assessed by the degree of its similarity to a stereotypical class member, has been found to lead to the following systematic biases in probability estimation:[64]

* Insensitivity to prior probability or base rate
* Insensitivity to the impact of sample size on the variance of the sampling distribution
* Misperception of the likelihood of different sequences resulting from a random process
* Insensitivity to the predictability of data

The neglect of the base rate was investigated a number of times, varying base rates, problem content, information order, and response mode.[65] The results confirmed the findings that base rates were ignored. When other experiments were used within subject experimental designs rather than between subjects, the findings showed that base rates were not ignored, in the sense that the subjects modified their judgments in the appropriate direction as the base rate was changed.[66]

Where the base rate was neglected, it was attributed to the fact that people lacked good schemata for working with probabilistic information,[67] and the "abstract, pallid, and remote" nature of the base rate contrasted to the generally "concrete, vivid, and salient" character of individuating information.[68]

In fact, three situations characterize the base rate fallacy case[69]:

1. People tend to rely on the base rate in making their judgments when case-specific evidence doesn't suggest a hypothesis (i.e., is not diagnostic and therefore not informative).[70]

2. People ignore the base rate when case-specific evidence strongly favors a particular hypothesis (i.e., is not diagnostic and therefore not informative).[71]

3. People rely on the base rates when the experimental case wording or format make

them appear causal[72] or specific.[73] This naturally follows from the findings that different framings of short cases will provide different results[74] and the suggestion by Tversky and Kahneman[75] that in the preliminary analysis of a decision problem, the decision maker frames the effective acts, contingencies, and outcomes: "Framing is controlled by the manner in which the choice problem is presented as well as by norms, habits and expectancies of the decision maker."[76]

Availability

Availability of information is argued to be an important clue that people use in making judgments. It has been considered as a bias whereby people make a probabilistic judgment on an event by the ease with which similar events are recalled. "A person is said to employ the availability heuristic whenever he estimates frequency or probability of the case with which instances or complications can be brought to mind."[77] That is, frequent events are easier to recall than infrequent ones, making availability a valid cue for the assessment of frequency and probability. Availability is also influenced by factors unrelated to likelihood, such as familiarity, recency, and emotional saliency and imaginability. S. Lichtenstein et al. asked their subjects to compare the frequency of occurrence of pairs of lethal events and found that they overestimated the relative frequency of diseases or causes of death that are much publicized.[78] What seems apparent is that emphasis on some aspects in the environment affects judgment by making it easier to recall instances and estimate their frequency.

Michael Ross and Fiore Sicoly postulated that an egocentric bias in availability of information in memory could produce biased attribution of responsibility for a joint product because of significant processes that may be operating to increase the availability of one's own contributions: selective encoding and storage of information, differential retrieval, informational disparities, and motivational influences.[79] Three experiments confirmed the prevalence of self-centered biases in availability and judgments of responsibility.

In everyday life these egocentric tendencies may be overlooked when joint endeavors do not require explicit allocations of responsibility. If allocations are stated distinctly, however, there is a potential for discussion, and individuals are unlikely to realize their differences in judgment could arise from honest evaluations that are differentially available.[80]

Confirmation Bias

It is an accepted normative view of scientific inference that disconfirmation and testing of alternative hypotheses have major roles. More particularly, Karl Popper's philosophy of science centers around the concept of disconfirmation or refutation.[81] He maintained that hypotheses can be disconfirmed only by evidence and never confirmed. J. R. Platt also argued that successive generations of alternative hypotheses should be disconfirmed—a strategy he labels "strong inference."[82]

Popper asserted that the purpose of science is not the verification but the falsification of theories.[83] The falsification can be achieved by deductive logic. If one adopts a rationalist view of humanity, then deductive logic is a necessary and natural part of human thought.[84] The behaviorist view would argue that the use of logical knowledge depends on whether or not the appropriate reinforcement contingencies have been applied.[85]

People are generally presented with conditional relationships between propositions that may be represented as "if p, then q," where p is the antecedent and q is the consequent. A typical deductive reasoning problem is to entertain alternative hypotheses with respect to the truth or the falsity of the rule. Given p, q, p' (not p) and q' (not q), the problem of deciding whether the rule "if p, then q" is true or false becomes a deductive reasoning problem. The selection may be accomplished using either a verification or falsification principle, depending on the degree of weight,[86] and as follows:

- A subject with no insight will select the options that verify the rule. That is, they will choose p or p and q.

- A subject with partial insight will appreciate the need to select potential falsifiers, but only choose options that could only verify. p' will be considered irrelevant because it should neither verify nor falsify. All other options will be chosen (i.e., p, q, and q') because they could either verify, falsify, or both.

- A subject with complete insight will select only the options that could falsify. That is, p and q' will be chosen.

Which strategies will be used has been the subject of experiments using either abstract or thematic problems, with the evidence showing only 10 percent of the subjects capable of solving the problem using the falsification principle.[87] The results were consistent with undergraduates as well as more sophisticated subjects (e.g., Ph.D. psychologists and statisticians)[88] and with abstract as well as thematic tasks.[89]

Which of these three strategies will be used by the accountant? The auditor's concern is mainly with verification—the examination of financial data for the purpose of judging the faithfulness with which they portray events and conditions. R. K. Mautz and H. A. Sharaf emphatically state the focus on verification:

In the business world, the act of verification is the trade of auditors, both internal and external. This philosophical truth about the necessity of verification is so well accepted that the business world has adopted a general practice of submitting such propositions to a verification process before they are given any serious consideration for many purposes. This verification consideration takes many forms; sometimes it is the continuous examination of procedures and data performed by an internal audit staff, sometimes the annual examination of an independent auditor, sometimes the investigation of an Internal Revenue Agent. Whatever the form, the importance and fact of verification are well accepted.[90]

Therefore, while deductive logic dictates the use of falsification in a deductive reasoning task, the emphasis on verification in auditing will lead the auditors to rely on a verification principle.

A. Belkaoui examined the use of logical knowledge in deductive reasoning by students and auditors.[91] One abstract and two thematic tasks were used and subjects were asked to test the truth or falsity of an implication rule. The results in the abstract test verified the dominance of the verification principle rather than the falsification principle for both students and auditors. No thematic effect was observed as the use of thematic effects showed a worsening of the falsification principle. In addition, the strong results on the dominance of the verification principle were found to be independent of the level of education, affiliation with a given accounting firm, position in the firm, years of experience as an auditor, years of application with the firm, or age of the subjects. While there is strong evidence both in accounting and psychology for this "confirmation bias," J. Klayman and Y.-W. Ha showed that many phenomena labeled confirmation bias are better understood in terms of a general "positive test strategy."[92] In addition, confirmation bias has meant different things to different researchers. Examples include the findings that people pay undue attention to the frequency of occurrence of two events, while underweighting instances in which one event occurs without the other;[93] the findings that people tend to discredit or reinterpret information counter to a hypothesis they hold;[94] and the findings that people may conduct "biased" tests that pose little risk of producing disconfirming results.[95]

Anchoring and Adjustment

In many situations, people make estimates by thinking of an internal value or "anchor" that is suggested by the formulation of the task or as a result of partial computation, and then make some adjustment to it to yield the final answer. This heuristic has been termed "anchoring and adjustment." For example, if a purchasing agent is asked to estimate next year's purchases, he may start with last year's purchases before making some adjustments to them to reflect new environmental conditions. Therefore, people starting from different anchors end up with different answers. In addition, this heuristic has been found to lead to the following systematic biases in probability estimation:[96]

- Insufficient adjustment
- Biases in the evaluation of conjunctive and disjunctive events—"the chain-like structure of conjunctions leads to overestimation, the funnel-like structure of disjunctions leads to underestimation"[97]
- Anchoring in the assessment of subjective probability distributions

P. Slovic also found evidence of anchoring in the subjective valuation of gambles.[98] Subjects finding a gamble basically attractive use the amount to win as an anchor, then adjust it downward to take into account the less-than-perfect chance of winning and the possibility of losing a small amount. The adjustment was insufficient and Slovic pointed out that it may be the reason why people price gambles inconsistently with straight choices between pairs of gambles where a monetary response is not required.

The anchoring heuristic was also observed in an experiment by M. Albert and H. Raiffa.[99] They asked subjects to give the 1st and 99th percentile values for various quantities of items. It amounted to asking the subjects to estimate the 98 percent confidence intervals for the population value of the various quantities. The evidence showed that, on average, the subject's 98 percent confidence intervals included the true value only 40–50 percent of the time.

The Conjunction Fallacy in Probability Judgment

The conjunction rule, a qualitative law of probability, specifies that the probability of a conjunction, $P(A \& B)$, cannot exceed the probabilities of its constituents, $P(A)$ and $P(B)$, because the extension (or the possibility set) of the conjunction is included in the extension of its constituents. In other words,

$$P(A \& B) \leq \min [P(A), P(B)]$$

But intuitive judgments of probability are generally not extensional. People instead use a limited number of heuristics. The natural assessments of representativeness and availability do not conform to the extensional logic of probability theory. "In particular, a conjunction can be more representative than one of its constituents, and instances of a specific category can be easier to retrieve than instances of a more inclusive category."[100]

One would expect, therefore, that representativeness and availability will make a conjunction appear more probable than one of its constituents. Indeed, Tversky and Kahneman present convincing evidence that people often violate the conjunction rule of probability theory when assessing the joint probability of two events.[101] They showed that both sophisticated and naive people, in many different substantive problems, often judge the conjunction of events to be larger than one of its components ("single violation") or as large as both of its components ("double violation"). Their experimental task included the following components:

A = the judged probability of an event A given model M

J = the judged probability of an event B given model M

$A \& J$ = the judged probability of the conjunction of A and J given model M

The violations to the conjunction rule were $B<J<A$ or $B<A<J$.

For example, they gave their subjects the following task: "Bill is 24 years old. He is intelligent, but unimaginative, compulsive, and generally lifeless. In school he was strong in mathematics. Please rank order the following statements by the degree to which Bill resembles the identical member of that class.''

• Bill is a physician, who plays poker for a hobby.
• Bill is an architect.
• Bill is an accountant. (A)
• Bill plays jazz for a hobby. (J)
• Bill surfs for a hobby.
• Bill is a reporter.
• Bill is an accountant who plays jazz for a hobby. (A & J)
• Bill climbs mountains for a hobby.

The risk included (1) a model M (the description of Bill), (2) an event A similar to the description (Bill is an accountant), (3) a dissimilar event J (Bill plays jazz for a hobby), and (4) the conjunction of the two events (event A and J: Bill is an accountant who plays jazz for a hobby). The subjects ranked the conjunctive event (A & J) as more probable than one of its constituents in this task as well as for other tasks in a variety of contexts using a number of different methods.

One explanation of this phenomenon may be derived from Tversky's feature-matching model, which suggests:[102]

$$S(a,b) = J(A\&B) - J(A-B) - J(B-A)$$

where

$$\begin{aligned} A\&B &= \text{the features that are common to both } A \text{ and } B \\ A-B &= \text{the features that belong to } A \text{ but not to } B \\ B-A &= \text{the features that belong to } B \text{ but not to } A \\ J &= \text{an interval scale measure of feature salience} \\ S &= \text{an interval scale measure of similarity} \end{aligned}$$

The model stipulates that the addition of a common feature to the stimuli produces an increase in their judged similarity and probability while the addition of a distinctive feature to either of the two produces a decrease in their judged similarity and probability. In the Tversky and Kahneman experiments the addition of event A with common features to the prototypical outcome of the description and event J with distinctive features led the subjects to rank conjunctive event ($A\&J$) as more probable than J but not more than A. H. J. Einhorn provides a more formal representation of the conjunction fallacy.[103] More examinations of judgments of event conjunctions were provided in various studies.[104]

Hindsight Bias

The hindsight bias or hindsight illusions were studied by B. Fischhoff[105] and Fischhoff and R. Byeth.[106] Basically, hindsight bias stipulates that subjects who have a knowledge that an outcome has occurred give that outcome a higher prior probability of occurrence than subjects who do not have any knowledge of the outcome. Fischhoff explains as follows:

In hindsight, people consistently exaggerate what could have been anticipated in foresight. They not only tend to view what has happened as inevitable, but also to view it as having appeared "relatively inevitable" before it happened. People believe that others should have been able to anticipate events much better than was actually the case. They even misremember their own predictions so as to exaggerate in hindsight what they know in foresight.[107]

In addition, subjects seem to be unaware of the influence of outcome knowledge on assessed probabilities. As stated by Fischhoff: "Making sense out of what he is told about the past seems so natural and effortless a response that one may be unaware that outcome knowledge has had any effect at all on him."[108]

Hindsight bias was observed in experiments by Fischhoff[109] employing psychotherapy cases, by Slovic and Fischhoff[110] employing the outcomes of scientific experiments, and by Fischhoff and Byeth[111], Fischhoff[112], and G. Wood[113], employing general knowledge events. It was also observed in a number of medical settings involving judgments by nurses,[114] patients,[115] surgeons,[116] and physicians.[117]

Various arguments were provided to explain the hindsight bias. First, that outcome knowledge restructures memory.[118] R. Hogarth, for example, states:

The knowledge that an event has occurred seems to restructure one's memory. Our memory of the past is not a memory of the uncertainties of the past, rather it is a reconstruction of past events in terms of what actually occurred. Furthermore, that past is structured in a way that makes some kind of coherent sense to the individual, for example, concerning the relationship between what actually happened and particular (but not all) antecedent events.[119]

Second, it stems from the difference between foresight and hindsight, with the first requiring more powers of imagination.

Prediction requires considerable powers of imagination and both the ability and willingness to entertain several hypotheses simultaneously. Keeping one's options open is not a tidy exercise and can induce considerable anxiety.

Postdiction or hindsight, on the other hand, requires little imagination and is an invitation to impose a causal structure on a sequence of past events. Furthermore, subjectively there is less uncertainty than in prediction problems concerning the events that "caused" what happened. One can believe any claim that seems plausible since it was seen to precede the event.[120]

Third, hindsight bias results from the limited availability of causal scenarios for alternative outcomes vis-a-vis scenarios for the reported outcome.[121]

Fourth, hindsight bias is a result of the individual's "fluency of diagnostic thinking."[122] In other words, outcome information makes possible the generation of a coherent story and what follows in terms of forward inference (i.e., prediction of outcomes) involves less uncertainty, given the reduction in the multiplicity of causation.

Fifth, hindsight bias is a result of motivating factors given that subjects, eager to preserve their self-images and how they are perceived by others, may be motivated to act as if they always knew what was going to occur.[123]

The hindsight bias raises a number of important issues with regard to judgments of the apparent failures (and successes) of others, distortions in memory, overcoming bias, and learning from experience.[124]

- With regard to judging others, hindsight makes it easier to judge the mistakes of others without considering that at the time a decision was made, it might have been quite reasonable.

- Distortions in memory result from hindsight bias. We may fail to blame people who make the wrong decision but get away with it.

- Fischhoff was able to "debias" distortions in memory caused by the knowledge of outcomes by giving the subject knowledge of the true outcomes following the false information provided earlier. That created a stimulus capable of overcoming hindsight bias.

- The hindsight bias raises questions concerning the ability of people to learn from experience and to make predictions.[125]

Illusory Correlation and Contingency Judgments

Illusory correlation refers to the belief that two variables covary when, in fact, they do not. L. J. Chapman defined it as "the report by observers of a correlation between two classes of events which, in reality, (a) are not correlated, (b) are correlated to a lesser extent than reported, or (c) are correlated in the opposite direction from that which is reported."[126] In fact, Chapman and Chapman provided subjects with information concerning hypothetical mental patients, which included a clinical diagnosis and a drawing of a person made by the patient.[127] The drawings and symptom statements were combined in such a way that "each drawing occurred as often with one statement as another."[128] Therefore, no relationship existed between drawings and symptom statements. The subjects were then asked to estimate the frequency with which each diagnosis (e.g., suspiciousness or paranoia) had been accompanied by various features of the drawings (e.g., peculiar eyes). The results showed that the subjects markedly overestimated the frequency of co-occurrence of pairs commonly believed to exist by society, such as suspiciousness and peculiar eyes. Similar results in

Exhibit 4.3
2 × 2 Joint Frequency Table

	Presence of Y	Absence of Y
Presence of X	a	b
Absence of X	c	d

illusory correlations were provided by Chapman and Chapman,[129] Golding and Rorer,[130] and Starr and Katkin.[131]

Illusory correlation studies point to the tendencies of finding nonexistent relationships.[132] Studies of contingency judgments, however, point to sensitivity to certain relationships and not to others. If X_1 and X_2 represent two events like the presence or absence of cloud seeding, and Y_1 and Y_2 represent two other events like the presence or absence of rain, then a contingency exists between X (cloud seeding) and Y (rain) to the extent that the probability of Y_1 given X_1 differs from the probability of Y_1 given X_2. A contingency exists between X and Y to the extent that $a/a+b$ differs from $c/c+d$. In contingency studies, subjects are generally asked to make a judgment J about the degree to which the variables X and Y covary. The normative or objective covariation, N, is measured by organizing the data in a 2 × 2 joint frequency rule as in Exhibit 4.3 and applying one of the following correct data-integration rules:

N_1 (difference in diagnosis) $= [a+d] - [b+c]$

N_2 (delta coefficient) $= [a/(a+b)] - [c/(c+d)]$

N_3 (contingency coefficient) $= [X^2/(n+X^2)]^{1/2})]$

N_4 (lambda coefficient) $= [\max(a,c) + \max(b,d) - \max(a+b, c+d)]/[n - \max(a+b, c+d)]$

N_5 (phi coefficient) $= [ad-bc]/[(a+c)(b+d)(a+b)(c+d)]^{1/2}$

The correlation between J, the judgment about the degree to which the variables X and Y covary, and the data integration rule N is a measure of accuracy. The results of experiments point to the following:

- Subjects fail to appreciate that all four frequencies in the table in Exhibit 4.3 are required.[133]

- Subjects make errors in estimating cell frequencies when factors unrelated to frequency influence the availability of data retrieved from memory or produced by imagination.[134]

- Subjects concentrate on the number of positive confirmatory data of a cell a and occasionally cell d, and ignore or underestimate the number of disconfirmatory data.[135]

• Studies of manipulatory task difficulty indicate that the covariation judgment accuracy decreases as establishing a data set becomes more difficult.[136]

Weber-Fechner Law

The Weber-Fechner law suggests that a just noticeable difference is uniquely related to the standard for which it was established. More explicitly, given a standard S and a just noticeable difference S, then

$$\text{change in } S/S = K \text{ for all } S$$

where

$$K = \text{constant}$$

In other words, the change in intensity of a stimulus that is necessary before it can be detected is a constant function of the amount of stimuli present. To measure the just noticeable difference, the method used is the method of constant stimulus differences. Under this method, subjects are presented with a standard, followed by a series of changes above and below the standard. The subjects are then asked to judge the pairs of stimuli. For the responses, three curves are drawn representing the relative frequency of judgments of larger, equal, and smaller for the different magnitudes of the comparison stimulus.

Accordingly, J. Rose et al. made the hypothesis that people do respond to data stimuli as to sense stimuli and these stimuli obey the Weber- Fechner law.[137] They asked the subjects to judge whether a stock should sell for more than, less than, or the same as a series of comparison stocks, based on comparison of earnings-per-share (EPS) figures. The results showed that judgments of numerical stimuli could be represented by the Weber-Fechner law. In effect, the Weber ratios ranged from 6.6 to 7.0 percent of the standard stimulus across two experiments and two standards.

John Dickhaut and Ian Eggleton continued this line of research on the Weber-Fechner law of examining comparative judgments of numerical information, especially accounting information.[138] Unlike the study by Rose et al., they manipulated the stated setting in which judgments were made, the sequence of data presentation, and the format in which standards and comparison stimuli were presented. The results showed that the subjects' perceptions of the data were consistent with the Weber-Fechner law. Examination of individual plots raised serious doubts about a similarity of the psychophysical process of comparing numerical stimuli. A second experiment was conducted followed by a questionnaire designed to elicit heuristics the subjects used in making similarity judgments. The results suggested that subjects used single decision rules, formulated either early in the task or possibly before the task was undertaken, applied inconsistently and defined as percentage functions of the expectations.

Magee and Dickhaut examined whether alternative compensation plans and the nature of the decision task condition the choice of heuristics.[139] Individuals' decision-making abilities in a cost-control setting were examined in an attempt to assess the effect of the compensation plan on these decisions. Based on an earlier study by Robert Magee,[140] they identified the heuristic to be used for each compensation plan. The results showed that alternative compensation plans condition the choice of heuristics. In addition, a questionnaire to elicit heuristics yielded results that were found to be related to differences in costs to the firm that would result from the different compensation plans. In short, alteration of the decision environment (specifically the compensation plan) influences the choice of heuristic and, ultimately, the costs incurred by an operating department.[141]

Other Heuristics

Various other heuristics have been extensively examined in psychology but not in accounting. There is a need for more accounting research to examine these untested heuristics in accounting. They include the following:

1. selective perception
2. frequency
3. concrete information
4. data presentation
5. inconsistency
6. conservatism
7. nonlinear extrapolation
8. law of small numbers
9. habit/"rules of thumb"
10. "best-guess" strategy
11. complexity in the decision environment
12. emotional stress in the decision environment
13. social pressures in the decision environment
14. consistency of information sources
15. question format
16. scale effects
17. wishful thinking
18. outcome-irrelevant learning structures
19. misperceptions of chance fluctuations (gambler's fallacy)
20. success/failure attributions
21. logical fallacies in recall

Exhibit 4.4
The Behavioral Foundations of Management Accounting

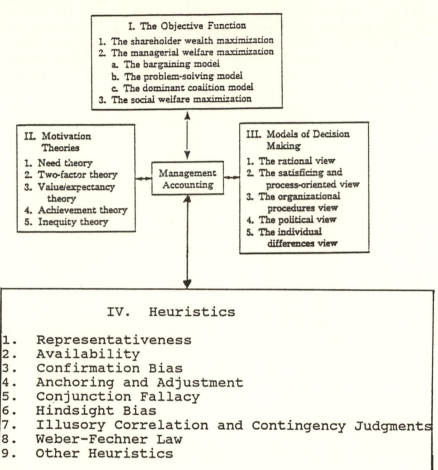

CONCLUSIONS

Management accounting rests on behavioral foundations. The type of objective function, motivation theories, heuristics, and the different models of decision making identify the factors likely to affect the behavior and performance of an individual within the organization (see Exhibit 4.4). First, management may either adopt the shareholder wealth maximization model, the managerial welfare model, or the social welfare model. The adoption of any model defines and restricts management to specific management techniques, attitudes, and behavior conducive to the accomplishment of the given objective. Second, the theories of motivation—namely, the need theory, the two-factor theory, the value/expectancy theory, the achievement theory, and the inequity theory—identify which environmental factors and management accounting techniques are susceptible to activate high performance or explain and describe the process of how desirable behavior may be initiated, encouraged, and even stopped. Third, the identification of the decision-making models employed by users in specific contexts may be of great help to the management accountant in adapting services to the users and the specific contexts. Five main perspectives of decision making were examined: the rational view, the satisficing process-oriented view, the organizational procedures view, the political view, and the individual differences view. Finally, the heuristics used by decision makers require different management reports in terms of informational content and format.

NOTES

1. Amitai Etzioni, *Modern Organizations* (Englewood Cliffs, N.J.: Prentice-Hall, 1964), p. 3.

2. Richard H. Hall, *Organizations: Structure and Process* (Englewood Cliffs, N.J.: Prentice-Hall, 1972), p. 9.

3. V. Buck, "The Organization as a System of Constraints," in J. D. Thompson (ed.), *Approaches to Organization Design* (Pittsburgh: The University of Pittsburgh Press, 1966), p. 109.

4. J. D. Thompson, *Organizations in Action* (New York: McGraw-Hill, 1967), p. 128.

5. C. Perrow, "The Analysis of Goals in Complex Organizations," *American Sociological Review* 26 (1961): 854–866.

6. Etzioni, *Modern Organizations*, p. 7.

7. Chapman M. Findlay and G. A. Whitmore, "Beyond Shareholder Wealth Maximization," *Financial Management* (Winter 1974): 25–35.

8. E. Solomon, *The Theory of Financial Management* (New York: Columbia University Press, 1963), p. 24.

9. W. Baumol, *Business Behavior, Value and Growth* (New York: Macmillan, 1964).

10. R. Marris, *The Economic Theory of Managerial Capitalism* (London: Macmillan, 1964).

11. A. Papandreou, "Some Basic Issues in the Theory of the Firm," in B. Haley (ed.), *A Survey of Contemporary Economics*, (Homewood, Ill.: Richard D. Irwin, 1952). Also, O. Williamson, *The Economics of Discretionary Behavior: Managerial Objectives in the Theory of the Firm* (Englewood Cliffs, N.J.: Prentice-Hall, 1964).

12. B. Branch, "Corporate Objectives and Market Performance," *Financial Management* (Summer 1973): 24–29.

13. Francine S. Hall, "Organizational Goals: The Status of Theory and Research," in J. Leslie Livingstone (ed.), *Managerial Accounting: The Behavioral Foundations* (Columbus, Ohio: Grid, 1975), pp. 1–29.

14. For an excellent presentation of these models, the reader is advised to examine the article by Hall in ibid.

15. Ibid., p. 17.

16. Ibid., p. 20.

17. Ibid., p. 23.

18. American Accounting Association, Committee on Measurement of Social Costs, "Report of the Committee on the Measurement of Social Costs, "*The Accounting Review*, Supplement to Vol. 69 (1974): 100.

19. Ibid., pp. 101–102.

20. M. R. Jones (ed.), *Nebraska Symposium on Motivation* (Lincoln: University of Nebraska Press, 1955), p. 14.

21. A. Maslow, "A Dynamic Theory of Human Motivation," *Psychological Review* 50 (1943): 370–373.

22. E. H. Caplan, *Management Accounting and Behavioral Science* (Reading, Mass.: Addison-Wesley, 1971), p. 49.

23. F. Herzberg, B. Mausner, and B. Snyderman, *The Motivation to Work*, 2nd ed. (New York: John Wiley, 1959).

24. Jacques E. Powers, "Job Enrichment: How One Company Overcame the Obstacle," *Personnel* (May-June 1972): 8.

25. Martin G. Evans, "Herzberg's Two-Factor Theory of Motivation," *Personnel Journal* (January 1970): p. 33.

26. K. Lewin, *Field Theory and Social Science* (New York: Harper, 1951).

27. V. H. Vroom, *Work and Motivation* (New York: John Wiley, 1964).

28. Ibid., p. 18.

29. L. W. Porter and E. E. Lawler, *Managerial Attitudes and Performance* (Homewood, Ill.: Irwin-Dorsey, 1968).

30. R. J. House, "A Path-Goal Theory of Leader Effectiveness," *Administrative Science Quarterly* 16 (September 1971): 321–338.

31. D. C. McClelland, *Personality* (New York:William Sloan, 1951); *The Achieving Society* (New York: Van Nostrand, 1961). Also, J. W. Atkinson, "Toward Experimental Analysis of Human Motivation in Terms of Motives, Expectancies, and Incentives," in J. W. Atkinson (ed.), *Motives in Fantasy, Action and Society* (New York: Van Nostrand, 1958).

32. J. W. Atkinson, "Motivational Determinants of Risk Taking Behavior," *Psychological Review* 64 (1957): 14.

33. E. Walster, E. Berscheid, and G. W. Walster, "New Directions in Equity Research," *Journal of Personality and Social Psychology* 25 (1973): 151–176. Also, J. S. Adams, "Toward an Understanding of Inequity," *Journal of Abnormal and Social Psychology* 22 (1968): 1045–1053.

34. Peter G. Keen and Michael S. Scott Morton, *Decision Support Systems: An Organizational Perspective*, Addison-Wesley Series on Decision Support (Reading, Mass.: Addison-Wesley, 1978), pp. 62–63.

35. G. T. Allison, *Essence of a Decision* (Boston: Little, Brown, 1971).

36. Ibid., p. 5.

37. Herbert A. Simon, *Administrative Behavior*, 2nd ed. (New York: Macmillan, 1957), p. 241.

38. J. G. March and H. A. Simon, *Organizations* (New York: John Wiley, 1958), p. 141.

39. Simon, *Administrative Behavior*, p. 272.

40. Ibid., p. 76.

41. R. M. Cyert and J. G. March, *A Behavioral Theory of the Firm* (Englewood Cliffs, N.J.: Prentice-Hall, 1963).

42. Ibid.

43. G. E. Clarkson, "A Model of Trust Investment Behavior," in Cyert and March, *A Behavioral Theory of the Firm*, Ch. 10.

44. John P. Crecine, "Governmental Problem Solving," in *A Computer Simulation of Municipal Budgeting* (New York, 1969).

45. Lair Aharoni, *The Foreign Investment Decision Process* (Boston, 1966).

46. P. R. Lawrence and J. W. Lorsch, *Organization and Environment* (Cambridge, Mass.: Division of Research, Harvard Business School, 1967).

47. Allison, *Essence of a Decision*, p. 144.

48. Ibid., p. 145.

49. Ibid., p. 146.

50. C. W. Lindblom, "The Science of Muddling Through, "*Public Adminstration Review* (Spring 1959): 79–88.

51. Kenneth R. Goldstein and Sheldon Blackman, *Cognitive Style: Five Approaches and Relevant Research* (New York: John Wiley, 1978), pp. 12–13.

52. T. W. Adorno, E. Frenkel-Brunswick, D. J. Levinson, and R. N. Sanford, *The Authoritarian Personality* (New York: Harper and Row, 1950).

53. J. Dermer, "Cognitive Characteristics and the Perceived Importance of Information," *The Accounting Review* (January 1973): 511–519.

54. M. Rokeach, *The Open and Closed Mind* (New York: Basic Books, 1960).

55. G. A. Kelly, *The Psychology of Personal Constructs*, 2 vols. (New York: W. W. Norton, 1955).

56. J. Bieri, "Cognitive Complexity and Personality Development," in O. J. Harvey (ed.), *Experience, Structure and Adaptability* (New York: Springer, 1966).

57. Jan H. B. Huysmans, "The Effectiveness of the Cognitive-Style Constraint in Implementing Operations Research Proposals," *Management Science* (September 1970): 94–95.

58. T. Mock, T. Estrin, and M. Vasarhelyi, "Learning Patterns, Decision Approach and Value of Information," *Journal of Accounting Research* (Spring 1972): 129–153.

59. O. J. Harvey, D. E. Hunt, and H. M. Schroder, *Conceptual Systems and Personality Organizations* (New York: John Wiley, 1961).

60. H. M. Schroder, M. J. Driver, and S. Streufert, *Human Information Processing* (New York: Holt, Rinehart and Winston, 1967).

61. Ibid., p. 37.

62. H. A. Witkin, R. B. Dyks, H. F. Faterson, D. R. Goodenough, and S. A. Karyn, *Psychological Differentiation* (New York: John Wiley, 1962). Also, H. A. Witkin, H. B. Lewis, M. Hertzman, K. Machover, P. B. Meisner, and S. Wagner, *Personality Through Perception* (New York: Harper, 1954).

63. D. Kahneman and A. Tversky, "Subjective Probability: A Judgment of Representativeness," *Cognitive Psychology* (July 1972): 431.

64. Ibid., pp. 430–454; D. Kahneman and A. Tversky, "On the Psychology of Prediction," *Psychological Review* (July 1973); A. Tversky and D. Kahneman, "Judgment Under Uncertainty: Heuristics and Biases," *Science* (September 1974): 1124–1131.

65. M. Bar-Hillel, "The Base Rate Fallacy in Probability Judgments," *Acta Psychologica* (October 1980): pp. 211–233; D. Lyon and P. Slovic, "Dominance of Accuracy

Information and Neglect of Base Rates in Probability Estimation,'' *Acta Psychologica* (January 1976): 287–298.

66. N. E. Airs and M. Maris, "Base-Rates Do Influence Social Judgments (But Not Optimally)'' (working paper, University of Michigan, 1978); M. Mavis and I. Dovalina, "Base-Rates Can Affect Individual Predictions'' (Working paper, University of Michigan, 1978).

67. R. E. Nisbett, R. Crandall, and H. Reed, "Popular Induction: Information is Not Necessarily Informative,'' in J. S. Carroll and J. W. Payne (eds.), *Cognitive and Social Behavior* (New York: Lawrence Erlbaum Associates, 1976).

68. R. E. Nisbett and E. Borgida, "Attribution and the Psychology of Prediction,'' *Journal of Personality and Social Psychology* (November 1975): 932–943.

69. D. Holt, "Evidence Integration in the Formation of Risk Assessments by Auditors and Bank Lending Officers'' (unpublished dissertation, University of Michigan, January 1984).

70. B. Fischhoff and M. Bar-Hillel, "Diagnosticity and the Base-Rate Effect,'' *Memory and Cognition* (July 1984): 402–410.

71. Ibid.

72. A. Tversky and D. Kahneman, "Evidential Impact on Base Rates,'' in D. Kahneman, P. Slovic, and A. Tversky (eds.), *Judgment under Uncertainty: Heuristics and Biases* (New York: Cambridge University Press, 1982), pp. 153–160.

73. Bar-Hillel, "The Base Rate Fallacy in Probability Judgments.''

74. P. Slovic, B. Fischhoff, and S. Lichtenstein, "Response Mode, Framing, and Information-Processing Effects in Risk Assessments,'' in R. Hogarth (ed.), *New Directions for Methodology of Social and Behavioral Science: Question Framing and Response Consistency*, no. 11, (San Francisco: Jossey-Bass, 1982), pp. 22–36.

75. A. Tversky and D. Kahneman, "Rational Choice and the Framing of Decisions,'' *Journal of Business* (October 1986).

76. Ibid., pp. 8251–8278.

77. A. Tversky and D. Kahneman, "Availability: A Heuristic for Judging Frequency and Probability,'' *Cognitive Psychology* 5 (1973): 208.

78. S. Lichtenstein, P. Slovic, B. Fischhoff, M. Layman, and B. Combs, "Perceived Frequency of Lethal Events,'' *Decision Research Report* 78–2 (Eugene, Ore.: Decision Research, a Branch of Perceptronics, Inc., 1978).

79. Michael Ross and Fiore Sicoly, "Egocentric Biases in Availability and Attributions,'' *Journal of Personality and Social Psychology* 37 (1979): 322–336.

80. Ibid., p. 336.

81. K. R. Popper, *Conjectures and Refutations* (New York: Basic Books, 1962).

82. J. R. Platt, "Strong Inference,'' *Science* 146 (1964): 347–353.

83. K. R. Popper, *The Logic of Scientific Discovery* (London: Hutchinson, 1959).

84. R. Revlin and R. E. Mayer, *Human Reasoning* (New York: John Wiley, 1987).

85. B. F. Skinner, *Beyond Freedom and Dignity* (London: Basic Books, 1963).

86. P. N. Johnson-Laird and P. C. Wason (eds.), *Thinking: Readings in Cognitive Science* (New York: Cambridge University Press, 1977).

87. J. S. Evans and B. T. Evans, *The Psychology of Deductive Reasoning* (London: Routledge and Kegan Paul, 1982).

88. R. M. Dawes, "The Mind, the Model and the Task,'' in F. Restel, R. M. Sliffrin, N. J. Castellan, H. R. Lindman, and D. B. Risoni (eds.), *Cognitive Theory*, vol. 1 (Hillsdale, N.J.: Erlbaum, 1975); R. A. Griggs and S. E. Ravesdall, "Scientists and the

Selection Task'' (unpublished manuscript, Department of Psychology, University of Florida, Gainesville, 1985); R. A. Griggs and J. R. Cox, ''The Elusive Thematic-Materials Effect in Wason's Selection Task,'' *British Journal of Psychology* 73 (1982): 407–420.

89. B. Fischhoff and R. Beyth-Maron, ''Hypothesis Evaluation from a Bayesian Perspective,'' *Psychological Review* (June 1983): 239–260; P. C. Vanduyne, ''Necessity and Contingency in Reasoning,'' *Acta Psychologica* (May 1976): 85–101.

90. R. K. Mautz and H. A. Sharaf, *The Philosophy of Auditing*, American Accounting Association Monograph No. 6 (Evanston, Ill.: American Accounting Association, 1961).

91. A. Belkaoui, ''Auditing and the Use of Logical Knowledge in Deductive Reasoning: An Experiment'' (unpublished manuscript, University of Illinois at Chicago, 1987).

92. Joshua Klayman and Young-Won Ha, ''Confirmation, Disconfirmation and Information in Hypothesis Testing'' (working paper, Graduate School of Business, University of Chicago, Center for Decision Research, February 1986).

93. H. R. Arkes and A. R. Harkness, ''Estimates of Contingency between Two Dichotomous Variables,'' *Journal of Experimental Psychology* (October 1983): 117–135.

94. C. Lord, L. Ross, and M. Legger, ''Biased Assimilation and Attitude Polarization: The Effect of Prior Theories on Subsequently Considered Evidence,'' *Journal of Personality and Social Psychology* (March 1979): 2098–2109.

95. M. Snyder, ''Seek and Ye Shall Find: Testing Hypotheses about Other People,'' in E. T. Higgins, C. P. Heiman, and M. P. Zamma (eds.), *Social Cognition: The Ontario Symposium on Personality and Social Psychology* (Hillsdale, N.J.: Erlbaum, 1981).

96. Tversky and Kahneman, ''Judgment under Uncertainty,'' pp. 1124–1131.

97. Ibid.

98. P. Slovic, ''From Shakespeare to Simon: Speculations and Some Evidence About Man's Ability to Process Information,'' *Research Monograph* (Oregon Research Institute, April 1972).

99. M. Albert and H. Raiffa, ''A Progress Report on the Training of Probability Assessors'' (unpublished manuscript, Harvard University, Graduate School of Business Administration, 1968).

100. A. Tversky and D. Kahneman, ''Extensional versus Intuitive Reasoning: The Conjunction Fallacy in Probability Judgment,'' *Psychological Review* (October 1983): 295.

101. Ibid., pp. 293–315.

102. A. Tversky, ''Features of Similarity,'' *Psychological Review* (February 1977): 327–352.

103. H. J. Einhorn, ''A Model of the Conjunction Fallacy'' (working paper, Center for Decision Research, University of Chicago, June 1985).

104. Frank J. Yates and Bruce W. Carlson, ''Conjunction Errors: Evidence for Multiple Judgment Procedures, Including 'Signed Summation,' '' *Organizational Behavior and Human Decision Processes* 37 (1986): 230–253; Dean M. Morier and Eugene Borgida, ''The Conjunction Fallacy: A Task Specific Phenomenon?'' *Personality and Social Psychology Bulletin* (June 1984): 243–252; John Uddo, Robert P. Abelson, and Paget H. Gross, ''Conjunctive Explanations: When Two Reasons are Better Than One,'' *Journal of Personality and Social Psychology* (March 1984): 933–943; A. Locksley and C. Stangor, ''Why vs. How Often: Causal Reasoning and Incidence of Judgmental Bias,'' *Journal of Experimental Social Psychology* (October 1984): 430–455.

105. B. Fischhoff, ''Hindsight Foresight: The Effect of Outcome Knowledge on Judg-

ment under Uncertainty," *Journal of Experimental Psychology: Human Perception and Performance* (May 1975): 288–299; "Perceived Informativeness of Facts," *Journal of Experimental Psychology: Human Perception and Performance* (May 1977): 349–358.

106. B. Fischhoff and R. Beyth, "I Knew It Would Happen: Remembered Probabilities of Once-Future Things," *Organizational Behavior and Human Performance* (February 1975): 1–16.

107. B. Fischhoff, "Debasing," in Kahneman, Slovic, and Tversky, *Judgment under Uncertainty*, p. 428.

108. Fischhoff, "Hindsight Foresight," p. 298.

109. Ibid.

110. P. Slovic and B. Fischhoff, "On the Psychology of Experimental Surprises," *Journal of Experimental Psychology: Human Perception and Performance* (November 1977): 544–551.

111. Fischhoff and Beyth, "I Knew It Would Happen."

112. Fischhoff, "Perceived Informativeness of Facts."

113. G. Wood, "The Know-It-All-Along Effect," *Journal of Experimental Psychology: Human Perception and Performance* (May 1978): 345–353.

114. T. Mitchell and L. Kalb, "Effects of Outcome Knowledge and Outcome Valence on Supervisors' Evaluations," *Journal of Applied Psychology* (October 1981): 604–612.

115. D. Pennington, D. Rutter, K. McKenna, and I. Morley, "Estimating the Outcome of a Pregnancy Test: Women's Judgments in Foresight and Hindsight," *British Journal of Social and Clinical Psychology* (November 1980): 317–323.

116. D. Detmer, D. Fryback, and K. Gassner, "Heuristics and Biases in Medical Decision-Making," *Journal of Medical Education* 53 (1978): 682–683.

117. H. Arkes, R. Wortmann, P. Saville, and A. Harkness, "Hindsight Bias among Physicians Weighing the Likelihood of Diagnoses," *Journal of Applied Psychology* (October 1981): 252–254.

118. R. Hogarth, *Judgment and Choice: The Psychology of Decisions* (New York: John Wiley, 1980).

119. Ibid., p. 102.

120. Ibid.

121. R. Nisbett and L. Ross, *Human Inference: Strategies and Shortcomings of Social Judgment* (Englewood Cliffs, N.J.: Prentice-Hall, 1980).

122. H. Einhorn and R. Hogarth, "Behavioral Decision Theory: Process of Judgment and Choice," *Journal of Accounting Research* (Spring 1981): 32–41.

123. Ross and Sicoly, "Egocentric Biases in Availability and Attribution," in Kahneman, Slovic, and Tversky, *Judgment under Uncertainty*, pp. 179–189.

124. Hogarth, *Judgment and Choice*, p. 103.

125. Fischhoff, "Debasing."

126. L. J. Chapman, "Illusory Correlation in Observational Report," *Journal of Verbal Learning and Verbal Behavior* (February 1967): 151.

127. L. J. Chapman and J. P. Chapman, "Genesis of Popular but Erroneous Psychodiagnostic Signs," *Journal of Abnormal Psychology* (June 1967): 193–204.

128. Ibid., p. 196.

129. L. J. Chapman and J. P. Chapman, "Illusory Correlation as an Obstacle to the Use of Valid Psychodiagnostic Signs," *Journal of Abnormal Psychology* (June 1969): 271–280.

130. S. L. Golding and L. G. Rorer, "Illusory Correlations and Subjective Judgment," *Journal of Abnormal Psychology* (June 1978): 249–260.

131. J. Starr and E. S. Katkin, "The Clinician as an Aberrant Actuary: Illusory Correlation and the Incomplete Sentences Blank," *Journal of Abnormal Psychology* (December 1969): 670–675.

132. H. M. Jenkins and W. C. Ward, "Judgment of Contingency between Responses and Outcomes," *Psychological Monographs: General and Applied*, No. 594 (1965); J. Smedsbund, "The Concept of Correlation in Adults," *Scandanavian Journal of Psychology* (Third Quarter, 1963): 165–173; J. Smedsbund, "Note on Learning, Contingency, and Clinical Experience," *Scandanavian Journal of Psychology* (Fourth Quarter, 1966): 265–266; W. C. Ward and H. M. Jenkins, "The Display of Information and the Judgment of Contingency," *Canadian Journal of Psychology* (September 1965): 231–241.

133. Nisbett and Ross, *Human Inference*.

134. Chapman, "Illusory Correlation in Observational Report"; Tversky and Kahneman, "Availability: A Heuristic for Judging Frequency and Probability"; R. Schweder, "Likeness and Likelihood in Everyday Thought: Magical Thinking in Judgments about Personality," *Current Anthropology* (December 1977): 637–658.

135. Chapman and Chapman, "Genesis of Popular but Erroneous Psychodiagnostic Observations"; "Illusory Correlation as an Obstacle to the Use of Valid Psychodiagnostic Signs."

136. Ward and Jenkins, "The Display of Information and the Judgment of Contingency"; Arkes and Harkness, "Estimates of Contingency," pp. 117–135; H. Shaklee and M. Mins, "Sources of Error in Judging Event Covariations: Effects of Memory Demands," *Journal of Experimental Psychology: Learning, Memory and Cognition* (May 1982): 208–224.

137. J. Rose, W. Beaver, S. Becker, and G. Sorter, "Toward an Empirical Measure of Materiality," supplement to *Journal of Accounting Research* (Spring 1970): 138–148.

138. John W. Dickhaut and Ian R. C. Eggleton, "An Examination of the Processes Underlying Comparative Judgments of Numerical Stimuli," *Journal of Accounting Research* (Spring 1975): 38–72.

139. Robert P. Magee and John W. Dickhaut, "Effects of Compensation Plans on Heuristics in Cost Variance Investigations," *Journal of Accounting Research* (Autumn 1978): 294–314.

140. Robert P. Magee, "A Simulation Analysis of Alternative Cost Variance Investigation Models," *Accounting Review* (July 1976): 529–544.

141. Magee and Dickhaut, "Effects of Compensation Plans," p. 307.

BIBLIOGRAPHY

The Objective Function

Anthony, Robert N. "The Trouble with Profit Maximization." *Harvard Business Review* (November–December 1960): 126–134.

Beams, Floyd A., and Fertig, Paul E. "Pollution Control Through Social Cost Conversion." *The Journal of Accountancy* (November 1971): 37–42.

Belkaoui, Ahmed. "The Impact of the Disclosure of the Environmental Effects of Organizational Behavior on the Market." *Financial Management* (Winter 1976): 26–31.

Cyert, Richard M.; March, James G.; and Starbuck, William H. "Two Experiments on Bias and Conflict in Organizational Estimation." *Management Science* (April 1961): 254–264.

Donaldson, Gordon. "Financial Goals: Management Versus Stockholders." *Harvard Business Review* (May–June 1963): 116–129.

Estes, Ralph W. "Accounting for Social Costs." *The Accounting Review* (April 1972): 284–290.

Findlay, Chapman M. and Whitmore, G. A. "Beyond Shareholder Wealth Maximization." *Financial Management* (Winter 1974): 25–35.

Lewellen, Wilbur G. "Management and Ownership in the Large Firm." *Journal of Finance* (May 1969): 299–322.

Linowes, David F. "Socio-Economic Accounting." *The Journal of Accountancy* (November 1968): 37–42.

Livingstone, J. Leslie (ed.). *Managerial Accounting: The Behavioral Foundations.* Columbus, Ohio: Grid, 1975.

Mobley, Sybil C. "The Challenges of Socio-Economic Accounting." *The Accounting Review* (October 1970): 762–768.

Schiff, Michael, and Lewin, Arie T. "Where Traditional Budgeting Fails." *Financial Executive* (May 1968): 55–62.

Williamson, O. *The Economics of Discretionary Behavior: Managerial Objectives in the Theory of the Firm.* Englewood Cliffs, N.J.: Prentice-Hall, 1964.

Motivation Theories

Adams, J. S. "Toward an Understanding of Inequity." *Journal of Abnormal and Social Psychology* 22 (1968): 1045–1053.

Caplan, E. H. *Management Accounting and Behavioral Science.* Reading, Mass.: Addison-Wesley, 1971.

Chung, Kae H. "Toward a General Theory of Motivation and Performance." *California Management Review* (Spring 1969): 81–88.

Herzberg, F.; Mausner, B.; and Snyderman, B. *The Motivation to Work*, 2nd ed. New York: John Wiley, 1959.

Maslow, A. "A Dynamic Theory of Human Motivation." *Psychological Review* 50 (1943): 370–373.

McClelland, D. C. *The Achieving Society.* New York: Van Nostrand, 1961.

Porter, L. W., and Lawler, E. E. *Managerial Attitudes and Performance.* Honewood, Ill.: Irwin-Dorsey, 1968.

Schein, Edgar. *Organization Psychology*, 2nd ed. Englewood Cliffs, N.J.: Prentice-Hall, 1970.

Vinacke, W. E. "Motivation as a Complex Problem." *Nebraska Symposium on Motivation.* Lincoln: University of Nebraska Press, 1962.

Vroom, V. H. *Work and Motivation.* New York: John Wiley, 1964.

Walster, E.; Berscheid, E.; and Walster, G. W. "New Directions in Equity Research." *Journal of Personality and Social Psychology* 25 (1973): 151–176.

Models of Decision Making

Allison, G. T. *Essence of a Decision*. Boston: Little, Brown, 1971.

Bariff, M. L., and Lusk, E. J. "Cognitive and Personality Tests for the Design of Management Information Systems." *Management Science* (April 1977): 820–829.

Cyert, R. M., and March, J. G. *A Behavioral Theory of the Firm*. Englewood Cliffs, N.J.: Prentice-Hall, 1963.

Dermer, J. "Cognitive Characteristics and the Perceived Importance of Information." *The Accounting Review* (January 1973): 511–519.

Goldstein, Kenneth, and Blackman, Sheldon. *Cognitive Style: Five Approaches and Relevant Research*. New York: John Wiley, 1978.

Huysmans, Jan H. B. "The Effectiveness of the Cognitive-Style Constraint in Implementing Operations Research Proposals." *Management Science* (September 1970): 92–104.

Keen, Peter G., and Scott Morton, Michael S. *Decision Support Systems: An Organizational Perspective*. Addison-Wesley Series on Decision Support. Reading, Mass.: Addison-Wesley, 1978.

Lindblom, C. W. "The Science of Muddling Through." *Public Administrative Review* (Spring 1959): 79–88.

March, J. G., and Simon, H. A. *Organizations*. New York: John Wiley, 1958.

Schroder, H. M.; Driver, M. J.; and Streufert, S. *Human Information Processing*. New York: Holt, Rinehart and Winston, 1967.

Simon, Herbert A. *Administrative Behavior*, 2nd ed. New York: Macmillan, 1957.

Sorter, George H.; Becker, Selwyn W.; Archibald, T. R.; and Beaver, W. "Corporate Personality as Reflected in Accounting Decisions: Some Preliminary Findings." *Journal of Accounting Research* (Autumn 1964): 183–196.

Heuristics and Biases

Belkaoui, A. "Auditing and the Use of Logical Knowledge in Deductive Reasoning: An Experiment." Unpublished Manuscript, University of Illinois at Chicago, 1987.

Belkaoui, A. *Human Information Processing in Accounting*. Westport, CT: Quorum Books, 1989.

Brichman, Thomas A. "An Effect of Hindsight on Predicting Bankruptcy with Accounting Information." *Accounting, Organizations and Society* (August 1988): 267–285.

Brown, Clifton E., and Solomon, Ira. "Effects of Outcome Information on Evaluations of Managerial Decisions." *Accounting Review* (July 1987): 564–577.

Dickhaut, John W., and Eggleton, Ian R. C. "An Examination of the Processes Underlying Comparative Judgments of Numerical Stimuli." *Journal of Accounting Research* (Spring 1975): 38–72.

Frederick, David M., and Libby, Robert. "Expertise and Auditors' Judgments of Conjunctive Events." *Journal of Accounting Research* (Autumn 1986): 270–290.

Gibbins, M. "Human Inference, Heuristics and Auditors' Judgment Processes." In *CICA Auditing Research Symposium*. Toronto: Canadian Institute of Certified Public Accountants (CICA), 1977.

Johnson, W. Bruce. " 'Representativeness' in Judgmental Predictions of Corporate Bankruptcy." *Accounting Review* (January 1983): 78–97.

Joyce, Edward J., and Biddle, Gary C. "Anchoring and Adjustment in Probabilistic Inference in Auditing." *Journal of Accounting Research* (Spring 1981): 120–145.
————. "Are Auditors' Judgments Sufficiently Regressive?" *Journal of Accounting Research* (Autumn 1981): 323–349.
Magee, Robert P. "A Simulation Analysis of Alternative Cost Variance Investigation Models." *Accounting Review* (July 1976): 529–544.
Magee, Robert P., and Dickhaut, John W. "Effects of Compensation Plans on Heuristics in Cost Variance Investigations." *Journal of Accounting Research* (Autumn 1978): 294–314.
Rose, J.; Beaver, W.; Becker, S.; and Sorter, G. "Toward an Empirical Measure of Materiality." Supplement to *Journal of Accounting Research* (Spring 1975): 38–72.
Swieringa, Robert; Gibbins, Michael; Larsson, Lars; and Lawson Sweeny, Janet. "Experiments in the Heuristics of Human Information Processing." Supplement to *Journal of Accounting Research* (1976): 159–187.

5

THE STRATEGIC FOUNDATIONS

Management accounting is built on strategic foundations. First, management accounting provides a framework and a language of discourse for the three stages of strategy: preenactment, resolution, and implementation. Second, the conduct of management accounting differs for different distinctions in the strategic process and the strategic decision-making process. Third, it works best when there is consequence between the design of management control systems and types of control strategies. Finally, the new area of strategic management accounting requires management accounting to focus on the firm's value added compared to its competitors and to monitor the firm's performance using strategic rather than tactical indicators. These relationships between strategy, strategic process distinctions, strategic archetypes, and strategic management accounting on one hand and management accounting on the other hand are exhibited in Exhibit 5.1 and explicated in this chapter.

NOTIONS OF STRATEGY

The Greeks refer to strategy as the "art of the general."[1] It evolved in the Harvard mold into an imaginative act of integrating numerous complex decisions.[2] A. D. Chandler, Jr. was the first to use strategy as a managerial tool.[3] He defined it as "the determination of the basic long-term goals and objectives of the enterprise and the adoption of courses of actions and the allocation of resources necessary for carrying out these goals."[4] The influence of this definition is clear in R. N. Anthony's depiction of strategic planning as "the process of deciding on objectives of the organization, or changes in these objectives, or the resources used to attain these objectives, and on the policies that are to govern the acquisition, use, and disposition of resources."[5] According to the last two

Exhibit 5.1
Management Accounting: The Strategic Foundations

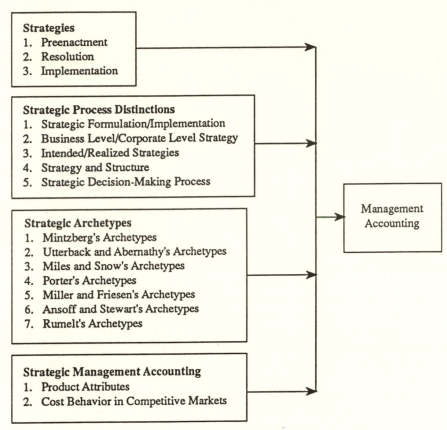

definitions, the concern of strategy is the link between the organization and its environment through both ends (objectives and goals) and means (courses of action and allocation of resources). Other theorists prefer to restrict strategy to only the objectives and goals and excludes the means to achieve them. C. W. Hofer and D. E. Schendel make the restriction by defining strategy as "the fundamental pattern of present and planned resource deployments and environmental interactions that indicates how the organization will achieve its objectives."[6] Another limitation is provided by M. E. Porter's concept of competitive strategy as "the search for a favorable competitive position in an industry. . . . [It] aims to establish a profitable and sustainable position against the forces that determine industry competition."[7] This school of thought is more in line with the argument that firms act to create their own environments by making a strategic choice regarding markets, products, technologies, desired scale of production, and so on. K. E. Weick refers to this concept as *environmental enactment*.[8] This interpretive view of organization assumes that organizations are socially constructed systems of shared meanings. The environment is neither objective nor perceived but enacted through the social interaction process of their organizational participants. As summarized by L. Smircich and C. Stubbart, "theories involving objective or perceived 'environments' envision concrete, material 'organizations' that are within, but separate from real material 'environments.' " The relationships between the two are expressed in terms of cause and effect. On the other hand, enactment theory abandons the idea of concrete, material "organizations/environments" in favor of a largely socially created symbolic world."[9] This view of enacted environment changes drastically the view of strategy and the role of the strategist from the old role of the one devoted to environmental scanning and data and fact collecting to a more imaginative and creative one best depicted as follows:

In the chaotic world, a continuous stream of ecological changes and discontinuities must be sifted through and integrated. Relevant and irrelevant categories of experience must be defined. People make sense of their situation by engaging in an interpretive process that forms the basis of their organized behavior. This interpretive process spans both intellectual and emotional realms. Managers can strategically influence this process. They can provide a vision to account for the streams of events and actions that occur—a universe within which organizational events and experiences take on meaning. The best work of strategic managers inspires splendid meanings.[10]

In any case the identification of strategies is needed to impose order in whatever environment. The decisions selected to be interpreted are then infused with meanings. What may happen is that different organizations will assign different meanings to a particular environmental event, resulting in different responses to similar environmental events. As stated by Jane Dutton and Susan Jackson;

"meanings attached to strategic issues are imposed by categories that decision makers employ to describe an issue. Categories are engaged by using linguistic labels. Two labels most frequently applied to strategic issues are focused on: threat and opportunity. Once applied, labels initiate a categorization process that affects the subsequent cognition and motivations of the decision makers; these, in turn, systematically affect the process and content of organizational actions.[11]

Accounting plays a role in the three stages of strategic change: preenactment, resolution, and implementation. Accounting provides "a framework for and a language of discourse [and] the power to establish and maintain the credibility of issue allocations through its authority structures, accountability measures, and performance evaluations."[12] Basically, strategies need to be framed in an accounting language and supported by the authority of accounting techniques, indicators, and reports.

STRATEGIC PROCESS

Strategic Process Distinctions

The strategic process is a complex phenomenon that calls for theoretical and practical distinctions. One distinction generally made is between *strategy formulation* and *strategy implementation*. Charles Snow and Donald Hambrick say "the advantage of making this distinction is that the cognitive aspects of strategy (formulation) can be viewed as an important phase apart from the action component (implementation).[13]

A second distinction made is between *business-level strategies* ("How should we compete in this business?") and *corporate-level strategies* ("What businesses should we be in?").[14] The difference between these two levels is explicated as follows:

The term business level refers to that level in an organization at which responsibility for the formulation of a multifunctional strategy for a single industry or product-market arena is determined; the term corporate level refers to the top level of the organization regardless of the number of industries in which it competes. Thus, for a multiindustry company, the business level normally would correspond to the divisional level. In a single product line company, however, the business and corporate level would be the same.[15]

The difference between the two strategies is important as corporate-level strategy precedes the enactment of the business-level strategy. In addition, the success of the business-level strategy in one period determines the corporate-level strategy in future periods. The two strategies are linked and equally important to each other's formulation and implementation.

A third distinction made by Mintzberg is between *intended strategy, deliberate strategy, realized strategy, unrealized strategy*, and *emergent strategy*.[16] Basically strategy is planned, qualifying as intended strategy, and if the exercise is successful they are realized strategies rather than unrealized strategies. If in addition a stream of decisions is made in a consistent way, it defines an emerging strategy that becomes a realized strategy. As stated by Mintzberg:

1. Intended strategies that get realized; these may be called *deliberate strategies*.
2. Intended strategies that do not get realized, perhaps because of unrealistic expectations, misjudgments about the environment, or changes in either during implementation; these may be called *unrealized* strategies.
3. Realized strategies that were never intended, perhaps because, as in (2), those that were got displaced along the way; these may be called *emergent* strategies.[17]

The difference between the intended and deliberate strategies on one hand and the emergent strategy on the other hand are a result of the differences between the teleological and the ecological views of strategy. The teleological view presumes that the strategic agenda is the sole responsibility of management. Under this perspective, management uses strategies to control the organization. It is a prescriptive view of the strategic process.[18,19] The ecological view presumes that the organization is a conflicting arena of different shareholders, each striving to impose and/or suggest an agenda. Under this view, strategy is the untamed of these organizational struggles, our expression of what the organization does rather than should do.[20,21] It is a descriptive approach similar to the emergent strategy approach. As stated by Jerry Dermer:

Thus, from an ecological perspective, the strategic agenda emerges from the reconciliation of conflicting rationalities, not from the imposition of management's global scheme.[22]

And because neither issues nor support can be controlled, managerial plans do not necessarily determine what the agenda contains. Consensus can originate anywhere and the role of "change entrepreneur" can be assumed by any shareholder with the motivation and ability to do so. Each change entrepreneur is free to operate within his/her own rationality, albeit constrained by the contingencies arising out of inescapable interdependencies. The dynamics of what determines the composition of the agenda is not the intentions of any particular player but rather the fit among concerns, capabilities and support. An issue gains the agenda when a concern is recognized, a resolution proposed and support sufficient to generate action aroused. This may be achieved through managerial control or it may be the result of other processes.[23]

Strategic Research

One important research theme has been to link strategy and structure of firms. The evidence is used to bolster either the argument "structure follows strategy" or the argument that "strategy follows structure."

The proposition that structure follows strategy followed from Chandler's historical analysis of 70 large American firms.[24] Basically, multiproduct growing firms solved their administrative problems by the implementation of new structures. The strategies adopted by these firms included either horizontal, vertical, or diversification in related or unrelated markets. Chandler maintained that a horizontal strategy called for a unitary structure, one characterized by manufacturing, sales and marketing, and finance departments; a vertical strategy called for a functional structure, one characterized by departments along discrete task lines; a diversification strategy called for a multidivisional structure, one in which a firm is organized into product divisions and each division contains a unitary structure. A heroic view of top management is presented. As stated by Robert Burgelman,

Chandler's case data suggest that multiple layers of management were involved in the strategic initiatives that produced the extensive diversification, and in response to which the new strategy and the new structure eventually emerged. The theoretical generalizations, however, collapse this strategic process into a top management activity. Even though the influence of lower levels in the determination of the context of the strategy is recognized, the major emphasis is on the role of top management.[25]

The proposition that strategy follows structure follows from J. L. Bower's study of strategy making as a multilayered process, spread over the management hierarchy.[26] The process is viewed as a culmination of a bottom-up and top-down multilayered process where strategy adopts itself to the particular structure of the firm. Top management role is less heroic moving to a new role. J. L. Bower and I. Doz state that "in contrast to strategy formulation as the critical direction-setting general management activity, this new process school of research suggested an alternative, that is, managing the strategic process."[27]

A second line of research has been connected with the strategic decision-making process. One line of research views strategic decision making as a linear, sequential, orderly activity originated by powerful executives. "It relies on rational techniques for analyzing environments and organizational resources, generating action alternatives and appraising these against unitary, consistent preferences."[28] A second line of research views strategic decision making as a disorganized, noisy, and uncoordinated activity resulting from the conflictual and political climates of firms, where primacy is given to personalities, power, context, and the untidiness of chance.[29]

STRATEGIC ARCHETYPES

Management accounting in general and management control systems in particular include formalized procedures for cost accumulation, product costing, budgeting, performance evaluation, and resource allocation. Business strategies define how a firm decides to compete in a given business and positions itself among its competitors. The strategy style adopted needs to be supported by adequate and appropriate management accounting techniques. Therefore, the strategic style chosen is an important determinant of the principles, techniques, and systems of management accounting adopted. The determination of the appropriate strategic style is important to both internal and external users of management accounting information of a given firm as it may show the nature of the "fit" between the strategic style and the management accounting system supporting its enactment, formulation, and implementation. Various models of strategic archetypes have been provided in the strategic management literature. They are explicated next.

Mintzberg's Strategic Archetypes

Mintzberg's model of strategic archetypes falls into three distinct groupings or modes: entrepreneurial, adaptive, and planning.[30] The *entrepreneurial mode* is modeled after the actions, attitudes, and behavior of the individuals who sought opportunity, founded firms, took bold decisions, focused on growth, and sought high uncertainty. Four characteristics are identified for the entrepreneurial mode of strategy-making:

1. In the entrepreneurial mode, strategy-making is dominated by the active search for new opportunities.
2. In the entrepreneurial organization, power is centralized in the hands of the chief executive.
3. Strategy-making in the entrepreneurial mode is characterized by dramatic leaps forward in the face of uncertainty.
4. Growth is the dominant goal of the entrepreneurial organization.[31]

The *adaptive mode* is modeled after the adaptive process characterized by C. E. Lindblom as "muddling through" or "disjointed incrementalism"[32] and used by R. M. Cyert and J. G. March.[33] Four characteristics are identified for the adaptive mode:

1. Clear goals do not exist in the adaptive organization; strategy-making reflects a division of power among members of a complex coalition.
2. In the adaptive mode, the strategy-making process is characterized by the "reactive" solution to existing problems rather than the "proactive" search for new opportunities.
3. The adaptive organization makes its decisions in incremental, serial steps.
4. Disjointed decisions are characteristic of the adaptive organization.[34]

The *planning mode* is modeled after the actions of the individuals whose analysis rests on systematic attainment of goals. Three characteristics are identified for the planning mode:

1. In the planning mode, the analyst plans a major role in strategy-making.
2. The planning mode focuses on systematic analysis, particularly in the assessment of the costs and benefits of competing proposals.
3. The planning mode is characterized above all by the integration of decisions and strategies.[35]

The characteristics and conditions of the three modes are summarized in Exhibit 5.2.

Utterback and Abernathy's Strategic Archetypes

James Utterback and William Abernathy's model of strategic types comprises three strategic types: performance-maximizing, sales-maximizing, and cost-minimizing.[36] The *performance-maximizing firm* faces an uncertain environment in which it is one of the first to introduce new products in the anticipation that new capabilities will expand customer requirements. As emphasized by Utterback and Abernathy,

a majority of innovations produced by performance-maximizing firms would be expected to be market-simulated with a high degree of uncertainty about their ultimate market

Exhibit 5.2
Characteristics and Conditions of the Three Modes

Characteristic	Entrepre-neurial Mode	Adaptive Mode	Planning Mode
Motive for Decisions	Proactive	Reactive	Proactive & Reactive
Goals of Organization	Growth	Indeterminate	Efficiency & Growth
Evaluation of Proposals	Judgmental	Judgmental	Analytical
Choices made by	Entrepreneur	Bargaining	Management
Decision Horizon	Long-Term	Short-Term	Long-Term
Preferred Environment	Uncertainty	Certainty	Risk
Decision Linkages	Loosely Coupled	Disjointed	Integrated
Flexibility of Mode	Flexible	Adaptive	Constrained
Size of Moves	Bold Decisions	Incremental Steps	Global Strategies
Vision of Direction	General	None	Specific
Condition for Use			
Source of Power	Entrepreneur	Divided	Management
Objectives of Organization	Operational	Nonoper-ational	Operational
Organizational Environment	Yielding	Complex, Dynamic	Predictable, Stable
Status of Organization	Young, Small or Strong Leadership	Established	Large

Source: H. Mintzberg, "Strategy Making in Three Modes." Copyright 1973 by The Regents of the University of California. Reprinted from the *California Managment Review*, Vol. 16, No. 2. By permission of The Regents.

potential. Technology to meet market needs may come from many sources. Innovation may often arise from unexpected sources or directions of inquiry. Performance-maximizing firms would be expected to rely more heavily on external sources of information, and on more diverse sources of information than would others.[37]

The *sales-maximizing firm* uses other firms' innovations to offer new product variation and features, thus reducing market uncertainty and ensuring more stable environments through the product differentiation. The *cost-minimizing firm* enters the market at the end of the product life cycle with less complex and less expensive products.

Miles and Snow's Strategic Archetypes

R. E. Miles and C. C. Snow's model of strategic archetypes comprises four strategic types: the defender, the analyzer, the prospector, and the reactor.[38] The first three are viewed as "stable" forms of organization, while the last one is viewed as essentially "unstable." Each type is assumed to have its own strategy for reacting to the environment and its own mix of strategy, technology, structure, and process that is consistent with the strategy.

Defenders are organizations that have narrow product-market domains. Top managers in this type of organization are highly expert in their organization's limited area of operation but do not tend to search outside of their domains for new opportunities. As a result of this narrow focus, these organizations seldom need to make major adjustments in their technology, structure, or methods of operation. Instead, they devote primary attention to improving the efficiency of their existing operations.

Analyzers are organizations that operate in two types of product-market domains—one relatively stable, the other changing. In their stable areas, these organizations operate routinely and efficiently through use of formalized structures and processes. In their more turbulent areas, top managers watch their competitors closely for new ideas, and then they rapidly adopt those that appear to be the most promising.

Prospectors are organizations that almost continually search for market opportunities, and they regularly experiment with potential responses to emerging environmental trends. Thus, these organizations often are the creators of change and uncertainty to which their competitors must respond. However, because of their strong concern for product and market innovation, these organizations usually are not completely efficient.

Reactors are organizations in which top managers frequently perceive change and uncertainty occurring in their organizational environments but are unable to respond effectively. Because this type of organization lacks a consistent strategy-structure relationship, it seldom makes adjustment of any sort until forced to do so by environmental pressures.[39]

Porter's Strategic Archetypes

M. E. Porter identified and defined three generic strategies:[40] cost leadership, differentiation, and focus strategies. *Cost leadership* focuses on the production of a standardized product at a low price for a high market share under conditions of economies of scale and tight cost control. As stated by Porter; "cost leadership requires aggressive construction of efficient-scale facilities, vigorous pursuit of cost reductions from experience, tight cost and overhead control, avoidance of marginal customer accounts, and cost minimization in areas like R&D, service, sales force, advertising, and so on."[41]

Differentiation focuses on the production of industry-unique products for loyal and relatively price-insensitive clientele, with emphasis on marketing and research.

Approaches to differentiating can take many forms: design or brand image (Fieldcrest in top of the line towels and linens; Mercedes in automobiles), technology (Hyster in lift trucks; McIntosh in stereo components; Coleman in camping equipment), features (Jenn-Air in electric ranges); customer service (Crown Cork and Seal in metal cans), dealer networks (Caterpillar tractor in construction equipment), or other dimensions.[42]

Focus strategy centers on the production of products that are needed by a defined buyer group, on a segment of the product line, or on a geographic market in the search of the appropriate niche. Porter says that

although the low cost and differentiating strategies are aimed at achieving their objectives industry-wide, the entire focus strategy is built around serving a particular target very well, and each functional policy is developed with this in mind. The strategy rests on the premise that the firm is thus able to serve its narrow strategic target more effectively or efficiently than competitors who are competing more broadly.[43]

Miller and Friesen's Archetypes of Strategy Formulation

D. Miller and P. H. Friesen examined undisguised cases of business organizations to look for simultaneous associations among a large number of variables to determine archetypes of strategic formulation.[44] Ten archetypes are identified. The successful archetypes are:

1. the adaptive firm under moderate challenge
2. the adaptive firm in a very challenging environment
3. the dominant firm
4. the giant under fire
5. the entrepreneurial conglomerate
6. the innovator

The failure archetypes are:

7. the impulsive firm
8. the stagnant bureaucracy
9. the headless giant
10. the aftermath

Each type is assumed to include the more intricate success and failure patterns characterizing firms. The attributes of the successful archetypes are shown in Exhibit 5.3, while those of the unsuccessful archetypes are shown in Exhibit 5.4.

Ansoff and Stewart's Strategic Archetypes

H. Igor Ansoff and John Stewart focused on the technology-based business and proposed a classification based on a differentiation between research and development, with an "R-intensive" type of firm that tends toward the basic and experimental, and a "D-intensive" type that tends toward commercial product design.[45]

The *R-intensive types* are assumed to display the following six characteristics:

1. They work with indefinite design specifications.
2. They tend to "broadcast" objectives and market data among technical people, rather than channel specific kinds of information to individuals.
3. They are nondirective in work assignments.
4. They maintain a continuous project evaluation and selection process.
5. They stress the perception of significant results.
6. They value innovation over efficiency.[46]

The *D-intensive types* are assumed to display these four characteristics:

1. Well-defined design specifications.
2. Highly directive supervision.
3. Sequential arrangement of tasks.
4. Vulnerability to disruption by change.[47]

Rumelt's Strategic Archetypes

R. P. Rumelt's methodology for the classification of diversification categories relies on three ratios: the specialization ratio, the related ratio, and the vertical ratio.[48] Each is based upon the proportion of revenues earned from various business activities.[49] The specialization ratio is used to define firms into the

Exhibit 5.3
Summary of Coping Methods Used by Each Archetype in Successful Subsample

		ENVIRONMENT		ORGANIZATION	STRATEGY MAKING
The adaptive firm under moderate challenge	S_{1A}	Dynamism Heterogeneity Hostility	(4–5)* (2–4) (5–6)	*Vigilant-Traditional* Delegation (6) Intelligence (5, 6, 5)** Strong Leader (Centralization, 6)	*Adaptive-Positive* Expertise(6) Proactiveness (6) Adaptiveness (6)
The adaptive firm in a very challenging environment	S_{1B}	Dynamism Heterogeneity Hostility	(5–7) (4–4) (4–6)	*Organic-Cerebral* Delegation-Centralization (6, 5) Intelligence (6, 7, 6) Technocratization (6)	*Assertive-Analytical* Product-Market Innovation (7) Proactiveness (7) Adaptiveness (6) Analysis (6)
The dominant firm	S_2	Dynamism Heterogeneity Hostility	(2–4) (2–3) (2–3)	*Hierarchical* Initial Strategy (6) Strong Leader (Centralization, 6) Resources (6)	*Extrapolation* Expertise (7) Integration (6) Innovation (6), Adaptiveness (6)
The giant under fire	S_3	Dynamism Heterogeneity Hostility	(4–6) (6–6) (3–6)	*Decentralized* Delegation-Centralization (7, 4) Intelligence (6, 6, 6) Technocratization (6)	*Incremental-Analytical* Analysis (6) Expertise (6). Conscious Strategy (6) Caution (proactiveness, 4)
The entre-preneurial conglomerate	S_4	Dynamism Heterogeneity Hostility	(4–5) (4–6) (4–4)	*Charismatic* Centralization (7) Delegation (6) Intelligence (6, 6, 6)	*Manipulation-Expansion* Analysis (6) Risk Taking (6) Proactiveness (6)
The innova-tors	S_5	Dynamism Heterogeneity Hostility	(5–6) (3–4) (5–5)	*Encephalized* Centralization (6) Initial Strategy (6)	*Innovation within Niche* Product-Market Innovation (7) Proactiveness (7) Expertise (6) Consciousness of Strategy (6)

* Figures in parentheses are modal scores for companies within each archetype; (4–5) means that the current dynamism score is 5, and that dynamism was scored 4 five years prior.
** Listed in order of scanning (5), controls (6), communication (5), which are all considered to be "intelligence" variables.
Source: Reprinted by permission of D. Miller and P. H. Friesen, "Archetypes of Strategy Formulation," *Management Science*, 24, no. 9 (May 1978): 929. Copyright 1978, The Institute of Management Sciences.

primary categories of either single business, dominant business, related business, or unrelated business. The related and vertical ratios are then used to subdivide firms into finer classifications.

The *specialization ratio* is defined as the proportion of the firm's revenues that is attributable to its largest discrete product market activity. The *related ratio* is defined as the proportion of firm revenues that is attributable to the largest group of businesses that are related to one another in some way. The *vertical ratio* is defined as the proportion of revenues attributable to all the by-products,

Exhibit 5.4
Summary of Coping Methods Used by Each Archetype in Unsuccessful Subsample

		ENVIRONMENT		ORGANIZATION	STRATEGY MAKING
The impulsive firm	F_1	Dynamism	(4–6)*	*Top Centered-Differentiated*	*Overextension*
		Heterogeneity	(3–6)	Centralization (7)	Risk Taking (7)
		Hostility	(3–7)	Low Intelligence (3, 1, 3)**	Proactiveness (6)
				(Key lack of controls)	Analysis (2)
				Differentiation (6)	
The stagnant bureaucracy	F_2	Dynamism	(2–5)	*Rigid-Bureaucratic*	*Ultra Conservatism*
		Heterogeneity	(2–2)	Centralization (6)	Conservatism (Risk Taking, 2)
		Hostility	(2–6)	Low Intelligence (2, 2, 1)	Proactiveness (1)
				(Obstructed communications)	Innovation (2)
				Internal Strife (Conflict, 7)	Adaptiveness (1)
					Traditions (6)
The headless giant	F_3	Dynamism	(3–5)	*Leaderless-Diversified*	*Muddling Through*
		Heterogeneity	(3–5)	No Leadership (centralization, 1)	Integration (1)
		Hostility	(3–6)	Divisions responsible for	Innovation (2)
				everything (delegation, 6)	Multiplexity (2)
				Low Intelligence (3, 2, 2)	Proactiveness (2)
				(low controls & communication)	Consciousness of Strategy (3)
					Traditions (6)
The aftermath	F_4	Dynamism	(3–5)	*Makeshift*	*Grafting + Groping*
		Heterogeneity	(2–3)	Past Trouble (initial	P.M. Innovation (5)
		Hostility	(4–6)	success of strategy, 2)	Integration (2)
				Centralization (6)	Risk Taking (5)
				Delegation (4)	
				Resource Availability (1)	

Source: Reprinted by permission of D. Miller and P. H. Friesen, "Archetypes of Strategy Formulation," *Management Science*, 24, no. 3 (May 1978): 929. Copyright 1978, The Institute of Management Sciences.

intermediate products, and final products of a vertically integrated sequence of manufacturing operations.

The primary diversification strategies and their subcategories are:

1. single business
2. dominant business as either
   a. dominant vertical
   b. dominant constrained
   c. dominant linked or
   d. dominant unrelated
3. related business as either
   a. related constrained or
   b. related linked
4. unrelated business as either

a. multibusiness or

b. unrelated-portfolio

A specialization ratio (SR) of less than .7 defines businesses as being either related or unrelated. If $.7 \leq SR < .95$, then the firm is classified as a dominant business. The firm is classified as a single business if $SR \geq .95$. A related ratio (RR) greater than .7 defines a related business. A vertical ratio (VR) greater than .7 defines a vertically integrated business.

Rumelt's ratios were used to classify firms as being in one of the three following categories:

1. Primarily dominant vertical firms. Vertically integrated firms ($VR \geq .7$) producing and selling different end products, no one of which contributes more than 94 percent of total revenues.
2. Related-constrained firms. Firms with $.7 \leq SR < .95$ and $RR \geq .7$, which have diversified by relating new businesses to a specific central skill or resource and in which each business activity is related to almost all the other business activities of the firm.
3. Unrelated business firms. Firms with $.7 \leq SR < .95$ and $RR < .7$, which have aggressive programs for the acquisition of new unrelated businesses.

STRATEGIC MANAGEMENT ACCOUNTING

John Shank and Vijay Govindarajan predicted that strategic accounting will supplant managerial accounting as a decisional framework because managerial accounting lacks strategic relevance.[50] While cost analysis provides an assessment of the financial impact of managerial decision alternatives, strategic cost analysis will provide cost data for the development of the right strategy necessary to gain competitive advantage. As stated by Shank and Govindarajan, "a sophisticated understanding of a firm's cost structure can go a long way in the search for sustainable competitive advantage. This understanding is what we refer to as 'strategic cost analysis.' "[51]

Underlying Shank and Govindarajan's concern is the failure of management accounting to explicitly consider strategic issues and concerns. Only strategic management accounting in general and strategic cost analysis in particular can fill that void.

Strategic cost analysis is broader than conventional cost analysis by bringing into the analysis the strategic elements necessary to gain a competitive advantage. As a result, accounting information gains an expanded role in the four stages of the strategic process: (1) formulation of strategies and stages, (2) communication of strategies, (3) development of tactics, and (4) implementation. That role is defined as follows:

At *stage 1*, accounting information is the basis for financial analysis, which is one aspect of the process of evaluating strategic alternatives. Strategies that are not feasible or do not yield adequate financial returns cannot be appropriate strategies.

At *stage 2*, accounting reports constitute one of the important ways that strategy gets communicated throughout an organization. The things that are reported are the things people will pay attention to. Good accounting reports are those that focus attention on the factors that are critical to success of the strategy adopted.

At *stage 3*, specific tactics must be developed in support of the overall strategy and then carried through to completion. Financial analysis, based on accounting information, is one of the key elements in deciding which tactical programs are most likely to be effective in helping a firm to meet its strategic objectives.

Finally, at *stage 4*, monitoring the performance of managers or business units usually hinges partly on accounting information. The role of standard costs, expense budgets, and annual profit plans in providing one basis for performance evaluation is well accepted in businesses worldwide. These tools must be explicitly adapted to the strategic content of the firm if they are to be measurably useful.[52]

Another working definition of strategic management accounting is provided by M. Bromwich as "the provision and analysis of financial information on the firm's product markets and competitor's costs and cost structures and the monitoring of the enterprises' strategies and those of its competitors in these markets over a number of periods."[53] With such a definition focusing on the provision of information concerning the firm's markets and on its competitors, Bromwich was successful in offering the vertical supports for the involvement of accountants in strategic management accounting. The first theoretical support for the involvement of accountants in strategic management accounting is provided by Bromwich.[54] This theoretical support is derived from the economic theory that sees economic goods as being a bundle of attributes. The accountant is asked to cost these attributes and monitor their performance over time. Information about a number of demand and cost factors pertaining to these attributes is deemed important for optimal decision making. As stated by Bromwich:

Accountants may play a role here in costing the characteristics provided by goods and in monitoring and reporting on these costs regularly. Similarly, they may be involved in determining the cost of any package of attributes which is being considered for introduction in the market. However, where a strategic perspective is adopted by accountants, costs may have to be considered in the context of demand factors because of the likely interplay between costs and demand in determining successful strategic conduct when considering product attributes.[55]

The second theoretical support is derived from the theory of contestable markets that gives the conditions for a firm's price and output strategy to be sustainable in the face of potential competition.

Following contestable market theory precepts, and the recommendation for monitoring cost advantages over rivals, strategic management accounting is oriented toward not only the cost structure of the firm but also the cost structures of all firms in the market and those likely to enter the market.

What follows from this concern with strategic management accounting is a complete restructuring of the role of accounting toward an active role in the strategic process and an essential means to help achieving economic success. Consequently, Shank and Govindarajan suggest the following key management questions to ask about any accounting idea:

- Does it serve an identifiable business objective? (facilitate strategy formulation . . . assess managerial performance.

- For the objective it is designed to serve, will the accounting idea enhance the chances of attaining the objective?

- Does the objective whose attainment is facilitated by the accounting idea fit strategically with the overall thrust of the business?[56]

CONCLUSIONS

As Exhibit 5.1 showed, management accounting needs to take the strategic concept into account to allow firms to achieve business success. It needs to adapt to various stages of the strategic process, the distinctions within the strategic process, the influence of strategic archetypes, and the new informational demands of strategic management accounting. As well stated by Bromwich,

there are good reasons why management accounting should be less introspectively concerned with enterprise costs and should adopt a more strategic perspective and become more concerned with markets and with the behavior of competitors. This is because costs and the other aspects of a firm's strategies are often highly inter-related and leaving corporate strategy to the strategists is likely not to capture the complete picture concerning enterprise strategic decisions.[57]

NOTES

1. B. H. Hart, *Strategy* (New York: Praeger, 1967).

2. K. R. Andrews, *The Concept of Corporate Strategy* (Homewood, Ill: Richard D. Irwin, 1971).

3. A. D. Chandler, Jr., *Strategy and Structure* (Cambridge, Mass.: MIT Press, 1962), p. 13.

4. Ibid.

5. R. N. Anthony, *Planning and Control Systems: A Framework for Analysis* (Cambridge, Mass.: Harvard University Graduate School of Business Administration, 1965), p. 27.

6. C. W. Hofer and D. E. Schendel, *Strategy Formulation: Analytical Concepts* (New York: West, 1978), p. 75.

7. M. E. Porter, *Competitive Strategy: Techniques for Analyzing Industries and Competitors* (New York: The Free Press, 1980), p. 1.

8. K. E. Weick, "Enactment Processes in Organization," in B. M. Staw and G. R. Salancik (eds.), *New Directions in Organizational Behavior* (Chicago: St. Clair Press, 1977).

9. L. Smircich and C. Stubbart, "Strategic Management in an Enacted World," *Academy of Management Review* (October 4, 1985): 727.

10. Ibid., p. 730.

11. Jane E. Dutton and Susan E. Jackson, "Categorizing Strategic Issues: Links to Organizational Action," *Academy of Management Review* (December 1, 1987): 77.

12. Jerry Dermer, "The Strategic Agenda: Accounting for Issues and Support," *Accounting, Organizations and Society* (February 1990): p. 74.

13. Charles C. Snow and Donald C. Hambricks, "Measuring Organizational Strategies: Some Theoretical and Methodological Problems," *Academy of Management Review* (May 4, 1980): 528.

14. Charles W. Hofer, "Towards a Contingency Theory of Business Strategy," *Academy of Management Journal* 18 (1975): 784–810.

15. Ibid., p. 784.

16. H. Mintzberg, "Patterns in Strategy Formulation," *Management Science* 24 (1978): 934–948.

17. Ibid., p. 945.

18. R. L. Achoff and F. E. Emery, *On Purposeful Systems* (Chicago: Aldine and Atherton, 1972).

19. A. Kuhn, *The Logic of Organization* (San Francisco: Jossey-Bass, 1982).

20. R. Dye, *Policy Analysis: What Governments Do, Why They Do It and What Differences It Makes* (University: University of Alabama Press, 1976).

21. H. Mintzberg and J. Walters, "On Strategies Deliberate and Emergent," *Strategic Management Journal* (March 1985): 25–37.

22. Dermer, "The Strategic Agenda," p. 69.

23. Ibid.

24. Chandler, *Strategy and Structure*.

25. Robert A. Burgelman, "A Model of the Interaction of Strategic Behavior, Corporate Context, and the Concept of Strategy," *Academy of Management Review* 8, no. 1, (1983): 62–63.

26. J. L. Bower, "Planning and Control: Bottom Up or Top Down Approach," *Journal of General Management* 1 (1974): 20–31.

27. J. L. Bower and I. Doz, "Strategy Formulation: A Social and Political View," in D. E. Schendel and C. W. Hofer (eds.), *Strategic Management* (Boston: Little, Brown, 1979), pp. 152–166.

28. Jeremy F. Dent, "Strategy, Organization and Control: Some Possibilities for Accounting Research," *Accounting, Organizations and Society* (February 1990): 8.

29. A. Pettigrew, *The Awakening Giant: Continuity and Change in ICI* (Oxford: Blackwell, 1985).

30. H. Mintzberg, "Strategy Making in Three Modes," *California Management Review* (Winter 1973): 44–53.

31. Ibid., pp. 45–46.

32. C. E. Lindblom, "The Science of 'Muddling Through,' " *Public Administration Review* 19 (1959), pp. 78–88.

33. R. M. Cyert and J. G. March, *A Behavioral Theory of the Firm* (Englewood Cliffs, N.J.: Prentice-Hall, 1963).

34. Mintzberg, "Strategy Making in Three Modes," pp. 46–47.

35. Ibid., p. 48.

36. James M. Utterback and William J. Abernathy, "A Dynamic Model of Process and Product Innovation," *OMEGA, The International Journal of Management Science* 3, no. 6 (1975): 639–656.

37. Ibid., p. 643.

38. R. E. Miles and C. C. Snow, *Organizational Strategy, Structure and Process* (New York: McGraw-Hill, 1978).

39. Ibid., p. 29.

40. Porter, *Competitive Strategy*.

41. Ibid., p. 35.

42. Ibid., p. 37.

43. Ibid., p. 38.

44. D. Miller and P. H. Friesen, "Archetypes of Strategy Formulation," *Management Science* (May 1978): 921–933.

45. H. Igor Ansoff and John M. Stewart, "Strategies for a Technology-Based Business," *Harvard Business Review* (November–December 1967): 71–83.

46. Ibid., p. 73.

47. Ibid., p. 74.

48. R. P. Rumelt, *Strategy, Structure and Economic Performance* (Cambridge, Mass.: Harvard University Press, 1974), pp. 29–32.

49. Ellen Pavlik and Ahmed Belkaoui, *Determinants of Executive Compensation* (Westport, Conn.: Greenwood Press, 1991).

50. John K. Shank and Vijay Govindarajan, "Making Strategy Explicit in Cost Analysis: A Case Study," *Sloan Management Review* (Spring 1988): 19–29.

51. Ibid., p. 19.

52. John K. Shank and V. Govindarajan, *Strategic Cost Analysis: The Evolution from Managerial to Strategic Accounting* (Homewood, Ill.: Richard D. Irwin, 1985), pp. xi–xii.

53. M. Bromwich, "The Case for Strategic Management Accounting: The Role of Accounting Information for Strategy in Competitive Markets," *Accounting, Organizations and Society* (February 1990): 27–46.

54. Ibid., p. 44.

55. Ibid.

56. Shank and Govindarajan, *Strategic Cost Analysis*, p. xii.

57. Michael Bromwich, *The Revolution in Management Accounting*, R. J. Chambers Research Lecture 1989 (Sydney: Accounting and Finance Foundation, 1985), p. 50.

BIBLIOGRAPHY

Allen, D. "Strategic Financial Management." In M. Bromwich and A. G. Hopwood (eds.), *Research and Current Issues in Management Accounting*. London: Pitman, 1986.

Andrews, K. R. *The Concept of Corporate Strategy*. Homewood, Ill.: Richard D. Irwin, 1971.

Ansari, S., and Euske, K. J. "Rational, Rationalizing and Reifying Uses of Accounting Data in Organizations." *Accounting, Organizations and Society* (March 1987): 549–570.

Argyris, C. *The Applicability of Organizational Sociology*. Cambridge: Cambridge University Press, 1972.

Armitage, H. M., and Langdon, W. E. "Management Accounting: The New Relevance." *CMA Magazine* (June 1988).

Atkinson, A. A. *Intra-firm Cost and Resource Allocations: Theory and Practice*. Toronto: Canadian Academic Accounting Association, 1987.

Baumol, W. J.; Panzar, J. C.; and Willig, R. D. *Contestable Markets and the Theory of Industry Structure*. San Diego: Harcourt Brace, Jovanovich, 1982; revised edition, 1988.

Berliner, C., and Brimson, J. *Cost Management in Today's Advanced Manufacturing: The CAM-I Conceptual Design*. Boston: Harvard Business School Press, 1988.

Bhimani, A., and Bromwich, M. "Accounting for Just-In-Time Manufacturing Systems." *CMA: The Management Accountants' Magazine*. Forthcoming.

Boland, R. J., and Pondy, L. R. "Accounting in Organizations: A Union of Natural and Rational Perspectives." *Accounting, Organizations and Society* (January 1983): 223–234.

———. "The Micro-Dynamics of a Budget Cutting Process: Modes, Models and Structure." *Accounting, Organizations and Society* (March 1986): 403–422.

Braybrooke, D., and Lindblom, C. E. *A Strategy of Decision*. New York: The Free Press, 1963.

Bromwich, M. "The Case for Strategic Management Accounting: The Role of Accounting Information for Strategy in Competitive Markets." *Accounting, Organizations and Society* (February 1990).

———. "Some Problems with Replacement Cost Asset Measurement for External Accounting Reports with Imperfect Markets." *Abacus* (December 1983): 148–161.

Bromwich, M., and Bhimani, A. *Management Accounting: Evolution Not Revolution*. London: CIMA, 1989.

Brown, R. H. "Bureaucracy as Praxis: Towards a Political Phenomenology of Formal Organizations." *Administrative Science Quarterly* (December 1978): 365–382.

Bruns, W. J., and Kaplan R. S. (eds.). *Accounting and Management: Field Study Perspectives*. Boston: Harvard Business School Press, 1987.

Brunsson, N. *The Irrational Organization*. New York: John Wiley, 1985.

Burgelman, Robert A. "A Model of the Interaction of Strategic Behavior, Corporate Context, and the Concept of Corporate Strategy." *Academy of Management Review* 8, no. 1 (1983): 61–70.

Chandler, A. D. *Strategy and Structure*. Cambridge, Mass.: MIT Press, 1962.

Channon, D. *The Strategy and Structure of British Enterprise*. New York: Macmillan, 1973.

Child, J. "Information Technology, Organizations, the Response to Strategic Challenges." in G. R. Carroll and D. Vogel (eds.), *Organizational Approaches to Strategy*. Cambridge, Mass: Ballinger, 1987, 29–46.

———. "Organization Structure Environment and Performance: The Role of Strategic Choice." *Sociology* (March 1972): 2–22.

Clark, J. M. *Studies in the Economics of Overload Costs*. Chicago: Chicago University Press, 1923.

Coates, J. B., and Longden, S. G. *Management Accounting in New and High Technology Growth Companies—CIMA Report*. London: CIMA, 1987.

Cohen, M. D.; March, J. G.; and Olsen, J. P. "A Garbage Can Model of Organizational Choice." *Administrative Science Quarterly* (February 1972): 1–25.

Cooper, R., "The Two-Stage Procedure in Cost Accounting—Part I." *Journal of Cost Management for the Manufacturing Industry* (Summer 1987): 39–45.

———. "The Rise of Activity-Based Costing—Part II." *Journal of Cost Management for the Manufacturing Industry* (Summer 1988): 45–54.

Cooper, R., and Kaplan, R. S. "How Cost Accounting Systematically Distorts Product Costs." In W. J. Bruns, and R. S. Kaplan (eds.), *Accounting and Management: Field Study Perspectives.* Boston: Harvard Business School Press, 1987, pp. 169–203.

Crozier, M. *The Bureaucratic Phenomenon.* London: Tavistock, 1964.

Dent, J. F. "Organizational Research in Accounting: Perspectives, Issues and a Commentary." In M. Bromwich and A. G. Hopwood (eds.), *Research and Current Issues in Management Accounting* (London: Pitman, 1986), pp. 143–178.

———. "Strategy, Organization and Control: Some Possibilities for Accounting Research." *Accounting, Organizations and Society* (February 1990): 3–25.

———. "Tensions in the Design of Formal Control Systems: A Field Study in a Computer Company." in W. J. Bruns and R. S. Kaplan (eds.), *Accounting and Management: A Field Study Perspective* (Cambridge, Mass.: Harvard Business School Press, 1987), pp. 119–145.

Dermer, J. *Management Planning and Control Systems.* Homewood, Ill.: Richard D. Irwin, 1977.

———. "The Strategic Agenda: Accounting for Issues and Support." *Accounting, Organizations and Society* (February 1990): 67–76.

Dess, G., and Davis, P. S. "Porter's Generic Strategies as Determinants of Strategic Group Membership and Organizational Performance." *Academy of Management Journal* (February 1984): 467–488.

Dyas, G. P., and Thanheiser, H. T. *The Emerging European Enterprise Strategy and Structure in French and German Industry.* New York: Macmillan, 1976.

Foster, G., and Horngren, C. T. "Cost Accounting and Cost Management in a JIT Environment." *Journal of Cost Management for the Manufacturing Industry* (Winter 1988): 4–14.

Fouraker, L. E., and Stopford, J. M. "Organization Structure and Multinational Strategy." *Administrative Science Quarterly* (March 1968): 47–64.

Franko, L. *The European Multi-Nationals.* New York: Greylock, 1976.

———. "The Move Toward a Multi-Divisional Structure in European Organizations." *Administrative Science Quarterly* (October 1974): 493–506.

Ginter, P. M.; Rucks, A. C.; and Duncan, W. J. "Planners' Perceptions of the Strategic Management Process." *Journal of Management Studies* (April 1985).

Gintzberg, M. J. "An Organizational Contingencies View of Accounting and Information Systems Implementation." *Accounting, Organizations and Society* (December 1980): 369–382.

Gordon, L. A., and Miller, D. "A Contingency Framework for the Design of Accounting Information Systems." *Accounting, Organizations and Society* (January 1976): 59–70.

Gordon, L. A., and Narayanan, V. K. "Management Accounting Systems, Perceived Environmental Uncertainty and Organization Structure: An Empirical Investigation." *Accounting, Organizations and Society* (December 1984): 33–48.

Govindarajan, V. J. "A Contingency Approach to Strategy Implementation at the Business Level: Integrating Administrative Mechanisms with Strategy." *Academy of Management Journal* (March 1988): 828–853.

———. "Appropriateness of Accounting Data in Performance Evaluation: An Empirical Examination of Environmental Uncertainty as an Intervening Variable." *Accounting, Organizations and Society* (February 1984): 125–136.

Govindarajan, V. J., and Gupta, A. K. "Linking Control Systems to Business Unit Strategy: Impact on Performance." *Accounting, Organizations and Society* (January 1985): 51–66.

Govindarajan, V., and Shank, J. K. "Making Strategy Explicit in Cost Analysis: A Case Study." *Sloane Management Review* (Spring 1988): 19–29.

Greenwood, R., and Hinings, C. R. "Organization Design Types, Tracks and the Dynamics of Strategic Change." In *Organization Studies* (March 1988): pp. 293–316.

Hall, D. J., and Saias, M. A. "Strategy Follows Structure." *Strategic Management Journal* (October 1980): 149–163.

Hambrick, D. C. "An Empirical Typology of Mature Industrial-Product Environments." *Academy of Management Journal* (March 1983), pp. 213–230.

———. "Environment, Strategy and Power Within Top Management Teams." *Administrative Science Quarterly* (February 1981): 253–276.

———. "Some Tests of the Effectiveness and Functional Attributes of Miles and Snow's Strategic Types." *Academy of Management Journal* (June 1983): 5–26.

Hannan, M. T., and Freeman, J. "The Population Ecology of Organizations." *American Journal of Sociology* (April 1977): 929–964.

Hayes, R., and Abernathy, S. J. "Managing Our Ways to Economic Decline." *Harvard Business Review* (October 1980): 67–77.

Hickson, D. J.; Butler, R. J.; Cray, D.; Mallory, G. R.; and Wilson, D. C. *Top Decisions: Strategic Decision Making in Organizations*. Oxford: Blackwell, 1986.

Hickson, D. J.; Hinings, C. R.; Lee, C. A.; Schneck, R. E.; and Pennings, J. M. "A Strategic Contingencies Theory of Intra Organizational Power." *Administrative Science Quarterly* (March 1971): 216–229.

Hiromoto, T. "Another Hidden Edge—Japanese Management Accounting." *Harvard Business Review* (July/August 1988): 22–26.

Hitt, M. A., and Ireland, R. D. "Relationships among Corporate Level Distinctive Competencies, Diversification Strategy, Corporate Structure and Performance." *Journal of Management Studies* (August 1986).

Hofer, C. W., and Schendel, D. E. *Strategy Formulation: Analytical Concepts* (New York: West 1978).

Howell, R. A., and Soucy, G. R. "Cost Accounting in the New Manufacturing Environment." *Management Accounting* (August 1987): 42–49.

Johnson, G. *Strategic Change and the Management Process*. Oxford: Blackwell, 1987.

Johnson, H. T. "Activity-Based Information: A Blueprint for World-Class Management Accounting." *Management Accounting* (June 1988): 23–30.

———. "Organizational Design Versus Strategic Information Procedures for Managing Corporate Overhead Cost: Weyerhauser Company 1972–1986." In W. J. Bruns and R. S. Kaplan (eds.), *Accounting and Management: Field Study Perspectives*. Boston: Harvard Business School Press, 1987, pp. 17–48.

Johnson, H. T., and Kaplan, R. S. *Relevance Lost: The Rise and Fall of Management Accounting*. Boston: Harvard Business School Press, 1987.

Jones, L. "Competitor Cost Analysis at Caterpillar." *Management Accounting* (October 1988): 32–38.

Kaplan, R. S. "Accounting Lag: Obsolescence of Cost Accounting Systems." In K. Clark and C. Lorenz (eds.), *Technology and Productivity: The Uneasy Alliance*. Boston: Harvard Business School Press, 1985, pp. 195–226.

————. *Introduction, Cost Accounting for the 90's: The Challenge of Technological Change Proceedings*. Montvale, N.J.: National Association of Accountants, 1986, pp. 7–10.

————. "Measuring Manufacturing Performance: A New Challenge for Managerial Accounting Research." *The Accounting Review* (April 1983): 686–705.

————. "One Cost System Isn't Enough." *Harvard Business Review* (January/February 1988): 61–66.

————. "Relevance Regained." *Management Accounting* (UK) (September 1988): 38–42.

————. "Yesterday's Accounting Undermines Production." *Harvard Business Review* (July/August 1984): 95–101.

Kobayashi, K. "Direct Costing for Pricing Custom-Made Products in Japan's Industries." In S. Sato, K. Sakate, G. G. Mueller, and L. H. Radebaugh (eds.). *A Compendium of Research on Information and Accounting for Managerial Decision and Control in Japan*. Sarasota, Fla.: AAA, 1982.

Lancaster, K. J. *Variety, Equity and Efficiency: Product Variety in an Industrial Society*. New York: Columbia University Press, 1979.

Lewis, A. *Overhead Costs: Some Essays in Economic Analysis*. London: G. Allen and Unwin, 1949.

Littler, D. A., and Sweeting, R. C. *Growth Business in High Technology Growth Companies—CIMA Report*. London: CIMA, 1987.

Lorange, P., and Vancil, R. F. *Strategic Planning Systems*. Englewood Cliffs, N.J.: Prentice-Hall, 1977.

Lorenz, E. H. "The Search for Flexibility: Subcontracting Networks in French and British Engineering." In P. Hirst and J. Zeitlin (eds.), *Reversing Industrial Decline?* Oxford: Berg, 1984, pp. 133–154.

Main, J. "The Trouble with Managing Japanese Style." *Fortune* (February 4, 1984).

Mason, R. D., and Mitroff, I. I. *Challenging Strategic Planning Assumptions*. New York: John Wiley, 1981.

McCall, M. W. "Making Sense with Nonsense: Helping Frames of Reference Clash." In P. C. Nystrom and W. H. Starbuck (eds.), *Prescriptive Models of Organization*. Amsterdam: North-Holland, 1977, pp. 111–123.

McHilhattan, R. D. "How Cost Management Systems Can Support the JIT Philosophy." *Management Accounting* (September 1987): 20–26.

Miles, R. E., and Snow, C. C. *Organizational Strategy, Structure and Process*. New York: McGraw-Hill, 1978.

Miller, D., and Friesen, P. H "Archetypes of Strategy Formulation." *Management Science* (May 1978): 921–933.

————. "Innovation in Conservative and Entrepreneurial Firms." *Strategic Management Journal* (October 1982): 1–27.

————. "Momentum and Revolution in Organizational Adaptation." *Academy of Management Journal* (October 1980): 591–614.

————. *Organizations: A Quantum View*. Englewood Cliffs, N.J.: Prentice-Hall, 1984.

————. "Porter's (1980) Generic Strategies and Performance: An Empirical Examination with American Data, Part 1: Testing Porter." *Organization Studies* (April 1986): 37–55.

————. "Strategy Making in Context." *Journal of Management Studies* (March 1977): 259–280.

Mintzberg, H. "Crafting Strategy." *Harvard Business Review* (July/August 1987): 66–75.

————. "Patterns in Strategy Formulation." *Management Science* 24 (1978): 934–948.

————. *The Structuring of Organizations*. Englewood Cliffs, N.J.: Prenctice-Hall, 1979.

Mintzberg, H. and McHugh, A. "Strategy Formulation in an Adhocracy." *Administrative Science Quarterly* (March 1985): 160–197.

Mintzberg, H.; Raisinghani, D.; and Theoret, A. "The Structure of 'Unstructured' Decision Processes." *Administrative Science Quarterly*, 21 (April 1976): 246–275.

Mintzberg, H., and Waters, J. A. "Tracking Strategy in an Entrepreneurial Firm." *Academy of Management Journal* (March 1982): 465–499.

Misawa, M. "New Japanese Style Management in a Changing Era." *Columbia Journal of World Business* (Winter 1987): 9–17.

Noreen, E. "Relevance Lost: The Rise and Fall of Management Accounting." *Accounting Horizons* (December 1987): 110–116.

Pennings, J. M. "Towards Convergence in Strategic Theory and Practice." In J. M. Pennings and Associates, *Organizational Strategy and Change*. San Francisco: Jossey-Bass, 1985, pp. 468–494.

Pettigrew, A. *The Awakening Giant: Continuity and Change in ICI*. Oxford: Blackwell, 1985.

————. *The Politics of Organizational Decision Making*. London: Tavistock, 1973.

Pfeffer, J. *Power in Organizations*. London: Pitman, 1981.

Pfeffer, J., and Moore, W. L. "Power in University Budgeting: A Replication and Extension." *Administrative Science Quarterly* (April 1980): 637–653.

Pfeffer, J., and Salancik, G. R. *The External Control of Organizations: A Resource Dependence Perspective*. New York: Harper and Row, 1978.

Porter, M. E. *Competitive Advantage: Creating and Sustaining Superior Performance*. New York: The Free Press, 1985.

————. *Competitive Strategy: Techniques for Analyzing Industries and Competitors*. New York: The Free Press, 1980.

Quinn, J. B. *Strategies for Change: Logical Incrementalism*. Homewood, Ill.: Richard D. Irwin, 1980.

Ranson, S.; Hinings, R.; and Greenwood, R. "The Structuring of Organizational Structures." *Administrative Science Quarterly* (April 1980): 1–17.

Roberts, John. "Strategy and Accounting in a U.K. Conglomerate." *Accounting, Organizations and Society* (February 1990): 107–126.

Rumelt, R. P. *Strategy, Structure and Economic Performance*. Cambridge, Mass.: Harvard University Press, 1974.

Salop, S. C. "Strategic Entry Deterrence." *American Economic Review* (May 1979): 335–338.

Scherer, F. M. *Industrial Market Structure and Economic Performance*. Chicago: Rand-McNally, 1970.

Schoenfeld, H. M. "The Present State of Performance Evaluation in Multinational Companies." In H. P. Holzer and H. M. Schoenfeld (eds.), *Managerial Accounting and Analysis in Multinational Enterprises*. Berlin: Walter de Gruyter, 1986, pp. 217–251.

Schonberger, R. I. "The Transfer of Japanese Manufacturing Management Approaches to US Industry." *Academy of Management Review* (March 1982): 479–487.

Seed, A. H. *Adopting Management Accounting Practice to an Advanced Manufacturing Environment*. Montvale, N.J.: National Association of Accountants, 1988.

Simmonds, K. "Strategic Management Accounting." *Management Accounting* (April 1981): 26–29.

Simmonds, Robert. "The Role of Management Control Systems in Creating Competitive Advantage: New Perspectives." *Accounting, Organizations and Society* (February 1990): 127–143.

Simons, R. "Accounting Control Systems and Business Strategy." *Accounting, Organizations and Society* (July 1987): 357–374.

Snow, C. C., and Hrebiniak, L. G. "Strategy, Distinctive Competence and Organizational Performance. "*Administrative Science Quarterly* (April 1980): 317–336.

Starbuck, W. H. "Congealing Oil: Intervening Ideologies to Justify Acting Ideologies Out." *Journal of Management Studies* (March 1982): 3–27.

———. "Organizations as Action Generators." *American Sociological Review* (March 1983): 91–102.

Starbuck, W. H., and Hedberg, B. L. T. "Saving an Organization from a Stagnating Environment." In H. B. Thorelli (ed.), *Strategy + Structure = Performance*. Bloomington: Indiana University Press, 1977, pp. 249–258.

Stopford, J. and Wells, L. *Managing the Multinational Enterprise*. London: Longman, 1972.

Suzuki, Y. "The Strategy and Structure of the Top 100 Japanese Industrial Enterprises 1950–1970." *Strategic Management Journal* (April 1980): 265–291.

Teece, D. J. "Applying Concepts of Economic Analysis to Strategic Management." In J. M. Pennings and Associates, *Organizational Strategy and Change*. San Francisco: Jossey-Bass, 1985.

Tsurumi, Y., and Tsurumi, H. "Value-Added Maximizing Behavior of Japanese Firms and Roles of Corporate Investment and Finance." *Columbia Journal of World Business* (Spring 1985): 29–35.

Utterbuck, James M., and Abernathy, W. J. "A Dynamic Model of Process and Product Innovation." *Omega* 3, no. 6 (1975): 639–656.

Vancil, R. F. *Implementing Strategy: The Role of Top Management*. Boston: Harvard Business School, Division of Research, 1982.

Vangermeesh, R. "Milestone in the History of Management Accounting." In *Cost Accounting for the 90's: The Challenge of Technological Change Proceedings*. Montvale, N.J.: National Association of Accountants, 1986, pp. 7–10.

Walsh, K.; Hinings, R.; Greenwood, R.; and Ranson, S. "Power and Advantage in Organizations." *Organization Studies* (March 1981): 131–152.

6

CONCLUSIONS

Various authors have criticized the limited scope usually given to management accounting. Generally, managerial accounting has taken the following forms:

1. Ad hoc approaches to single-instance decision situations simplified to involve only one or two variables—for example, make or buy decisions.
2. An expansion of cost accounting technique—for example, cost planning and control.
3. A more or less conventional approach to budgetary planning and control.[1]

Managerial accounting has . . . addressed itself mainly to the problems of sub-optimization, and has largely worked outside the scheme of the "continuous data gathering" system. It is rather obvious that this has been due largely to the fact that present accounting systems do not provide adequate structure to enable the gathering of enough pertinent managerial data from routine accounting records.[2]

This lack of adequate structure is mainly due to the failure to recognize the conceptual foundations of management accounting as a guide for the development and evaluation of management accounting techniques. As pointed out in this book, management accounting rests on accounting, problem and decisional, organizational, behavioral, and strategic foundations. The incorporation of these five foundations in management accounting will provide the adequate structure that will enable the gathering of enough pertinent managerial data for internal problem solving.

The *accounting foundations* include basic and secondary objectives, qualitative characteristics, and concepts as an accounting framework within which techniques may be evaluated. Management accounting techniques will be judged in terms of their conformity to this "emerging management accounting theoretical structure."

The *problem and decisional foundations* include the frameworks for determining the types of problems, the needed information, the types of decisions taken and decision centers, and defining the role of management element accounting in decision making.

The *organizational foundations* include the elements of organizational structure most prevalent and essential to a proper functioning of a management accounting system and the theories of organization essential to an identification of the significant elements that approximate the patterning and order in organizations. They define the role and scope of management accounting in the organization and the techniques, approaches, and philosophies it may espouse in order to provide adequate services to the organization.

The *behavioral foundations* include various concepts—namely, the objective function in management accounting, motivation theories, models of decision making, and heuristics, which identify factors and situations that influence individual behavior and performance and suggest avenues for management accounting to adapt its services.

The *strategic foundations* show a congruence between the strategic process, types, and decision making, and the conduct of management accounting in general and strategic management accounting in particular.

These conclusions point to the possibility of formulating a model of the nature, elements, and determinants of the conceptual foundations of management accounting. Such a model would represent a first step toward the development of a combinatorial theory of management accounting. More explicitly, the scope and conduct of management accounting in a given organization rests on the five conceptual foundations discussed in this book. Management accounting systems will differ from one another on the basis of the extent of appreciation and the incorporation of these foundations, their determinants, and their elements in the design of the system.

Each of these foundations may be characterized by appropriate determinants. Hence, the accounting foundations are determined by the extent to which management accounting techniques are derived from an accounting conceptual framework. The problem and decisional foundations are determined by the problem formulation process and the information and decision systems frameworks. The organizational foundations are determined by the theories of organization and the elements of organizational structure. The behavioral foundations are determined by the objective function, the motivation theories, the heuristics, and the models of decision making. The strategic foundations are determined by the strategic process and the strategic archetypes. Each of the determinants of the conceptual foundations depends on the set of variables or elements of the foundations, which will characterize by their implementation the resulting management accounting system.

NOTES

1. Hector R. Anton, "Activity Analysis of the Firm: A Theoretical Approach to Accounting (Systems) Development," in H. R. Anton and P. Firmin (eds.), *Contemporary Issues in Cost Accounting* (Boston: Houghton Mifflin, 1966), p. 293.

2. Hector R. Anton, "Some Implications of Information Theory for Business Organizations." *Revista Internazionale Di Science Economiche E Commerciale* (Milan) 9 (1962): 3.

INDEX

Abernathy, W., 145
Abstract individual styles, 115
Acceptability, standard for information, 12
Accountability, responsibility of a management accountant, 14
Accountants: roles in managerial and in financial accounting, 3. *See also* Management accountants
Accounting foundations, 1–29
Accounting information system (AIS), 26
Accuracy, expression as precision and reliability, 10
Achievement theory of motivation, 109–10
Activity center, defined, 48
Adams, S., 110
Adaptability in using data, 12
Adaptive mode for strategy making, 145
Adhocracy, 64–65
Adjustment in making judgments, 120–21
Adorno, T. W., 114
Aggregation of data, 11
Agre, G. P., 32
Albert, M., 121
Allison, G. T., 111, 114
Allocation of resources as an objective of management accounting, 3

American Accounting Association (AAA), 1; Committee on Concepts and Standards-Internal Planning and Control, 10; Committee on Courses in Managerial Accounting, 13; Committee on Courses in Managerial Accounting, report of, 15; Committee on Managerial Decision Models, 9–10; Committee on Measurement of Social Cost, 103–4; educational recommendations, 4; Management Accounting Committee, 7; Statement of Basic Accounting Theory, 9–10
Analytical techniques, and decision structure, 42
Analytic cognitive style, 115
Analyzability dimension of technology, 81
Analyzers as strategic archetypes, 147
Anchoring and adjustment task formulation, 120–21
Ansoff, H. I., 149
Ansoff and Stewart's strategic archetypes, 149
Anthony, R. N., 25, 37, 40, 139
Anthony framework, 37, 40
Archetypes, strategic, 144–52
Argyris, C., 77

Atkinson, J. W., 109
Authoritarianism, and decision making, 114
Authority: bases of, in Weberian theory, 73; of staff, 65; Weberian views of, 71–72
Availability of information, and probabilistic judgment, 118

Bargaining model for managerial maximization, 102
Base rate fallacy, 117–18
Behavioral foundations, 87–138
Belkaoui, A., 120
Biases for simplifying judgment problems, 116–27
Bieri, J., 115
Bitner, L. N., 16
Blumenthal, S., 48
Blumenthal framework, 48, 50
Boundaries as an organizational characteristic, 56
Bounded rationality, principle of, 111–12
Boutell, W., 12
Bower, J. L., 144
Boyd, V., 2–3
Branch, B., 102
Bromwich, M., 153
Buck, V., 100
Budgets, 62
Bureaucratic authority, 72
Burgelman, R., 143
Business environment, incorporation into managerial accounting, 3
Business-level strategies versus corporate-level strategies, 142
Byeth, R., 123

Caplan, E. H., 106
Certificate in Management Accounting (CMA), 5
Chandler, A. D., Jr., 139, 143
Chapman, J. P., 124
Chapman, L. J., 124
Charismatic authority, 72
Choice as a part of problem solving, 40, 41
Clarkson, G. E., 113

Classical organization structure, 74–76
Cognitive styles: complexity, and decision making style, 115; and decision making, 114
Communication: formal theoretical concept of, 13; as a function of management accounting, 9
Comparability of data, 11
Competence standards, 5
Competitive game in organizations, 114
Competitive strategy, 140
Computers, and information manager role for management accountants, 4
Concepts of management accounting, 8, 13–15
Conceptual framework, management accounting as a, 24, 26
Concise information system, 80
Concrete individual styles, 115
Confidentiality, 5
Confirmation bias, 118–20
Congruence, between personal and company objectives, 77
Conjunction fallacy in probability judgment, 121–22
Consensus in environmental strategies, 143
Consistency of information, 11
Constraints: cognitive styles as, 115; independent, on organizational units, 113; open and closed, on a problem, 32; organizational, provided by the environment, 60; in the rational view of decision making, 111; social, on organizational goals, 103
Contestable markets, and strategic management accounting, 153–54
Contingency model: for the design of management accounting, 79–81; studies, and covariation, 125
Continuity as an organizational characteristic, 56
Control: operational module, Blumenthal framework, 48; and the operative (worker) level, 76; and organizational structure, 62–65; as a planning function, 14; relationship of management accounting to, 8–9; responsibility of a

management accountant, 14. *See also* Management controls; Operational control

Controllers: independence of, 71; organizational roles of, 66–67; role in design and operation of the control system, 67–71

Control system: design and operation of, 67–71; as a response to the environment, 85

Corporate-level strategies versus business-level strategies, 142

Cost accounting: versus management accounting, 3–6; scope of, 4–5

Cost analysis, strategic, 152

Cost behavior, 14

Cost leadership strategy, 148

Cost minimization: as an objective of cost accounting, 3; as a strategy, 147

Cost reduction, and management accounting, 3

Cowan, D. A., 34–35

Crecine, J., 113

Crisis, organizational plasticity in, 73

Cursory information system, 80

Cyert, R. M., 10–11, 113, 145

Data as stimuli, 126

Davidson, H. J., 10–11

Dearden, J., 45

Dearden framework, 45–47

Decision centers: defined, 48; as links among activity centers, 48

Decision environment, and problem constraints, 32–34

Decision maker, perceptions of, and problem structure, 36

Decision making: harmonizing the accounting system with, 12; information for internal, 4; and management accounting, 2; models of, 110–16; as a response to a gap between actual performance and goals, 45; strategic process, 144; support for, 31. *See also* Preferences

Decisions, programmed versus nonprogrammed, 41–42

Decision Support Systems, 44

Deductive logic: and auditing, 120; and a rationalist model, 119

Defenders as strategic archetypes, 147

Delay attribute of timeliness, 12

Deliberate strategy, defined as the outcome of an intended strategy, 142

Departmentalization, 60–61

Dermer, J., 114, 143

Design: organizational, 79–89; as a phase of problem solving, 40–41

Dickhaut, J. W., 126, 127

Dickson, W. J., 76

Differentiation in decision making, 115

Differentiation strategy, 148

Diffuse information system, 80

D-intensive strategies, 149

Disjointed incrementalism (muddling through), 145

Dissatisfiers, 106–7; and job context, 106

Diversification strategies, 151–52

Division structure, role of controllers in, 71

Dogmatism, and decision making, 115

Dominant coalition: model for managerial maximization, 103; in the organizational procedures view, 113; role in defining organizational goals, 100

Dominant vertical firms, 152

Doz, I., 144

Drabeck, T., 56

Dual economy, models of sectorial economic differentiation, 86–87

Dutton, J., 141

Ecological view of strategy, 143

Education, suggested course material, 15–16

Efficiency as the measure of productive processes, 74

Eggleton, I., 126

Egocentric bias, and availability of information, 118

Einhorn, H. J., 122

Elaborate information system, 80

Emergent strategies as unintended realized strategies (outcomes), 142

Entrepreneurial mode for strategy making, 144–45

Environment: complexity of, and infor-
mation processing, 115; and control
systems, 85–87; material versus so-
cially created, 141; role in natural sys-
tem theory, 78
Environmental enactment, 140–41
Equilibrium in natural system theory, 78–
79
Estrin, T., 115
Ethical standards for management ac-
countants, 5–6
Etzioni, A., 99–100
Evaluation, responsibility of a manage-
ment accountant, 14
Ewusi-Mensah, Kweka, 85–86
Expectations, and motivation, 107
External environment, states of, 85–86
External reporting, responsibility of a
management accountant, 14

Fairness: and neutrality of information,
12; as a norm in behavioral modules,
110
Falsification principle, 119
Fayol, H., 75
Feature-matching model, 122
Feedback: nonlinear, in business organi-
zations, 45; in the planning process, 14
Field dependence, and decision making,
115–16
Financial accounting versus management
accounting, 2–3
Financial Executives Institute, 67
Financial system: basis in the flow of
dollars in the organization, 46; and
management control, 46
Fischhoff, B., 123
Flamholtz, E. G., 85
Flexibility: as an attribute of management
accounting, 3; in using information, 12
Focus strategy, 148
Formulation: as the cognitive aspect of
strategy, 142; strategic, 148
Forrester, J., 45
Forrester framework, 45
Frame of reference: for management ac-
counting, 2–3; management accounting
as a, 7

Frameworks: for management accounting
in the contingency model, 79–81; for
organizational problems, 36–49; for
strategic change, 141
Friesen, P. H., 148
Function, departmentalization by, 61
Functional authority of the controller, 67–
70
Functional unit, defined, 48

Gambling, anchoring and adjustment heu-
ristics, 120–21
Gantt, H., 74
Generally accepted accounting principles
(GAAP), 2
Gilbreth, F., 74
Goal conflicts, among organizational
units, 113
Goals: definitions of organizational, 100;
organizational, decision making as a
means to, 45; specificity and formali-
zation in the rational perspective, 73.
See also Objectives
Golding, S. L., 125
Golembiewski, R., 55
Gordon, L. A., 79
Gorry, G. A., 42–44
Gorry-Scott Morton framework, 42–44
Gouldner, A. W., 73
Govindarajan, V., 71, 152, 154
Group norms: in organizations, 77; and
setting of standards, 77

Ha, Y.-W., 120
Hall, R., 100
Hambrick, D., 142
Harvey, O. J., 115
Hass, E., 56
Hawthorne studies, 77
Hegelian Inquiring System, 34
Henning, D., 70
Herzberg, F., 106
Heuristic cognitive style, 115
Heuristics for simplifying judgment prob-
lems, 116–27
Hierarchy of needs, 104, 106
Hindsight bias, 123–24
Hofer, C. W., 140

Hogarth, R., 123
Homans, G., 56
House, R. J., 108
Human relations theory, 76–77
Huysmans, Jan, 115

Illusory correlation, 124–26
Implementation as the action aspect of
    strategy, 142
Incentive, success as, 109
Incremental change in the political model
    of decision making, 114
Incumbency as the basis of authority, 73
Individual differences model of decision
    making, 114–16
Individuals, roles under bureaucratic au-
    thority, 72
Inequity theory of motivation, 110
Information: from accounting, 2; behav-
    ioral impact on users of, 4; definition
    in accounting, 13; as a dimension of
    systems activity, 46; qualitative charac-
    teristics of, 9–12; relationship of man-
    agement accounting to, 9; relevance
    and user receiving position, 10; re-
    quirements by decision category, An-
    thony model, 40
Information systems: closed loop feed-
    back in, 45; matching styles with tech-
    nologies, 79–80; organizational,
    modules of, 48, 50; properties of, 10
Integration in decision making, 115
Integrative complexity, and decision-
    making style, 115
Integrity, standards of, 6
Intelligence as a phase of problem solv-
    ing, 40
Intended strategies, and their outcomes,
    142
Interval attribute of timeliness, 12

Jackson, S., 141
Job satisfaction, two-factor theory, 106–7

Kahn, R., 56
Kahneman, D., 118, 121–22
Kantian Inquiring System, 34
Katkin, E. S., 125

Katz, D., 56
Keen, P. G., 44
Kelly, G. A., 115
Khandwalla, P. N., 86
Kilmann, R. H., 33–34
Klayman, J., 120
Krupp, S., 60

Lawler, E. E., 108
Lawrence, P. R., 113
Learning of motives for achievement, 109
Leavitt, H., 81
Legitimate authority as the source of so-
    cial behavior, 71–72
Lewin, A. Y., 71
Lewin, K., 107
Lichtenstein, S., 118
Likert, R., 77
Lindblom, C. E., 114, 145
Line managers, relationships with staff,
    65–66
Linguistic labels, and strategic planning,
    141
Location, departmentalization by, 61
Logistics system: information in, 46; and
    operational control, 46
Long-range plan, relationship between the
    organization and environment in, 40
Lorsch, J. W., 113

Machine, the organization as, 73
Machine bureaucracy as a component of
    divisionalized organizations, 64
Machine Bureaucracy, The (Mintzberg),
    62–63
Macintosh, N. B., 79
Magee, R. P., 127
Management: role in adapting strategy
    and structure, 143–44; role in the
    shareholder wealth maximization
    model, 101; role in the teleological
    view of strategy, 143
Management accountants: responsibilities
    of, 14–15; role as facilitator, 31; roles
    in satisficing or organizational proce-
    dures models, 113
Management accounting: in a bureau-
    cratic structure, 73–74; constraints of

information users' cognitive styles,
116; versus cost accounting, 3–6; as a
decision support system, 44; defined,
1; versus financial accounting, 2–3, 7–
8; goals for information presentation,
and problem structure, 43–44; implication of expectancy theory for, 108–9;
implications for the SOWM, 103; implications of achievement theory for,
110; role and structure by technology,
85; role in classical theory, 76; role in
human relations theory, 77; role in natural system theory, 78; strategic, 152–
54; system defined, 13
Management Accounting, Committee on,
definition by, 6
Management and the Worker, 77
Management controls: centers of, Blumenthal framework, 48; and competition, 86; decision requirements of, 44;
and the financial system, 46; modules
for, Blumenthal model, 48. *See also*
Control
Management information, role of man-
agement accounting in, 67
Management information system, role of
organizational systems in, 48
Managerial welfare maximization model,
101–3
Managers, role in the managerial welfare
maximization model, 101–2
March, J. G., 113, 145
Maslow, A., 104, 106
Mathematical model for expressing oper-
ational control, 40
Mautz, R. K., 119
May, E., 77.
McClelland, D. C., 109
McGregor, D., 77
Measurement, definition in accounting,
13
Membership, organizational, 56
Merchant, K., 85
Merton, R., 73
Michels, R., 78
Miles, R. E., 147
Miles and Snow's strategic archetypes,
147

Miller, D. A., 79, 148
Miller and Friesen's strategic archetypes,
148
Mintzberg, H., 62, 63–64, 142, 144
Mintzberg's strategic archetypes, 144–45
Mitroff, I. I., 32–33
Mock, T., 115
Models, impact on perceptions, 111
Moseley, R., 70
Motivation: goal congruences and, 12; for
personal success, 109; theories of,
104–10
Motivation hygiene, 106
Motivators, satisfiers as, 106
Muddling through, 145
Multidisciplinary approach, 4, 25

National Association of Accountants
(NAA): Certificate in Management Ac-
counting program of, 4–5; definition of
management accounting by, 6–7
Natural system theory, 78–79
Need theory of motivation, 104, 106
Neutrality of data, 11
Normative models for modern cost ac-
counting, 4

Objective functions: of cost accounting
and management accounting, 3; in
management accounting, 99–104; and
relevance, 10
Objectives: of accounting information, 2;
of the CMA program, 5; congruence
between personal and organizational,
77; of management accounting, 8–9,
31; mutuality of, 10; organizational,
40; relevance of, 10; and strategy, 139.
See also Goals
Objectivity: of data, 11; standards for
management accountants, 6
Official goals, 100
Open systems, organizations as, 56
Operating systems management, relationship of management accounting to, 9
Operational control: defined, 40; and the
logistics system, 46; system, decision
requirements of, 44. *See also* Control;
Management controls

Operative goals, 100

Optimal choices, and rational decision making, 111

Optimal organizational efficiency in classical theory, 75

Organizational design, 79–89

Organizational foundations, 55–98

Organizational performance, suggested outputs for measuring, 103–4

Organizational personality, 78

Organizational problem areas, relationship of management accounting to, 8

Organizational procedures model of decision making, 113

Organizational structure: activities grouped into units, 48; dimensions of, 62; divisionalized, 64; the machine bureaucracy, 63; the professional bureaucracy, 63–64; simple (nonstructure), 62–63; work centered and authoritarian, classical view, 74

Organization chart, hierarchical, 60

Organizations: classification by technology, 81, 85; defined, 56; definition of, and goals of, 100; formal and informal, 76–77

Parsons, T., 78

Participative management, 77

Paton, W., 1

Performance auditing, 4

Performance-maximizing strategy, 145–46

Performance reports, 62, 77

Perrow, C., 81, 100

Personal service organizations, organizational structure of, 63–64

Personnel system, information in, 46

Planning: defined, 14; long-range, attributes of information for, 11; by management accounting, 61–62; relationship of management accounting to, 8; responsibility of a management accountant, 14; short-range, and financial accounting systems, 11

Planning mode for strategy design, 145

Platt, J. R., 119

Political model of decision making, 113–14

Pollard, W. B., 16

Popper, K., 118–19

Porter, L. W., 108

Porter, M. E., 140, 148

Porter's strategic archetypes, 148

POSDCORB, 74–75

Positive test strategy versus confirmation, 120

Precision, defined, 10–11

Prediction, 123

Predictive ability of accounting data, 3–4

Preferences: and personal behavior, 107. See also Decision making

Price, J., 73

Principles of Scientific Management, 74

Probability: as a factor in motivation, 107; representativeness in assessment of, 117; of success, and personal motivation, 109

Probability judgment: conjunction fallacy in, 121–22

Problem: classification on the structured/ill-structured continuum, 34; conditions for existence of, 32; decisional foundations for, 37–49; definition of, 31–32; foundation of, 32–34; identification as deviation from goals, 32; well-structured, example, 36

Problem foundations, 31–54

Problem solving: model for managerial maximization, 102–3; the recognition process, 34; Simon model of, 40; stages of, 31–37

Process, departmentalization based on, 61

Process-oriented model of decision making, 112–13

Product, departmentalization based on, 61

Profit maximization, objective function for management accounting, 3

Program budgets, 4

Programming, centralization of, 46

Prospectors as strategic archetypes, 147

Public interest accounting, 104

Qualitative characteristics for management accounting, 8

Raiffa, H., 121
Ratio, vertical, 150–51
Rational model of decision making, 111–12
Rational perspective theory, 71–74
Reactors as strategic archetypes, 147
Realized strategy, 142
Real time, defined for distribution and use of information, 12
Reinforcement contingencies, and logical use of information, 119
Reitman, W. R., 32, 34
Related ratio, 150–51
Related-constrained firms, 152
Relatedness of businesses, defined in terms of specialization ratio, 152
Relationships: defining organizational structure, 60–62; equity in, as a motivating factor, 110; staff and line, 65–66
Relevance as an attribute of management accounting, 3
Reliability, defined, 10–11
Reporting functions of accounting, internal routine, special, and external, 2
Representativeness as a heuristic, 117–18
Research, role under Porter's generic strategies, 148
Research strategy versus development strategy, 149
Responsibility, and job enrichment, 107
Responsibility accounting, 62
R-intensive strategies, 149
Risks, 102; and personal goals, 109
Roethlisberger, F. J., 76
Rokeach, M., 115
Role perceptions, impact on performance, 108
Rorer, L. G., 125
Rose, J., 126
Rosenzweig, K., 70
Ross, M., 118
Rumelt, R. P., 149
Rumelt's strategic archetypes, 149–50

Sales-maximizing strategy, 147
San Miguel, J. G., 71

Sathe, Vijay, 67
Satisficing model of decision making, 112–13
Satisfiers, 106–7
Schendel, D. E., 140
Schiff, M., 71
Schroder, H. M., 115
Scientific management, 74–76
Scott Morton, M. S., 42–44
Selznick, P., 78
Shank, J., 152, 154
Shannon, C., 13
Sharaf, H. A., 119
Shareholder wealth maximization model, 101
Sicoly, F., 118
Silverman, D., 85
Simon, H. A., 40–42, 111
Simon framework, 40–42
Singerian-Churchmanian Inquiring System, 34
Slovic, P., 120
Smircich, L., 141
Snow, C. C., 142, 147
Social accounting, 105
Social welfare maximization model, 103–4
Solomon, E., 101
Specialization ratio, 149–50
Stability: as an organizational characteristic, 56; of organizations, and strategic archetype, 147
Staff, relationships to line managers, 65–66
Standard Industrial Classification System, 81
Standard operating procedures as a standard response to well-structured problems, 36
Standards for accounting information, relationship of management accounting to, 9–10
Starr, J., 125
Statement of Basic Accounting Theory on the decision-making functions, 1–2
Stewart, J., 149
Stimuli, data as, 126

Strategic accounting, 152–54
Strategic archetypes, 144–52
Strategic cost analysis, 152
Strategic foundations, 139–54
Strategic management accounting, working definition of, 153
Strategic planning, 40; decision requirements of, 44
Strategic process, 142–44
Strategic research, 143–44
Strategies: defined, 139; for defining problems under complexity and uncertainty, 33–34; definition, Greek classical, 139
Structure, organizational, 55–71
Stubbart, C., 141
Subjective probability. *See* Probability judgment
Subjective rationality, 112
Symbolic world as the organizational environment, 141
System, definition for management accounting, 13

Tactical programs, role of financial analysis in designing, 153
Taylor, D., 2–3
Taylor, F., 74
Taylor, R. N., 32, 34, 36
Technical competence as the basis of authority, 73
Techniques of management accounting, 8; responsibility of a management accountant, 15–16, 17
Technology, impact on accounting system design, 81–85
Teleological view of strategy, 142–43
Thematic Apperception Test (TAT), 109
Theory of management accounting, 6
Thompson, J. D., 56, 100
Tiessen, P. A., 79

Timeliness of information, 12
Topologies of organizations, 56–59
Traceability of data, 11
Traditional authority, 72
Treasurer, roles of, 67–69
Tversky, A., 118, 121–22
Two-factor theory of motivation, 106–7

U-Curve Hypothesis, 115
Understandability, standard for information, 12
Uniformity of data, 11
Unrelated firms, 152
Utterback, J., 145
Utterback and Abernathy's strategic archetypes, 145, 147

Valences, personal utilities as, 107
Value/expectancy theory of motivation, 107–9
Variability dimension of technology, 81
Variance as a measure of verifiability, 11
Variance analysis: example, 16, 18–23
Vasarhelyi, M., 115
Verifiability of data, 11
Verification, role of auditors, 119–20
Vroom, V. H., 107

Walster, E., 110
Waterhouse, J. H., 79
Weaver, W., 13
Weber, M., 71
Weber-Fechner law, 117, 126–27
Weick, K. E., 140
Western Electric Company, 77
Witkin, H. A., 115–16
Wood, G., 123
Woodward, J., 81
Work: as a dimension of systems activity, 46; satisfiers relating directly to, 106

About the Author

AHMED RIAHI-BELKAOUI is Professor of Accounting at the College of Business Administration, The University of Illinois at Chicago, and Chairman of the Cultural Studies and Accounting Research Committee, American Accounting Association (Internal Accounting Section). Riahi-Belkaoui is also a member of the editorial board of several professional journals and is the author of seventeen previous Quorum books and co-author of two more.